365 Meditations for Couples

Sally D. Sharpe, Editor

Amy Valdez Barker and Richard Barker II, Lloyd and Clare Doyle,
Tim and Becky Eberhart, Warren and Mary Ebinger,
Kwasi Kena and Safiyah Fosua,
Kel and Ellen Groseclose, Robert and Jeanette Lauer,
Ulrike and Clifton Guthrie,
Daon and Monica Johnson,
James Chongho and Karen Eunsook Kim,
Bill and Katie Treadway, John and Ginny Underwood

DIMENSIONS
FOR LIVING
NASHVILLE

365 MEDITATIONS FOR COUPLES

Copyright © 2003 by Dimensions for Living

This book is printed on recycled, acid-free, elemental-chlorine–free paper.

Library of Congress Cataloging-in-Publication Data

365 meditations for couples / Sally D. Sharpe, editor ; Amy Valdez Barker . . . [et al.].
  p. cm.
  ISBN 0-687-06384-1 (pbk. : alk. paper)
  1. Spouses—Prayer-books and devotions—English. 2.
Marriage—Religious aspects—Christianity—Meditations. 3. Devotional calendars. I. Title: Three hundred sixty-five meditations for couples.
II. Sharpe, Sally D., 1964- III. Barker, Amy Valdez.
  BV4596.M3A13 2003 242'.644—dc21

                                                                      2003001654

All scripture quotations, unless otherwise indicated, are taken from the New Revised Standard Version of the Bible, copyright ©1989, Division of Christian Education of the National Council of the Churches of Christ in the United States of America. Used by permission. All rights reserved.

Scripture quotations marked RSV are from the Revised Standard Version of the Bible, copyright 1946, 1952, 1971 by the Division of Christian Education of the National Council of the Churches of Christ in the United States of America. Used by permission. All rights reserved.

Scripture quotations noted KJV are from the King James Version of the Bible.

Scripture quotations marked CEV are from the Contemporary English Version, © 1991, 1992, 1995 by American Bible Society. Used by permission.

Scripture quotations marked NLT are from the Holy Bible, New Living Translation, copyright © 1996. Used by permission of Tyndale House Publishers, Inc., Wheaton, Illinois 60189. All rights reserved.

Scripture quotations marked TEV are from the Today's English Version—Second Edition. Copyright © 1992 by American Bible Society. Used by permission.

Scripture quotations marked NIV are from the HOLY BIBLE, NEW INTERNATIONAL VER-SION®. Copyright 1973, 1978, 1984 by International Bible Society. Used by permission of Zondervan Publishing House. All rights reserved.

Scripture quotations marked *The Message* are from THE MESSAGE. Copyright © Eugene H. Peterson, 1993, 1994, 1995. Used by permission of NavPress Publishing Group.

Scripture quotations marked TLB are from *The Living Bible* © 1971. Used by permission of Tyndale House Publishers, Inc., Wheaton, Illinois 60189. All rights reserved.

Scripture quotations noted JBP are from J. B. Phillips, *The New Testament in Modern English*, published by Macmillan. Copyright © J. B. Phillips, 1958, 1959, 1960, 1972.

Scripture quotations noted AMP are from the Amplified Bible, Old Testament, copyright © 1965, 1987 by the Zondervan Corporation. The Amplified New Testament, copyright © 1954, 1958, 1987 by the Lockman Foundation. Used by permission.

03 04 05 06 07 08 09 10 11 12—10 9 8 7 6 5 4 3 2 1

MANUFACTURED IN THE UNITED STATES OF AMERICA

CONTENTS

INTRODUCTION

"To have and to hold, from this day forward, for better—for worse, for richer—for poorer, in sickness and in health, to love and to cherish, till death do us part."

*M*ore than likely, you and your spouse exchanged vows similar to these on your wedding day. And if yours was a Christian ceremony, your vows were pledged in God's name. According to the *New World Dictionary*, a vow is "a solemn promise or pledge, especially one made to God, dedicating oneself to an act, service, or way of life." It is a sacred covenant, a binding agreement. Yet despite the seriousness of the commitment, half of all marriages in the United States today end in divorce, with an average duration of only seven years. Those who were children of divorce are 50 percent more likely to divorce than their counterparts from intact families (divorcemagazine.com). Unfortunately, Christians fare no better in the statistics according to the Barna Research Group.

In a culture where divorce is so prevalent, how can we beat the odds? I believe Jesus gave us the answer when he said, "But from the beginning of creation, 'God made them male and female.' 'For this reason a man shall leave his father and mother and be joined to his wife, and the two shall become one flesh.' So they are no longer two, but one flesh. Therefore what God has joined together, let no one separate" (Mark 10:6). The key lies in the words *one flesh*. Rather than creating woman from the dust of the ground, God created her from the man's flesh and bone. This illustrates so beautifully that a man and woman symbolically become one flesh in marriage, which is a mystical union of two individuals' hearts and lives—a union that God takes very seriously, as we see throughout the Bible. The goal in marriage, then, is not friendship or even compatibility; it is nothing less than oneness. *And this is possible only in partnership with God.* In other words, God must be the glue that "joins us together." If we keep God in the center of our lives—both as individuals and as married couples—then our marriages will not only survive but will actually thrive!

7

This book is intended for just that purpose. Twelve Christian couples offer biblical guidance, practical insights, personal stories, and words of encouragement for the challenging journey of marriage. Though they write in a variety of styles and draw from a multitude of life experiences, they share a common purpose: to help you strengthen your relationship as you become one in union with God—as you keep God in the center of your lives. Some of the couples have been married for only a few years and some have been married for decades, but all know firsthand both the difficult "work" and tremendous blessings of married life; and all know the loving, gracious God who makes it possible for two to become one—and remain one.

You may be newly married, or you may have been together for many years. A shared devotional time may be old hat to you, or you may be embarking on a totally new experience. In any case, these devotions will enrich your relationship and deepen your spiritual intimacy. Because the book is not tied to a specific calendar year, it doesn't matter if you begin in January or July. You'll find a consistent format throughout. Each brief devotion begins with a passage of scripture and ends with a prayer. In addition, each devotion includes "Talk It Over" questions and/or suggestions to help you discuss the insights you've gained and apply them to your relationship.

There are several ways to use this book. You might want to start each day with a shared devotion. If that doesn't work for you, you might read the scripture and devotion separately during the day and come together at the end of the day for discussion and prayer. Or you might opt for a regular devotional time once or twice a week, choosing from the devotions provided for that week. The important question is not *when* or *how* you structure your time together but simply *if.* If you will commit to a regular devotional time together, you can be assured that God will be working, for Jesus promised that "where two . . . are gathered in my name, I am there among them" (Matthew 18:20). May your marriage be richly blessed!

Sally D. Sharpe, Editor

ABOUT THE WRITERS

Richard and Amy Valdez Barker (AUGUST) live in Lake Mills, Wisconsin, where they are raising their first child. Richard is in the field of information technology management. Amy is currently serving as Youth Coordinator of the Wisconsin Annual Conference of The United Methodist Church. They both enjoy long walks, long naps, and visiting God's creation all over the world.

Lloyd and Clare Doyle (APRIL) live in Waverly, Tennessee, where Lloyd is pastor of First United Methodist Church. Clare is a full-time mother and a freelance writer. In addition to contributing to *365 Meditations for Teens,* she has been a regular writer for the curriculum resource *LinC (Living in Christ)*. Lloyd and Clare enjoy performing music, traveling, woodworking, needlework, sports, and being together. They are the parents of two children, Elizabeth, age ten, and Allen, age seven.

Becky and Tim Eberhart (SEPTEMBER) live in Mitchell, South Dakota, where Becky is pastor at First United Methodist Church and Tim is chaplain at Dakota Wesleyan University. Although both grew up in the Midwest, they met and fell in love in Nashville, Tennessee, as classmates at Vanderbilt Divinity School. They share a love of God's good creation, a vision of faithful living that includes both personal and social holiness, and a desire for authentic Christian community. Their son, Henry Thomas, brings laughter, learning, and clarity to their lives.

Warren and Mary Ebinger (FEBRUARY) have been married fifty-one years and are the parents of three children and three grandchildren. Warren, a retired pastor who currently serves as pastor of outreach at Woodside United Methodist Church in Silver Spring, Maryland, and Mary, a certified counselor, lead marriage enrichment retreats based on their book *Do-It-Yourself Marriage Enrichment*. They also were contributors to *365 Meditations for Families*. Through the years they have been involved in missions work in the Dominican Republic, Jamaica, Grenada, Alaska, Puerto Rico, and Zimbabwe, as well as in flood-ravaged parts of Georgia and Iowa.

9

Kel and Ellen Groseclose (JANUARY) live in Wenatchee, Washington. They were high school sweethearts and recently celebrated their fortieth anniversary. They are the parents of six adult children and are blessed by the addition of nine grandchildren. They enjoy being home together, going to baseball games, eating out, camping in their travel trailer, and visiting with family. Kel writes in his journals, plays old-time fiddle tunes, and digs in his small garden. Ellen makes quilts for each family member, reads mystery novels, and is the family "communications center."

Clifton and Ulrike Guthrie (JUNE) enjoy life in Bangor, Maine, with their two young children, balancing family life with work as a seminary professor and religious books editor, respectively.

Daon and Monica Johnson (MARCH), native Marylanders, now reside in Nashville, Tennessee. Daon is a fitness manager at the Delta Health and Adventure Club in Nashville, in addition to serving as the associate pastor for the Springfield Parish of The United Methodist Church. Monica, who teaches sign language to the hearing and leads a Spirit Led Women's Ministry for the Springfield Parish, is the domestic engineer of the Johnson household. Daon and Monica have been married for three years and are the proud parents of Walter, Caleb, and Lisa-Nicole.

Safiyah Fosua and Kwasi Kena (MAY) are both ordained clergy members of the Greater New Jersey Annual Conference. Currently, Safiyah serves as the Director of Invitational Preaching Ministries of the General Board of Discipleship and Kwasi serves as the Director of Field Services for the General Commission on United Methodist Men. Prior to their current appointments, Safiyah and Kwasi spent four years in Ghana West Africa as missionaries. The couple has two adult sons and one grandson. Both Safiyah and Kwasi enjoy reading, traveling, and being with their grandson.

James Chongho and Karen Eunsook Kim (OCTOBER), who make their home in Atlanta, have been married more than twenty years and have four children who provide much inspiration and joy. James is a United Methodist pastor serving Korean Church of Atlanta. Previously he was a campus minister in Chicago for fifteen years. Karen Eunsook is a licensed social worker and works for the Department of Labor as a compliance officer. James is the author of *Temptation to Conform and Call to Transform:*

10

Anthology of Stories of Faith in the Korean-American Context, written in Korean, and *Signs of Promise, Seeds of Hope,* Advent meditations for college students.

Robert and Jeanette Lauer (DECEMBER) live in San Diego, where they are research professors at Alliant International University. Robert also is an ordained minister. They are active in their church, frequently speak to groups on topics related to marriage and family, and hold weekend marriage enrichment seminars. Together they have written seventeen books, including *Becoming Family: How to Build a Stepfamily That Really Works; The Play Solution: How to Put the Fun and Excitement Back into Your Relationship;* and *Love Never Ends: Growing Together in Faith and Marriage.* Robert and Jeanette have three children and five grandchildren.

Bill and Katie Treadway (NOVEMBER) live in the Nashville, Tennessee, area with their two children. Katie is an ordained minister in the Cumberland Presbyterian Church, and Bill is an editor in electronic publishing at Upper Room Ministries of The General Board of Discipleship of The United Methodist Church. In addition to spending time with their children, Katie loves to start craft projects, browse bookstores, and play classical piano. Bill enjoys hiking and reading all kinds of books; and listening to Americana music. Both dream of the day when they can invest their time together traveling with a canine companion.

John and Ginny Underwood (JULY) live in Nashville, Tennessee, with their three-year-old daughter, Avery, and their newest addition, Alyssa, born in February 2003. Both are originally from Oklahoma and are members of the Oklahoma Indian Missionary Conference of The United Methodist Church. They represent the Seminole, Comanche, and Kiowa tribes of Oklahoma. Ginny is managing editor for the public information office of United Methodist Communications. John is currently receiving manager at Garden Ridge and hopes to put his teaching license to work for Native American children. They have been married nine happy years.

IRRITATIONS AND IDIOSYNCRASIES

Kel and Ellen Groseclose

January 1 ~ God Chooses People with Idiosyncrasies

God chose what is foolish in the world to shame the wise . . . what is weak in the world to shame the strong.

—1 Corinthians 1:27

*G*od obviously appreciates people with character; and character comes with unique personalities; and personalities always include their share of idiosyncrasies. It's apparently part of God's plan. It started with the first humans in the Garden and hasn't stopped since. Each of us is a one-of-a-kind individual with quirks and peculiarities. It's what makes us special.

God chose Moses, who had difficulty communicating; Elisha, who was touchy about his baldness; and Job, who was an expert at pouting. Ruth apparently had a stubborn streak; Martha was fussy; Mary was impractical; and John the Baptist had interesting eating and clothing habits. You could probably find at least one idiosyncrasy in every biblical personality.

If God used imperfect people then, there's hope for us now. God can turn our weaknesses into strengths. This month we'll consider ways to cope creatively with those annoyances and eccentricities we all seem to have.

Lord, you create us with such interesting variations. Teach us to appreciate them in ourselves and in each other. Amen.

Talk It Over: *With kindness and thankfulness, discuss your idiosyncrasies with your partner.*

January 2 ~ No Fine Print

"I have come to call not the righteous but sinners to repentance."
—Luke 5:32

God's love for us, expressed so completely in Jesus Christ, is unconditional. There are no fine print, escape clauses, or exclusionary language. We are totally accepted, including our quirks and irritating habits. Jesus had a special affinity for persons who admitted their imperfections and expressed their need for his saving grace. He welcomed despised tax collectors, people with physical infirmities, noisy children, beggars, lepers, outcasts, wayward sons and daughters. Folks who thought they were perfect were the ones Jesus had difficulty reaching with his love.

When we behave self-righteously, we cut ourselves off from the fullness of Christ's redemptive, creative, and transforming power. When we focus on each other's irritating habits, we limit the flow of love between us and we may miss the depth of joy our relationships offer.

O Lord, as Jesus accepted persons who came to him honestly and openly, may we be receptive and compassionate to one another in all our dealings. Amen.

Talk It Over: *Using concrete examples, thank each other for ways your spouse may have recently expressed unconditional love.*

January 3 ~ Put the Sandpaper Away

This priceless treasure we hold . . . in a common earthenware jar—to show that the splendid power of it belongs to God and not to us.
—2 Corinthians 4:7 (JBP)

One of our favorite television programs is *Antiques Roadshow* on PBS. Hardly a show goes by without an expert appraiser explaining to someone, "If you hadn't refinished this furniture, it would be worth ten times more."

Our spirits are housed in clay pots, these human bodies, to remind us of our dependence upon God. Who we are inside, our hearts and minds and souls, are priceless treasures. They're our eternal heritage.

We need to put away that coarse sandpaper, that can of varnish and paint remover, and strive to see each other as God's beautiful originals. Outward signs of wear and tear only serve to add value to our lives. Those lumps and bumps help us more clearly show forth God's glory and grace.

O God, may we see each other as you see us: persons of infinite worth housed in common packages with plain wrapping. Amen.

Talk It Over: *Think of a challenge you've shared that has made you stronger and more loving as a couple.*

January 4 ~ Don't Keep Score

If you kept a record of our sins, who could escape being condemned? But you forgive us, so that we should reverently obey you.
—Psalm 130:3-4 (TEV)

We citizens of the modern world seem to enjoy keeping score: tallying our caloric intake, weighing ourselves every day, checking our investment portfolios, and keeping track of the latest sports scores. That's all well and good. But when we begin adding up and remembering every little wrong done to us, or keeping a journal account of our spouse's irritating habits, we've gone too far. Even the Almighty wipes our slate clean for the mistakes we've made, when we seek forgiveness.

It's important to balance our checkbook and keep records of taxes paid. Grocery lists are helpful. But when it comes to people's errors and idiosyncrasies, we should practice forgetfulness and cultivate a poor memory. It's God's way to live.

Patient God, may we embody your forgiving and forgetting nature in all our relationships. Amen.

Talk It Over: *Talk about your feelings when someone won't let you forget a past mistake you've made—and when you feel forgiven and are allowed freely to move forward.*

January 5 ~ God Is Realistic

Don't quarrel with anyone. Be at peace with everyone, just as much as possible.
—Romans 12:18 (TLB)

I'm thankful the scriptures understand how human we are. We're encouraged to live in harmony with others, but it comes with a codicil: "just as much as possible." That's not an escape clause, or an easy way out when the going is tough. Rather, God is realistic and understands the complexities of our human condition. It's important to know that being sweet or compassionate can't fix everything. Eccentricities can be charming. Idiosyncrasies are unique qualities that add energy and even good humor to relationships.

But God also gives us discernment to know when minor irritations move into the realm of major problems—when it's not just mere grouchiness but is actually abusive behavior. Our pragmatic God expects us to tolerate and even laugh about the small problems, but to seek help and safety about those that may be more serious.

O wise God, thank you for your gifts of honesty and courage. Amen.

Talk It Over: *Discuss the apostle Paul's words when he said that we should speak the truth in love (Ephesians 4:15a).*

January 6 ~ Don't Borrow Trouble

"Give your entire attention to what God is doing right now, and don't get worked up about what may or may not happen tomorrow."
—Matthew 6:34a (The Message)

When the two of us began this writing project, we decided to make lists of our own idiosyncrasies. At first, neither of us was convinced we had any. But after reflection, we both ended up with long litanies of rather strange behaviors. We then decided it was better not to see these complete listings. We trashed them because it's healthier to deal with irritating habits one at a time. God has promised to walk with us step by step.

Human frailties are so common and numerous their full weight could easily overwhelm us. When it comes to borrowing trouble, there's certainly no shortage of people willing to lend it. But there's a far better way:

God's way. "God will help you deal with whatever hard things come up when the time comes" (Matthew 6:34*b* The Message). Amen!

O God, this particular couple wouldn't have survived this long without your daily help. Amen.

Talk It Over: *Thank God together for being with you every moment of every day.*

January 7 ~ Content with Who You Are

"You're blessed when you're content with just who you are—no more, no less. That's the moment you find yourselves proud owners of everything that can't be bought."
—Matthew 5:3 (The Message)

We are more likely to be blessings to others when we feel good about ourselves. We also tend to notice each other's shortcomings more frequently when we're struggling with our own problems. There's much wisdom found in the Beatitudes of Jesus (Matthew 5:1-12). He was a great spiritual teacher in part because he was such an astute student of human nature. He knew then and still knows today what's in people's hearts.

If we're going to bless others, and especially our spouses, we must first come to terms with ourselves. Before we're able to share peace, we must experience it personally. When we find fault with people around us, it probably means we need to do some good old-fashioned soul searching.

Dearest Friend and Companion, remind us of how loved and blessed each of us is. Amen.

Talk It Over: *Reflect silently on today's text; then talk about how much contentment, or lack of it, each of you is experiencing.*

January 8 ~ Filled with Peace

Oh! May the God of green hope fill you up with joy, fill you up with peace, so that your believing lives . . . will brim over with hope!
—Romans 15:13 (The Message)

An effective method for getting rid of negative thoughts is to fill your mind with positive thoughts. When the God of green hope fills your soul with joy, sorrow will still visit but won't stay as long. If your spirit overflows with peace, there won't be much room for conflict or trouble. These latter realities will hang around, waiting for opportunities that never come as long as you're brimming over with hope.

Rather than listing irritating habits and complaining about how many each other has, how much better to review our pleasant qualities. When we're busy praising, we don't have time for finding fault. It's not a matter of whether we'll experience annoyances. We will. What counts is how we respond to them. By staying green and growing, we'll hardly even notice our partner's weaknesses.

Dear God, fill us to the brim with joy and peace and hope. Amen.

Talk It Over: *Find something green and growing in your spouse/your relationship; then discuss how it came to be that way.*

January 9 ~ The Lost Art of Listening

Guard your steps when you go to the house of God; to draw near to listen is better than the sacrifice offered by fools.

—*Ecclesiastes 5:1*

This verse from the Hebrew Bible is proper etiquette for worshipers in the Temple. They are advised to approach God with openness and a readiness to listen. It's wisdom that's equally applicable to our human relationships. How many times could we have avoided an argument by following this simple suggestion? If we were slower to talk and quicker to listen, wouldn't others feel more affirmed and valued?

We live in a society filled with noise: car stereos blaring, sirens wailing, television sets droning on, people yelling. We've learned to raise our voices in order to be heard above the constant cacophony. There's little we can do to turn down the volume of the world around us; but we can seek to become better listeners. Active listening is a rare gift. We might even call it a blessed idiosyncrasy.

18

O Still Small Voice, slow us down and hush our voices that we may listen. Amen.

Talk It Over: *Take turns listening to each other; no interruptions allowed.*

January 10 ~ An Inside Job

*God can do anything, you know—far more than you could ever imagine. . . .
He does it not by pushing us around but by working within us, his Spirit deeply
and gently within us.*

—*Ephesians 3:20 (The Message)*

The mighty God of the universe—who flung the stars to the farthest reaches, who brought forth massive mountains and created deep seas—this God of unlimited power chose to work "gently and deeply within" us human creatures. How much easier simply to bark out the orders and demand we obey; to give us no choice in the matter. But this God of profound love deals with us tenderly, desiring our love in return.

What is it about us finite, two-legged ones who walk upright on the earth's crust that causes us to push around others of our kind; to take offense at each other's differing ways; to grow impatient with idiosyncrasies so common to our race? Can you not hear God's chosen One saying, "Children, go thou and work deeply within"? (paraphrase of Luke 10:37*b*).

Gentle God, remind us that love is always an inside job. Amen.

Talk It Over: *Share experiences of times when God worked gently within you.*

January 11 ~ The Gift of Not Noticing

*[Love] is not irritable or touchy. It does not hold grudges and will hardly even
notice when others do it wrong.*

—*1 Corinthians 13:5c,d (TLB)*

Ellen has the gift of not noticing life's minor distractions. As the mother of a large family (six children), she managed to ignore the usual chaos,

19

responding as needed when trouble was brewing. Kel, however, never quite learned that skill and frequently got frustrated. Everyone survived, and all our offspring have become productive adults.

When it comes to the strange, annoying quirks of those we love, an efficient way of coping is simply not to notice. Even if we are aware of each other's imperfections, we certainly don't need to dwell on them. Love accomplishes what nothing else in the world ever can. It brings laughter out of tension, hope out of disappointment, and joy out of sorrow.

God, may your love fill us so completely that there'll be room left only for goodness and beauty. Amen.

Talk It Over: *If either of you is nursing a grudge, find a creative or humorous way to defuse it.*

January 12 ~ Fresh Every Day

The steadfast love of the LORD never ceases, his mercies never come to an end; they are new every morning; great is your faithfulness.
                                                                    —*Lamentations 3:22-23*

Some things are best when they're fresh: carrots just dug from the garden, chocolate chip cookies still warm from the oven, small children soft and damp from the bathtub, coffee brewed moments before the first sip. But far better than these is God's steadfast love and mercy, which are new every morning.

It's a good thing the Spirit of God gives us a fresh start each day. We grow weary from work, tired from worry, cranky from enduring the faults of others, and stale from failing to recharge our spiritual batteries. As the sun rises faithfully each morning, so does God's grace, all fresh and pure, delivered right to our doorstep.

O God of the ages and of eternity, your love is forever sweet and new. May it keep our spirits fresh every day, all day. Amen.

Talk It Over: *Discuss ways to handle times when your souls feel parched and dry. Share ways you've experienced God's refreshing power.*

20

January 13 ~ O Taste and See

O taste and see that the LORD is good.

—Psalm 34:8a

The old saw, "The way to a person's heart is through their stomach," is only partially correct. True, if you put a bowl of mint chocolate-chip ice cream in front of us, we'd purr like kittens. But our other senses work just as well. Following an animated discussion about tracking mud through the freshly mopped kitchen, or why the curling iron is still plugged in, a hug has marvelous healing powers. A bouquet of roses from the garden, with their beauty and fragrance, goes a long way toward solving arguments. The sound of gentle words such as "I'm sorry" or "I love you" can soften even the hardest hearts. Holding hands while going for a walk employs all our human senses, especially if you tuck a bit of food in your pocket.

The psalmist was wise. Tangible expressions of caring such as tasting and seeing both connect us to God and bring us together as a couple.

O You whose Word became flesh, touch us with your love. Amen.

Talk It Over: *Take turns expressing your caring in a small, tangible way.*

January 14 ~ Wisdom of the Ages

We can always "prove" that we are right, but is the Lord convinced?
—Proverbs 16:2 (TLB)

The writer of Proverbs, purportedly Solomon, was a person of wisdom. When it came to spouses, he knew a great deal. Some things simply can't be improved, so reflect on these gems from Proverbs as paraphrased in the *Living Bible.*

A soft answer turns away wrath, but harsh words cause quarrels. (15:1)
Gentle words cause life and health; griping brings discouragement. (15:4)
It is better to eat soup with someone you love than steak with someone you hate. (15:17)
Love forgets mistakes; nagging about them parts the best of friends. (17:9)

Any story sounds true until someone tells the other side and sets the record straight. (18:17)

It is hard to stop a quarrel once it starts, so don't let it begin. (17:14)

In the end, people appreciate frankness more than flattery. (28:23)

Thank you, God, for making your Word so plain. Teach us now to follow it. Amen.

Talk It Over: *Choose one of these proverbs and illustrate its truth from your experiences as individuals or a couple.*

January 15 ~ Listening to God When It Counts

Be sure you do not refuse to hear the voice of God!

—Hebrews 12:25 (JBP)

When we most need to hear a word from God, we are often least receptive to it. When we're upset or irritated, convinced we're right and the other person is wrong, or fussing that our carefully constructed world is falling apart, we aren't likely to pause long enough to listen to our spouse. We probably aren't going to stop and pray about it either. The two people offering this advice are among those who don't follow it. Confession is good for the soul, isn't it?

Calming down in a crisis isn't easy. Listening when we're upset or angry is tough. Yet if we don't, might we be refusing to hear the voice of God? Looking at it from this perspective, that next argument just might produce more light and less heat.

O God, help us keep our ears and hearts open even when our mouths are going fast and furious. Amen.

Talk It Over: *Think back to your last heated discussion. How good were your listening skills? Were you able to hear God's still small voice?*

January 16 ~ Prime Rib or Broccoli?

If you eat meat, eat it to the glory of God and thank God for prime rib; if you're a vegetarian, eat vegetables to the glory of God and thank God for broccoli.

—Romans 14:6 (The Message)

22

As parents of six children, we can tell you that no two have the same tastes. It was nearly impossible to prepare a meal they'd all eat. Without running a cafeteria, we tried not to force our food preferences on them. We wanted to honor each as an individual. It's the same with spouses. We hopefully share many common traits and interests, but we will surely have a number of significant differences, too.

In a marriage, one may be a morning person; the other definitely not. One turns the thermostat up; the other turns it down. One knows the precise bank balance; the other's not even sure where the bank is. God has gone to considerable effort to make each of us unique. The least we can do is honor that.

Lord, we thank you for creating us as individuals—well, most of the time. Amen.

Talk It Over: *Think of ways your differences can become strengths.*

January 17 ~ Let's Hear It for Courtesy

You should all be of one mind living like brothers [and sisters] with true love and sympathy for one another, generous and courteous at all times.
                                                             —1 Peter 3:8 (JBP)

The more closely we share life together, the more thoughtful and considerate we need to be. The old days are gone forever, when men spread their cloaks over mud puddles to help women cross the street. That's healthy for both sexes. Shared kindness, however, is a virtue that makes our lives together sweeter. Courtesy should always be in vogue. Generosity with our time and attention isn't just frosting on the cake. It's a concrete way of expressing caring. Love isn't love unless it's shared in down-to-earth ways.

Rather than pick at others' faults, how much better to compliment them for their strengths. Most courtesies are simple and easily accomplished—a door held open, dirty clothes picked up, dinner dishes cleared from the table. The hard part isn't in the doing; it's in the motivation.

Gentle Creator, inspire us to be courteous in all our relationships. Amen.

Talk It Over: *Recall a recent courteous act you gave to or received from your partner.*

January 18 ~ Life Is So Everyday

Whatever happens, make sure that your everyday life is worthy of the gospel of Christ.

—*Philippians 1:27 (JBP)*

Life is lived in the realm of "everyday." It's where work is done, tears are wiped, laughter is heard, and love is shared. It's where hearts are broken and mended. In marriage, it's what starts when the honeymoon is over. The old gospel hymn looks forward to the "sweet by and by." That's an important part of our faith. Until that day arrives, however, we must find ways to live in the challenging here and now. The goal is not merely to survive but to prosper, to find meaning and joy in each moment.

Relationships are nurtured on a daily basis. If we primarily focus on each other's failures, our joy will soon fade. We need to plan for the future yet live in the present. It's a delicate balancing act requiring God's constant guidance.

God of grace, nudge us when we need a push; hold us when we need a lap; and keep us alive each and every day. Amen.

Talk It Over: *Discuss the "places" in your day where you discover joy.*

January 19 ~ The Old Boomerang Effect

"Don't pick on people, jump on their failures, criticize their faults—unless, of course, you want the same treatment. That critical spirit has a way of boomeranging."

—*Matthew 7:1-2 (The Message)*

These are Jesus' words of wisdom from the Sermon on the Mount. Using contemporary language, they ring as true today as they did nearly two millennia ago. How we talk about and treat others does eventually "come home to roost." If we're bitter or grouchy, people will, at least, tiptoe around us and perhaps choose to avoid us entirely.

A critical spirit has a way of boomeranging. So, too, does an affirming spirit. There's obviously no guarantee if we act respectfully that others will return our goodness in kind. However, it's certainly worth a try. In the process, we may learn to be kinder to ourselves. When a hug is given, one is received; laughter is infectious; joy begets joy. Crankiness may boomerang, but loveliness multiplies.

God, may kindness rule our lives so we'll never have to duck when the boomerang of ill-temper returns to its sender. Amen.

Talk It Over: *Take turns overwhelming each other with as many kind words as possible.*

January 20 ~ Real Rest

"Are you tired? Worn out? Burned out on religion? Come to me. Get away with me and you'll recover your life. I'll show you how to take a real rest."
                                                          —Matthew 11:28 (The Message)

When the daily grind exhausts us, we're more likely to say things we don't mean and hurt people we love. We're not angry; we're bone weary. This verse reads like a travel agency advertisement. But this offer is the genuine article. It's free for the taking because it comes from our Savior.

Jesus recognized our human tendency to allow the constant pressures, demands, and stresses to get to us. We can't seem to recover by ourselves. They don't make bootstraps big enough. The answer is to take frequent emotional/spiritual retreats. They need not be lengthy or expensive—a few moments of quiet prayer in the car; a walk at dawn; arranging flowers from the garden; a warm bath; a good book.

Dear Jesus, thanks for your offer of real rest. Help us put it to use more often. Amen.

Talk It Over: *Give yourselves permission to rest for a moment. Be silent; close your eyes; breathe deeply; hold hands if you wish.*

January 21 ~ Got Character?

Suffering produces endurance, and endurance produces character, and character produces hope, and hope does not disappoint us.
                                                          —Romans 5:3b-5a

25

Achieving true Christian character takes time, a little testing, a pinch of hardship, a bit of struggle, and a ton of patience. Mix these together and you've got the ingredients for character. Along with it comes a recipe for hope that does not disappoint us. Sorry, there are no quick fixes, shortcuts, or instant results when it comes to character.

We all have habits that others find irritating. A few of our idiosyncrasies, no doubt, cause our friends some serious head scratching. Of course, their little quirks may do the same to us. But look at it this way: we're all in this character-building business together. Though it's not easy, take comfort that we're heading in the right direction.

Lord, may we move through times of testing and struggle by growing stronger, better, and closer to you. Amen.

Talk It Over: *The Greek word for character refers to the process of refining metal. Review experiences where you as a couple endured the "refiner's fire." Did you emerge from it stronger? Why or why not?*

January 22 ~ No Performances, Please

"Be especially careful when you are trying to be good so that you don't make a performance out of it. It might be good theater, but the God who made you won't be applauding."

—Matthew 6:1 *(The Message)*

There are well-meaning Christians who make careers out of being good. That is, they're righteously rigid, inflexible with others, and basically joyless about it. They may be judgmental with those they think aren't working as hard as they to achieve goodness. If you don't have clenched jaws and ever-present beads of perspiration, you must not be serious about this life of faith.

The One we seek to follow never made a performance out of being good. He was humble and always seemed to find a way to give others the credit. While the religious leaders of his day pranced around on stage, Jesus walked the dusty back roads teaching, healing, and loving. "Go and do likewise."

O God, since we all have a long journey ahead, help us serve you humbly and accept each other graciously. Amen.

Talk It Over: *Trace the highlights of your spiritual quest as a couple, noting the peaks and valleys.*

January 23 ~ Our Lives Count for Plenty

"Do you want to stand out? Then step down. Be a servant. If you puff yourself up, you'll get the wind knocked out of you. But if you're content to simply be yourself, your life will count for plenty."

—Matthew 23:11-12 (The Message)

We want our lives to count for something. Jesus' prescription, however, seems backward compared to prevailing definitions of success. He teaches that we win not by gaining but by giving, not by standing up but by stepping down. Pretending to be something we aren't or trying to camouflage our limitations doesn't cut it when it comes to God.

Once we've learned to accept ourselves as we are—weaknesses and strengths, irritating and lovely habits alike—we've taken a giant step toward making our lives count for plenty. That's a necessary prelude for receiving and using the gifts God has given us.

O Lord, don't let us get puffed up with ourselves. Fill our sails with the wind of your Spirit, and help us truly enjoy the journey. Amen.

Talk It Over: *Recall a time in your relationship as a couple when you stood out by stepping down.*

January 24 ~ Surrounded by Joy

Therefore, since we are surrounded by so great a cloud of witnesses, let us also lay aside every weight and the sin that clings so closely, and let us run with perseverance the race that is set before us.

—Hebrews 12:1

We're surrounded! Usually we're surrounded by noise, clutter, telephone solicitations, and vehicles during rush hour. In this case, we're encircled by the saints of God. What a joyful experience! We draw inspiration and strength from those dear souls who've come before us, who know exactly what we're going through. Many we may have known and loved; others are persons we never had the privilege of meeting.

This great cloud of witnesses is God's gift to the community of faith. What comfort it brings to know in our struggles, tensions, and even in our minor squabbles, that we are not alone. God's saints surround us with understanding and love.

Encompassed about by your saints, O God, may we look always to Jesus, the pioneer and perfecter of our faith. Amen.

Talk It Over: *With thanksgiving, name persons you've loved and admired deeply who are surely part of your cloud of witnesses.*

January 25 ~ Tend to Your Knitting

So tend to your own knitting. You've got your hands full just taking care of your own life before God.

—Romans 14:12 (The Message)

In today's vernacular, we might say, "Get a life." Relationships go better when partners criticize less and do their own "knitting"—that is, take care of their own daily duties. To nag those closest to us is counterproductive, always. Our task is to meet our own responsibilities faithfully and pleasantly, and to give others the space to fulfill theirs. We all experience frequent lapses. After all, we are human.

In knitting, mistakes are best caught early and attended to quickly. The longer one waits, the more there'll be to undo. So it is with couples. When the relationship gets balled up, don't wait until it's hopelessly tangled. Attend to the problem, then get on knitting your lives together with God and each another. You'll end up with a beautiful tapestry of love.

You who knit us together before birth, give us patience with each other as we continue the good work you began. Amen.

28

Talk It Over: Discuss how it feels when someone else tries to tend to your "knitting."

January 26 ~ In Tune with Each Other

Let the peace of Christ keep you in tune with each other, in step with each other. None of this going off and doing your own thing.
—Colossians 3:15 (The Message)

Anybody who's attended a grade school orchestra concert knows something about dissonance. The children are just beginners, and the listeners are mostly family members who dearly love them. But out of tune is still out of tune. A great deal of practice will help those young violin and clarinet players.

As a couple, being out of harmony with each other isn't a one-time performance. It's a 24/7 proposition. Staying in tune involves good communication skills. We cannot continue to make beautiful music unless there's a great deal of listening, forgiveness, and patience. And above all else, it depends on both partners having regularly scheduled "tune-ups" with God.

Gracious One, tune our hearts to sing your praises so that we may ever be in harmony with you and with each other. Amen.

Talk It Over: List several ways you stay in tune with each other. How do you handle any discordant notes between you?

January 27 ~ Something Greater

"I tell you, something greater than the temple is here. . . . Something greater than Jonah is here! . . . Something greater than Solomon is here!"
—Matthew 12:6, 41c, 42c

When we hold a newborn child in our arms, gaze into a brilliant night sky, or experience music that gives us goose bumps, we're in the presence of something greater than we are. What delight to be swept up in the majesty of God. It lifts us above the trenches of faith where our daily lives are so often lived.

Basking in God's glory helps put our worries and disappointments in perspective. The Light of the World doesn't remove those daily irritations, but fills us with grace so they really don't matter anymore. Something greater than our personal struggles is here. Something greater than our human institutions is here. Something greater than the world's travail is here. What is there left to say but "Hallelujah"?

When we are trapped by our problems, O God, overwhelm us with your beauty, bowl us over with your joy, and inundate us with your love. Amen.

Talk It Over: *List and celebrate those things that take your breath away.*

January 28 ~ Pray About Everything

Don't worry about anything; instead, pray about everything; tell God your needs and don't forget to thank Him for His answers.
—Philippians 4:6 (TLB)

Don't stew and fret: pray. Don't nag or scold: pray. Prayer should be our first line of defense rather than our last resort. God creates us as unique individuals, complete with fascinating quirks, eccentricities, and all kinds of peculiar mannerisms. It may be part of God's plan to keep us growing spiritually and to test our faith.

Prayer is the primary way of connecting to our Creator. Prayers don't have to be lengthy. For busy people, short and direct are best. When you're on the job, try "OTJ" prayers. When you feel an argument coming, pause and offer a quick prayer of thanksgiving for your spouse. When there's more month than money, more tasks than clock, more responsibilities than energy, pray for strength. Don't tune God out; tune God in.

Thank you, Lord, for inviting us to pray about anything and everything. Amen.

Talk It Over: *Pray together for your relationship either silently, or if you're comfortable, aloud. Don't hurry; savor the moment.*

January 29 ~ Straight for the Goal

I leave the past behind and with hands outstretched to whatever lies ahead I go straight for the goal—my reward the honor of my high calling by God in Christ Jesus.

—Philippians 3:13b-14 (JBP)

It's hard to leave the past behind, both for positive and negative reasons. Letting go of old joys and hurts is difficult. But it's necessary in order to embrace the present and move ahead. It's not how fast we move; it's the direction we're going. This verse leaves no doubt about our destination— going straight for the goal of following Christ.

It's nearly impossible to move forward if you keep looking back. Driving down a busy street while focused on the rearview mirror is dangerous. Jesus used an image of plowing crooked furrows while staring over your shoulder. Dwelling on the past will slow or halt your emotional and spiritual growth as a couple.

By forgetting ancient mistakes and accomplishments, we're set free to move forward with renewed enthusiasm.

God, grant us cherished memories of the past, confidence in the present, and courage to move toward the future. Amen.

Talk It Over: *Discuss this familiar saying: "Let go; let God."*

January 30 ~ Revel in God

Celebrate God all day, every day. I mean, revel *in him!*

—Philippians 4:4 (The Message)

We twenty-first-century citizens often act as though celebrations are nothing but fun and games. In truth, they're significant statements that life is precious, community is wonderful, and God is good. This doesn't mean we never experience times of depression, disappointment, or sorrow. But even when life is tough, there are still ample reasons to rejoice. God's Spirit is our constant companion. God's wisdom is always available. God's love is ours forever.

31

We're not talking about elaborate gatherings or huge parties. Reveling in God can be done quietly as a couple—lighting a candle and remembering Christ, who is the light of the world; breaking bread together with a lunch of peanut butter and jelly sandwiches; blowing soap bubbles into the wind; laughing and singing and praying together. Celebrating God with each other will surely lift our spirits and put joy in our hearts.

O God, teach us to rejoice and celebrate life even as your Son, Jesus, did. Amen.

Talk It Over: *Recall the most memorable, healing, or joyful celebrations you've experienced in your life together.*

January 31 ~ Life Depends on It

Go after a life of love as if your life depended on it—because it does.
—1 Corinthians 14:1a (The Message)

Love isn't an added attraction; it's the main feature. Love isn't gravy; it's meat and potatoes. Love isn't fluff; it's substance, the very heart of life. We need to receive and share it with all our being. When other persons are on their best behavior, go after love. When they're irritating and unlovable, go after love. Love takes the initiative, not waiting for the other to make the first move. Go after love in the short term and over the long haul.

It's true. Our lives depend on love. We're not talking only about eternity. Our goal is to fill every moment of every day with love. God, the great lover of the cosmos, is realistic and knows well our human limitations; yet God calls us to be forever caring and compassionate. Don't wait for love. Go for it!

God, you created us in your image. Since you are love, then so are we. Amen!

Talk It Over: *Take turns reading aloud 1 Corinthians 13:4-7, if possible from several different translations. Share your insights.*

February

THE POWER OF COMMUNICATION

Warren and Mary Ebinger

February 1 ~ The Words You Speak

Reckless words pierce like a sword.

—*Proverbs 12:18a (NIV)*

"Sticks and stones may break my bones, but words can never hurt me." Perhaps you remember saying this as a child, or have heard it said to you. Of course, it is not true. Words sometimes hurt more than we realize. Both your choice of words and the emotion with which you speak them can be either hurtful or helpful. That's why communication can either "make or break" a marriage. Perhaps nothing has more power in your marriage relationship than the way in which you communicate with each other. This month we'll consider some basic and yet extremely effective ways to improve your communication and, therefore, your marriage.

One of the simplest ways to begin improving your communication is simply to be more careful in your conversations with each other, not allowing words or expressions to get out of control. Many couples fail to realize that verbal abuse is as hurtful psychologically as physical abuse is to the body. In contrast, kind words spoken lovingly can make an amazing difference in how one feels and can have healing power.

God of love and kindness, help us share words with each other that are loving and kind, and forgive us for the times when our words have hurt each other. Amen.

33

Talk It Over: For a few moments, reflect together on times when words you spoke to each other may have hurt, sometimes without you realizing it. What can you do to change your choice of words or the way you speak to each other?

February 2 ~ Happy Talk

A happy heart makes the face cheerful, but heartache crushes the spirit.
> —*Proverbs 15:13 (NIV)*

Someone who is happy shows a cheerful face. One who acts happy often becomes happy in the process. The Old Testament mentions the words *happy* and *cheerful.* Jesus tells us not to "be anxious" in his Sermon on the Mount, and "blessed" is sometimes interpreted as "happy."

One night Doug asked Ellen, "What was the happiest part of today?"

"I was angry most of the day. I can't think of anything," Ellen replied irritably.

"I know, but this morning we saw tiny green tomatoes in our garden and the bright yellow and purple pansies."

"I liked that," Ellen admitted, "and when you suggested fast food after my busy day at work."

No matter what type of day we have, there is always something good if we try to find it.

Lord, help us as a couple to be happy, and to make an effort even when it may be difficult. Amen.

Talk It Over: At the end of the day, take turns telling about the happiest part of your day. Try this several times a week, even on difficult days. It can become a helpful practice in your life.

February 3 ~ Speaking with Love

If I speak in the tongues of mortals and of angels, but do not have love, I am a noisy gong or a clanging cymbal.
> —*1 Corinthians 13:1*

Our very voices—the tone, level, pitch, intensity—often say more than the words we speak. That is why the apostle Paul urges us to be careful how we talk to each other. Without love in our voices, they become merely noise, a clanging sound, causing stress and creating a barrier to good communication. Have you both experienced this sometimes?

The conversations we have, whether a few minutes or an hour, reflect our feelings inside. When love is at the center of our feelings, the words we speak are translated to our partner in a way that results in a spirit of helpful sharing, allowing us to make the best decisions and understandings possible, whatever the subject of conversation.

Dear God, your Son spoke in words of love and called us to do so. May this be our goal today. Amen.

Talk It Over: *Check each other's voice in this way. Share one sentence relating to something you would like your partner to do for you. First speak without love in your voice; then say the same sentence with love. Can you hear the difference?*

February 4 ~ Compliments

Her children rise up and call her happy; her husband too, and he praises her.
—Proverbs 31:28

Complimenting your spouse is the best "reward" you can give for what he or she does. We easily give compliments to those with whom we work, to our neighbors, and to friends; yet often we take those closest to us for granted. One way to change this pattern is to think of at least one thing each day you can say in a complimentary way to your partner. Sometimes you might want to express this compliment in the form of a telephone call or a note left on the kitchen counter or an e-mail message. Remember, however, that compliments should be genuine and sincere, not superficial or artificial. If you give the compliment to your spouse face-to-face, offering a hug or kiss afterward is like icing on the cake. Sharing such a compliment when children or relatives are present can mean even more. It is a way to say, "Thank you," and "I love you" at the same time.

Dear God, may we always be aware of ways we can express our appreciation to each other with loving words. Amen.

February 5 ~ Listening to Each Other

Listen, for I have worthy things to say.

—Proverbs 8:6a

Are you listening to me?

We often ask this when our spouses seem preoccupied, respond routinely, or begin speaking before really hearing what is being said. Answering before listening is foolish, but it is also one of the common ways that communication breaks down and misunderstandings occur.

One way of dealing with this is called "active listening." Here's how it works. Your partner might say, "I thought we might drop Carrie off at church for choir at 7:00; then we could go to the Simpson's for the Dessert Fellowship and she could ride home with Jan." The other might then say, "Are you saying that . . . (repeat exactly what the first said)? Is that right?" Practicing this can lead to good listening patterns.

Lord, you hear all that we say to you. Help us listen to what we're saying to each other. Amen.

Talk It Over: Take a few minutes to try active listening. Try this several times during the day. Let it become a habit in your daily conversations.

February 6 ~ Finding the Way

It is not good to have zeal without knowledge, nor to be hasty and miss the way.
—Proverbs 19:2 (NIV)

"We've been driving for three hours. Shouldn't we be there by now?"

"I'm sure we're on the right road. It's just taking a little longer than I thought."

"We've never come this way before. Did you look at the map?"

"Who needs a map? Charlie gave me good directions on the phone for a shortcut."

"I can't believe this is happening. You never look at a map! Next time I'm going to drive!"

"You got us lost the last trip we took. You were driving so fast you missed the turn off the interstate. Another time you were actually looking at the map while driving. We almost ran off the road! Remember that?"

Does any of this sound familiar? Unfortunately, many couples argue in the car—as well as in other places—because of carelessness or impatience. Knowing the way is more important than getting to our "destination" in a hurry. It's true with life, too. We need a map before going off in all directions.

Thank you, God, for your Word, which shows us the way, and for your Son who is the Way, the Truth, and the Life. Amen.

Talk It Over: *Reflect together on a time when you were really lost. How did you find the way? Is there any need for direction right now in your life?*

February 7 ~ Notes of Love

And this is his command: to believe in the name of his Son, Jesus, and to love one another as he commanded us.
—1 John 3:23 (NIV)

Many letters in the Bible talk about love—generally about everyone "loving one another." The Bible also emphasizes love between a man and a woman. At times, we show more loving care to others than we do to our spouses, yet the commandment holds true for marriage.

When was the last time you wrote a note to express your love for your spouse? It's a great way to nurture your marriage. Adapt some great passages of Elizabeth Barrett Browning, Shakespeare, or Kahlil Gibran. Even Napoleon and King Henry VIII wrote beautiful love letters. Be creative in your "delivery"—a handwritten letter on beautiful stationery or a note left in a lunch bag, in the car, or on his or her pillow. Or write a poem titled "Why I Love You" or "Ten Reasons Why I Married You." Make it special by writing in calligraphy, rolling it as a scroll, and tying it with ribbon. Though it takes only moments to do, this special gift will be cherished through the years.

Lord, help us be more intentional about writing letters of love as well as speaking words of love.

Talk It Over: *Talk about love letters or notes you have given each other in the past. Surprise each other with one this week!*

February 8 ~ Smile

"Love each other as I have loved you."

—John 15:12 (NIV)

A couple who visited Calcutta asked Mother Teresa what they could do to make their lives better. She told them simply to smile at each other. That, she said, would help them have greater love for each other (from *A Gift From God,* Mother Teresa as quoted in *A Guide to Prayer for Ministers and Other Servants,* Reuben P. Job and Norman Shawchuck, The Upper Room, Nashville, Tennessee, 1983, p. 171).

Did you ever notice that when you smile at a sales clerk, you usually get a smile back; talking to a baby frequently causes smiles and gurgling; and saying "Excuse me" when you accidentally bump into a stranger often brings the friendly response, "That's all right"?

Do you smile more at people at work and total strangers yet not at those you love? A smile is a way to communicate your love. Do you need to practice more?

Lord, help us be kind and show our love to each other with smiles, gentle words, and kind deeds.

Talk It Over: *Talk about using some silent signal, such as touching the corner of your mouth, whenever you feel a need for a smile from your spouse.*

February 9 ~ Patience

Love is patient, love is kind.

—1 Corinthians 13:4 (NIV)

Patience is defined as a gift of the Spirit. Are you patient in relating to each other? Complex schedules cram too much into too short a time and may lead to questions and comments such as, "Where have you been? You said you'd be home an hour ago!" "Aren't you ready yet? We're going to be late!" "When are you going to get that faucet fixed? It has been dripping for a month!"

Recognize that there are often valid reasons for delays and unfinished tasks, and practice patience. Can you share some responsibilities, rather than constantly complain? Perhaps you can make changes in your schedules or revise your expectations.

Ask God to help you be patient, but don't expect results immediately! Be patient and kind to each other.

Lord of life and love, when we become impatient with each other, help us remember that true love is patient and kind.

Talk It Over: *Take time now or later to role-play a situation from the past in which one or both of you were impatient. Reverse roles. Discuss how your responses could have been different.*

February 10 ~ Always and Never

Instead, speaking the truth in love, we will in all things grow up into him who is the Head, that is, Christ.
—*Ephesians 4:15 (NIV)*

"Always" and "never" may get mixed into your conversations when you are upset with each other. It happens almost automatically. Yet, it is completely unfair to generalize in this way. Perhaps you have found yourself saying, "You are always late," or "You are never on time." These tend to put the other person down by suggesting a hopeless pattern of poor time management or an attitude of not caring.

"Speaking the truth in love" means avoiding the blaming words and trying to work out a plan for helping the situation. That is love. Remember that no one is beyond change. Speaking the truth in love gives both of you the opportunity to change your own patterns and to be understanding when the other is caught by the pressure of time.

Lord, help us today to speak the truth about feelings or concerns in love rather than in harshness and blame. Amen.

Talk It Over: *Spend a few minutes now or later in the day reviewing the ways you can speak more kindly in a constructive rather than destructive critique of each other's actions. Then agree to be willing to look and listen for the words "always" or "never" in your comments to each other. You could even treat it as a game.*

February 11 ~ Let It Go

But this one thing I do: forgetting what lies behind and straining forward to what lies ahead, I press on toward the goal.

—Philippians 3:13-14

Sometimes we carry unkind words or hurt feelings from the past into the present. It's like excess baggage. This can make us heavy in heart and mind. Just as the apostle Paul recognized that he had to let go of his past (which was not very pleasant to recall), so also must we. We must recognize unhappy experiences for what they were, and then let them go.

Letting go isn't easy. You'll need each other's caring support. First, talk about the when, why, and where of the hurt, and then, through forgiving and accepting forgiveness, place the past where it should be—in the past. If the hurt relates to others in the past, determine if anything needs to be said or done, and then let it go.

Too much awaits you today and tomorrow to let the past cloud the sky of the future.

God of all time, forgive us when we allow past experiences to prevent possibilities of joy and the fullness of love here and now. Amen.

Talk It Over: *Discuss one thing from your past—your past individually or as a couple—that needs to be erased from the present.*

February 12 ~ Bills to Pay

Let no debt remain outstanding, except the continuing debt to love one another.

—Romans 13:8 (NIV)

"How in the world did our credit card balance get so high?"

"I haven't used it for anything but groceries and incidentals. It's all there on the monthly statement. Check it out for yourself."

"Some of your incidentals must have really added up! Did we need all these?"

"You should talk! What about those tickets you charged for that football game?"

When we charge too much on credit cards or spend too much in any other way, it causes friction and resentment, as well as difficulty in paying off remaining balances.

Look at accumulated bills together. Most people find that a budget is the only way to manage money. If you have not worked out a budget, try it.

O God, we know you meet our needs in ways beyond what we deserve. Help us plan carefully so we may meet the financial needs of our family and do it with love. Amen.

Talk It Over: *Take a few moments right now to set a time when you can look over your income and expenditures for an average month. Agree that this will be a priority. Let go of any blame or anger you may have.*

February 13 ~ The Presence of the Spirit

"Love your neighbor as yourself."

—*Matthew 19:19 (NIV)*

We need loving communication with God and others. What value is it if we tell God of our thanks and love in our morning prayers and fail to give this to others, especially our loved ones? God intends us to love other people—*as we love ourselves.*

God made us—a remarkable creation. Yet, as counselors, we often hear, "I love my family, but I don't like myself." Is this what God wants? Why are we dissatisfied with ourselves? What do we need to change? Get rid of guilt? Ask forgiveness? Do we need to forgive ourselves? Sometimes it is more difficult to love ourselves than to love others. But to truly love others, we must respect ourselves, too.

The Holy Spirit within us can fill us with love for others and ourselves. Then we must communicate this love.

41

Lord, come fill us with your love and help us love others as ourselves in loving communication.

Talk It Over: *Talk about any difficulty you might have loving yourselves and how you can truly have the spirit of love, especially with those who are hard to love.*

February 14 ~ Be Mine

My lover is mine and I am his [or hers].

—Song of Songs 2:16 (NIV)

Valentine's Day: a time to say or send messages of love to each other—words sometimes accompanied by flowers, chocolates, hearts made of all kinds of material.

On our bathroom mirror is a stuffed red heart superimposed on a larger red heart, with this message at the center: "Be Mine." It has been there for a year—since last Valentine's Day. Neither one of us has even talked about moving it. Guests have come and gone, but the hearts stay.

"Be Mine" must never be a selfish claim on the other, but a personal interpretation of Jesus' words to truly love each other—to communicate our feelings fully. Let your life reflect the love you have for each other, and tell it in words or other expression on this Valentine's Day. Then you will be your true self.

Thank you, God, for the privilege of sharing life so intimately with each other that the word mine *becomes both of us. Amen.*

Talk It Over: *Plan a candlelight dinner at home or at a cozy restaurant. If you have children, arrange for a baby-sitter. As you enjoy the meal, tell each other how much more you enjoy the feeling of belonging to the other—"the two becoming one."*

February 15 ~ Plan Together

But the married man is anxious about the affairs of the world, how to please his wife, and his interests are divided.

—1 Corinthians 7:33-34a

There's a romantic song that ends, "We'll always be together." Yet the hectic pace of life often leaves little time for couples to be together—alone.

One husband always wanted his wife to go bicycling with him. "Why should I go with him? I like to do other things," she would say. She finally went a short way with him on her bicycle one day, and they ended up taking longer, fun trips together. Another husband took his wife on some business trips. They enjoyed exploring different places together. Another couple in their seventies decided to go on a hot-air balloon trip. You might enjoy taking classes together in cooking, dancing, or yoga; or simply reading a book together. The possibilities are endless. Be creative!

Lord, a man and a woman are to be together. Help us look at our time together more creatively. Amen.

Talk It Over: *Brainstorm things you can do together. Try some different things, even if one of you is more excited about an idea than the other, and decide to enjoy each thing you do together.*

February 16 ~ Eat Together

Jesus said to them, "Come and have breakfast."
—John 21:12 (NIV)

Jesus liked to eat—at a wedding; with Zachaeaus; with his friends Mary, Martha, and Lazarus; with his disciples. It is important to eat together as a family when there are children. However, couples need to schedule special times when they can plan to have a meal alone.

Sharing food brings you together. It may be soup and sandwiches at home for lunch, a carefully packed picnic lunch in the park, an inexpensive meal from a drive-in on a busy night, a romantic candlelit dinner prepared at home, or a beautiful expensive restaurant. It matters not.

What does matter is that you enjoy the food and share together the events of the day, or words of love in between the simplest of food, and know this a time to cherish together. This can be communication at its best.

Lord, you liked to eat with your friends; help us enjoy the simplest of meals with your spirit with us. Amen.

Talk It Over: Make a list of places and times where you can share a meal alone together. Then pencil in some "dates" on your calendar. Arrange for childcare if necessary. Consider having "faith talks" or a devotional time together during or after your meal.

February 17 ~ Hidden Fears

Perfect love drives out fear.

—1 John 4:18 (NIV)

Ever since we were children, we have experienced fears. Uncertainties and anxieties of life affect us also as adults. Sometimes we hide these fears inside. We do not want to reveal or discuss them. However, talking about fears—dealing with them honestly and openly—is important to your marriage.

Tell each other what you fear. Why are you afraid? What can you do about it? Do not simply dismiss your partner's fear as "silly." Some fears go back to childhood. Allow time to share how you feel. Be understanding as you listen. In addition to sharing with each other, you may want to talk about certain fears with your pastor or a counselor.

Remember, fears may affect your relationship without you realizing it. This is why it is so important for you to tell each other about your fears.

Dear God, help us to remember Jesus' words about "not being afraid" and to trust you to help us work through any fear. Amen.

Talk It Over: Each of you take a few moments to list one concern or fear you have at the present time. Then arrange a time to discuss these fears soon. Remember that God can help you work through whatever you fear.

February 18 ~ I Told You So!

[Love] does not rejoice at wrong, but rejoices in the right.

—1 Corinthians 13:6 (RSV)

We are tempted to say these words when poor decisions were made or too much money was spent without each other's consent. The decision or expenditure brings both disappointment and resentment. "I told you so!" we say, placing blame.

Some people almost delight in saying, "I told you so!" as if proving a point. The apostle Paul tells the Christians in Corinth, however, that love does not follow such a pattern of scolding or blaming. Rather, there is a need for understanding and caring in the midst of disappointment. Instead we might say, "I'm sorry it turned out this way. What can we do about it?"

Dear God, forgive us when a decision causes regrets. Help us find ways to deal with it, rather than condemning what was done. Grant us your peace. Amen.

Talk It Over: *Think together and share one such instance when you could have responded in a better way than you did. How would you express yourself now?*

February 19 ~ I'm Sorry

Be kind to one another, tenderhearted, forgiving one another, as God in Christ has forgiven you.

—Ephesians 4:32

"I'm sorry" are two very important words in any relationship, especially the marriage relationship. These words are often hard to say, however, because of feelings that keep us from recognizing some fault we have— from wanting one's own way to saying words that hurt deeply. Being sorry, however, is not merely saying two words. It is doing something about the wrong. It is making it right, if possible, or determining not to repeat it.

Sometimes you may say, "I'm sorry" casually, without really meaning it. It then becomes simply punctuation in the middle of a sentence, with little intention to do something about it. Being sorry means asking for forgiveness. In marriage, this is always a two-way street, requiring the injured partner to say, "I forgive you" in return. Only then can you meet at the intersection of words and feelings and restore love in the process.

Dear God, help us to be truly sorry when we have hurt the one we love, and help us to say it. Amen.

Talk It Over: Share a time when each of you was truly sorry and recall the difference it made when your spouse forgave you.

February 20 ~ Saying Thank You

Give thanks in all circumstances, for this is God's will for you in Christ Jesus.
—1 Thessalonians 5:18 (NIV)

Saying thank you to God is something we are expected to do. Saying thank you to each other is not always expected and often is considered unnecessary in our homes. Yet it is a response that means so much if said with genuine meaning after something good has been done or said.

We politely say thank you to others in the office, at church, or even at the checkout counter, but unfortunately, we often forget to say thank you to each other. Of course, saying thank you in a sarcastic or hurtful way after someone has done something displeasing to you is obviously *not* a good idea. Yet, an appropriate thank you can make such a difference. Speaking our thanks—to God and to each other—is what Christ taught us to do.

God of every good gift, thank you for this day. Help us express thanks to each other more often, because this is what it means to have a thankful heart. Amen.

Talk It Over: Tell about some of the times when you were especially thankful for something your partner did or said. Did you say thank you?

February 21 ~ First Things First

"Seek first his kingdom and his righteousness, and all these things will be given to you as well."
—Matthew 6:33 (NIV)

One of the toughest tasks is not doing the things you think have to be done but, instead, waiting to talk together about priorities and agree on them. How do we really know what God wants us to be doing as the highest priority—especially when so many of our commitments are on a fixed schedule of payments, time, and job responsibilities? Perhaps it would be helpful to list your priorities. Then you can decide what changes need to be made. Ask God, "How can we put your kingdom first with all these responsibilities?" Be open to God's guidance.

Sometimes this can lead to major disagreements. Who is in charge anyway? Can God actually grant us the other things we need if we put his ideas and Jesus' teachings first? Maybe we haven't really tried to do it that way. Is this the message God has for this very day?

Dear God, this is tough. Help us to understand what it means to seek you first and to listen to you—not only to each other. Amen.

Talk It Over: *Discuss briefly your priorities and how God may be calling you to change them. Remember to respect each other's viewpoints.*

February 22 ~ Our Children

Train children in the right way, and when old, they will not stray.
—Proverbs 22:6

Children are a gift from God and a challenge to care for, guide, train, and send forth. If you have children now, or hope to be parents someday, or are reaching out in love in some way to other children, there are guidelines from God's Word to help you.

Couples often disagree about house rules, discipline, curfews, and privileges versus responsibilities of children at different ages and stages. If you are struggling with opposing views about raising children or relating to children who have left the nest or returned, be sure to talk about them. Do not allow children of any age to place you in a position of taking sides or favoring one over another. Most important, let your love for them be genuine. This requires "modeling love" on the part of both of you.

God, you are our parent. We are your children. Help us express unconditional love to our children just as you care for us. Amen.

Talk It Over: *What is one concern you have in relating to your children or those*

in the larger circle of family and friends? How can you respond together to con-
vey love and understanding?

February 23 ~ Our Parents

"You know the commandments . . . honor your father and mother."
—Mark 10:19 (NIV)

"Why do we have to go see your mother every Sunday afternoon?"

"Because she's lonely ever since my dad died last year."

"What about *my* dad? He's been alone for five years now."

"We've never been close to your dad. He doesn't take any interest in our children, and besides, he has a lot of friends in Toledo."

Have you ever disagreed about matters related to in-laws and other family members? Though every couple's family dynamics are different, there are always issues and concerns that need to be considered. This involves time and, in some cases, financial planning for elderly parents.

It is important to talk about options and to stay open to each other's feelings. There are no easy answers. Remember, however, to focus on your immediate family—whether there's just the two of you or children as well—knowing there will be enough love to go beyond!

Thank you, God, for our parents and the love they have given us. Show us the way to honor them—whether they are living in the present or only in our memories. Amen.

Talk It Over: *Discuss how you can keep contact with your parents and other relatives. Be creative. Talk about how you can express love to them and receive love from them.*

February 24 ~ There's No Time

There is a time for everything, and a season for every activity under heaven.
—Ecclesiastes 3:1 (NIV)

Do you ever wonder if there's really enough time for everything that has to be done? Many couples are caught in a time bind that seems to allow no opportunity to really talk together except about immediate concerns of the day. Work schedules, family responsibilities, and church or community commitments seem to leave little to no time to talk about things of the heart.

What can we do about it? Even those couples who lead the busiest lives somehow find time to talk together if they see this as a high priority. Yet it is so common for most of us to slip into routine patterns that use up all the available time. This sometimes includes long hours at the computer or even in front of the television.

The key to finding the time is in your hands, and it can open new doors to understanding and love.

Thank you, God, for each day—for twenty-four hours to spend. Help us find time within these hours to talk together and to talk with you. Amen.

Talk It Over: *Take a few minutes now to set a time when you will reserve thirty minutes to talk all by yourselves. Adjust this time frame if necessary, but agree that it will happen.*

February 25 ~ A Time to Laugh

[There is] a time to weep and a time to laugh.

—Ecclesiastes 3:4 (NIV)

Taking ourselves too seriously diminishes the joy and fun of marriage. There may be serious concerns that face us, some with deadlines, yet there is such a need for laughter in the midst of everything else—often as a release of the tensions of the day. Laughter has been called "good medicine for the soul." It can be a source of communication all its own.

Mornings may not be a time you laugh, although some studies show that fifteen minutes of laughter are as beneficial as thirty minutes of calisthenics. Joy and laughter are closely intertwined. Weeping may bind us together, too, but laughter sets us free, for the moment, from sadness. As the psalmist has written, "Weeping may remain for a night, but rejoicing comes in the morning" (Psalm 30:5b NIV). Let there be laughter!

49

O God, you must have a great sense of humor as you observe the comedy of life. Therefore, we ask you to help us see the lighter side, to laugh a little, and to love a lot. Amen.

Talk It Over: *What can you laugh about? Tell a quick story or read a favorite comic strip. Call each other sometime today to tell something funny that happened.*

February 26 ~ When It's Hard to Pray

"Bless those who curse you, pray for those who mistreat you."

—*Luke 6:28 (NIV)*

"I'm so mad at my manager! Just because I was late a few times, he took away my overtime pay, and you should have heard what he called me!"

"That's not right! Is there anything you can do to change his mind?"

"Maybe I'll just quit. He's always treated me this way!"

"You can't do that. We need the money! Maybe we should pray for him."

"Are you serious? How can I pray for that guy? You always think prayer is the answer! Do you really believe God cares about this?"

"Of course I do. First, I think you should pray for yourself. Ask God to show you what to do and what to say."

"You don't know what he's like! How can you ask me to pray for him?"

Have you had a conversation along these lines? Prayer really does work. It's the highest form of communication.

Dear God, help us remember to turn to you in tough times. Amen.

Talk It Over: *Share together a time you found help in dealing with difficult people through prayer. Is there a similar concern facing you now?*

February 27 ~ Sad Times

Jesus wept.

—*John 11:35 (NIV)*

50

For better, for worse; in sickness and in health—these words were part of your wedding vows. Every marriage has its share of sadness, whether it's in relation to grieving the loss of parents or others, moving or saying good-bye to friends, or dealing with sickness or other hardships.

One couple, before they married, had a difficult time talking about the death of the man's sister. "If we can't talk about this now, how are we going to share anything similar to this once we are married?" they asked us one day in a counseling session. Both of them knew that sadness and sickness would come. Finally, they broke down with tears and talked about their great loss.

Some years later, the couple told us that this particular crisis brought them closer together and made them better able to face the difficult times in their lives.

Joy and sorrow are part of every life. You need a strong marriage in order to share both the happy and the sad times.

Lord, you had happy times, but you also had sad times in your life. We thank you that you were triumphant. Help us face troubled times with courage and be thankful for joyful times. Amen.

Talk It Over: *If you have already had sad or tragic times in your marriage, how have you faced them? What, if anything, would you do differently? Share how you will cope with loss, death, or other difficult challenges in the future.*

February 28 ~ Tomorrow

"Who of you by worrying can add a single hour to his life?"
                                        —Matthew 6:27 (NIV)

There is a difference between worrying about tomorrow and planning for tomorrow. We make schedules for the day and special times, and this is good—unless we tend to worry about it.

A wife was diagnosed with a rare disease, and she and her husband talked about how difficult it was to realize they would have a shorter time together than they had thought. They felt sad, but then they began to plan what they wanted to do together in the time that was left. They brainstormed and came up with a long list, such as enjoying flowers and plants, taking a hot-air balloon trip, playing their favorite games, and eating more chocolate. Some were realistic. Some were dreams. Instead of worrying about the future, they changed their outlook to make it a creative time together.

What do you worry about? Is it important? Can you do something about it?

Lord, help us not to worry but to live each moment with you in our plans. Amen.

Talk It Over: *Do you worry unnecessarily? Share valid concerns and those you can eliminate. Make lists separately of all you want to do in your lifetime and then discuss which things are possible.*

February 29 ~ Remembering

I thank my God every time I remember you.
—Philippians 1:3 (NIV)

Looking back at life experiences brings into focus our memories of good times and not-so-good times. Pausing to remember and reflect on the happiest moments often recreates the feelings we shared at those times. As the apostle Paul wrote letters to the people he had known and worked with, he thanked God for the memories.

It is important to talk together about your memories, the good times you have shared through the years. Reviewing special days of celebration is helpful for the health and wholeness of your marriage. It is a way of communicating your feelings for each other and your gratitude to God.

Dear God, as we remember good times, help us be more thankful than ever for each other and for your blessings during our marriage. Amen.

Talk It Over: *Take a few moments now to name one special memory each of you has of your life together. Walk into the rest of this day with these joyful memories on the "computer screen" of your mind.*

March

A HEALTHY BALANCE

Daon and Monica Johnson

March 1 ~ Feeding the Mind, Body, and Spirit

Be well-balanced . . . be vigilant and cautious at all times, for that enemy of yours, the devil, roams around like a lion roaring, seeking someone to seize upon and devour.

—1 Peter 5:8 (AMP)

There was a time in my life when I was busy from sun up 'til sun down. My morning began so rushed that I didn't make time to pray. The lack of intimacy with God in the morning did not allow me to become equipped for the struggles that I often endured in marriage. In addition to the morning rush, I did not have time to eat properly. As a result, I had low energy and low patience. I had difficulty showing the fruit of the Spirit toward my mate. When we are not taking the time to feed our spirit (intimacy with the Father), feed our minds (meditating on scriptures), and feed and our bodies (proper nutrients), the enemy is able to invade our marriages.

"Thriving" couples are intentional and careful in how they feed their spirits, minds, and bodies. They seek to maintain a healthy balance—in their personal lives and in their marriage. This month we'll consider disciplining ourselves to spend time with God and our mate. As a result, we can maintain a healthy life-style that exemplifies Christ to others and a marriage filled with contentment.

Father, help me to daily feed my spirit, mind, and body so that my life and my marriage maintain a healthy balance. Amen.

Talk It Over: *Discuss with your spouse where the enemy has been able to successfully attack your marriage.*

March 2 ~ Healthy Discipline

Beloved, do not imitate evil, but imitate good. He who does good is of God; he who does evil has not seen (discerned or experienced) God—has enjoyed no vision of Him and does not know Him at all.

—3 John 1:11 (AMP)

As a child, I admired my mother's way of loving my dad. Especially in the bad times, her love always remained unconditional. She imitated Christ's love. Eventually, I drifted away from her example and began to love others only if they earned my love.

Once I gave God full authority over my life, making Jesus my Lord and Savior, I began to change my life-style to once again imitate my mother's teaching. The more I studied the Word and got to know Christ, to see him and experience him, the more I became like him. Now others around can imitate me because I am disciplined about studying and imitating Christ's unconditional love.

Lord, forgive me for those times when I lack the discipline to be an example of your love for my mate and others to imitate. Amen.

Talk It Over: *Discuss whether your love imitates the unconditional, merciful love that God gives to you.*

March 3 ~ Body and Soul

Beloved, I pray that you may prosper in every way and [that your body] may keep well, even as [I know] your soul keeps well and prospers.

—3 John 2 (AMP)

Daon is a health fitness trainer and is very intentional about keeping his physical body in shape. However, the scripture also tells us to keep our soul (mind, will, and emotions) healthy and prospering.

Although Daon's outside looks healthy, he could suffer internally if he does not daily renew his mind by meditating on scriptures. Life inflicts pain, stress, and negativity upon our minds. It is important for us to daily commune with God and meditate on the Word of God (Romans 12:2). Setting aside time to meditate on the Word allows us to spend quality time with God—alone as well as with our mate.

Father, forgive me for neglecting my soul. Teach me how to meditate on your Word. Amen.

Talk It Over: How often do you meditate on the scriptures as individuals and as a couple? The Word is like medicine to the body. Take some time to refresh as you meditate on the Word with your mate.

March 4 ~ In His Time

"We hoped for peace but no good has come, for a time of healing but there was only terror."

—*Jeremiah 8:15 (NIV)*

It is the Heavenly Father's will for us to put our hope in him. However, sometimes the answer to our prayers seems to tarry. I came to realize that my prayers for my mate or myself would not change a particular situation instantly. The scripture says that even when we put our hope in God, a time of what feels like terror may come before the healing is manifested. If the answer to our prayers should tarry, we should rest in knowing that it will come to pass in God's time. It is important to hold fast to God's promises in order to maintain wholeness and to be anchored during our times of waiting.

Father, give us a heart that will not become hopeless when our prayers tarry. Amen.

Talk It Over: If your mate becomes ill or your marriage needs healing, it is easy to become anxious. The Father doesn't work on our timetable, but he's in control of our situation. We must pray for patience and for wisdom on how to pray the Father's will.

March 5 ~ Speak Life

Death and life are in the power of the tongue: and they that love it shall eat the fruit thereof.

—Proverbs 18:21 (KJV)

Marriage can be a time of testing when we do not see eye-to-eye with our spouse. It can even tempt us to speak negatively about our mate. For example, I have a confidant who is a Christian and a prayer intercessor. She holds me accountable for my Christian walk, including being a wife. While talking with her once, I found myself sharing negative things about my mate. God had to show me that anything negative I spoke was death unto my husband. I've learned to speak life to the negative situations in my marriage and allow God to heal them.

God, teach me how to speak life into my marriage by speaking positively about my mate. I desire for my tongue to nourish the lives around me. Amen.

Talk It Over: *Are you using your tongue to kill the destiny of your marriage? Take some time to think about the things you speak about your mate and your marriage. If it doesn't bring life, it brings death.*

March 6 ~ Are You Willing to Make a Change?

Pay attention, my child, to what I say. Listen carefully. Don't lose sight of my words. Let them penetrate deep within your heart, for they bring life and radiant health to anyone who discovers their meaning.

—Proverbs 4:20-22 (NLT)

It is important to know what the Word of God says about marriage. It is of even greater importance to know that marriage is a ministry. I've learned that the Father has used my marriage to make me more holy,

56

more like him. Being married means making daily adjustments. As God's Word speaks to me and instructs me how to love and be a helpmate, I keep God's Word hidden in my heart. I am willing to make a change for a healthy marriage and, ultimately, a prosperous ministry.

God instructs us to never lose sight of his words and to hide them within our hearts.

Father, help me make the adjustments necessary to have a healthy marriage. Amen.

Talk It Over: What have you hidden in your heart? Search the scriptures for understanding about marriage. Attend a marriage seminar to enhance your knowledge. Always be willing to make necessary changes.

March 7 ~ Heart Guard

Above all else, guard your heart, for it affects everything you do.
—Proverbs 4:23 (NLT)

As a result of a tragic car accident, I laid on my back for several weeks in the Shock Trauma Unit. Often the enemy would attempt to speak doubt and fear to my heart. Although I was unable to physically lift a Bible to read God's Word, his Word was hidden in my heart. Not only had I memorized scriptures in previous years, but I also was able to put the Word to work in my life. It became a vital instrument in maintaining my peace and hope. David tells us in Psalm 119:11, "I have hidden your word in my heart that I might not sin against you" (NIV).

We guard the Word in our heart. The enemy tells us to doubt God's healing and wholeness in our marriages and within our bodies, yet the Holy Spirit will quicken us with the Word. He will remind us of the promises of God and encourage our hearts from sinning.

Dear God, please show me, by your Spirit, how to guard my heart and to put your Word to work in my life that I may not sin against you. Amen.

Talk It Over: Are you intentional about studying God's Word and guarding your heart from the sin of doubt, fear, worry, and other lies from the enemy? Discuss ways you may encourage one another in this effort.

March 8 ~ A Good Cry

O LORD my God, I cried unto thee, and thou hast healed me.
—Psalm 30:2 (KJV)

Crying is an emotional response to grief, sorrow, pain, fear, anger, or despair. In Psalm 30:2, David cries to God in the midst of pain or possibly a sickness that seems to have afflicted the emotional monarch. God's response to David's tears is to extend his healing hand into David's situation, providing health and healing.

Even though it has been reported that women cry five times more than men in similar situations, the benefits of crying for both genders—both medical and spiritual—have been well documented. Shouldn't God also respond to a couple who cries out to him for the healing of their marriage? their ailing parent(s)? their wayward child?

Lord, help us share our grief, sorrow, pain, and fear with each other and with you. We anxiously await the touch of your healing hand in our lives. Amen.

Talk It Over: *Take some time to become aware of your hidden emotions as well as the emotions of your spouse. Trust each other with your intimate emotional secrets so that healing and wholeness may flourish within your marriage.*

March 9 ~ Robbers, Murderers, and Vandals

"The thief cometh not, but for to steal, and to kill, and to destroy: I am come that they might have life, and that they might have it more abundantly."
—John 10:10 (KJV)

Ever since Cain murdered Abel, crime has been a problem that has plagued society. Murders, burglaries, vandalism, and even terrorism are the featured headlines in most news programs. However, as shocking and alarming as the statistics are, we believe that the greatest crime plaguing our society is divorce.

With the breakdown and devaluing of marriages in our society, there has been a corresponding decline in the effectiveness of our families to produce healthy citizens. Unhealthy citizens do not have the ability to pro-

58

duce a healthy society. Since our marriages are being stolen, murdered, and vandalized spiritually, we can only expect the same to occur in our streets as well.

O God, make us aware of the enemy's attempts to vandalize our marriage. Provide us with the arsenal to withstand his attacks. Amen.

Talk It Over: *Many marriages suffer because they are robbed of their wholeness. Ask yourself and your spouse in what ways the enemy has attacked your wholeness (body, spirit, or soul), thus destroying your ability to experience life/health within your marriage.*

March 10 ~ Home Security System

And no terrible disasters will strike you or your home.
—Psalm 91:10 (CEV)

We recently purchased a home security system to protect ourselves and our valuables against the potential attack of unwanted intruders. Our security system has several motion detectors placed in strategic zones in our home. To turn our system on or off, we must enter a secret code. When the security of our home is compromised, an alarm sounds and authorities are notified.

I am now considering a security system for my marriage! This security system will protect our marriage against unwanted intruders. This security system will have "motion detectors" placed in three strategic zones in our marriage: time zone, touch zone, and talk zone. Unlike the home security motion detectors, however, which sound an alarm when any motion is detected, these detectors will sound an alarm when *no* motion is detected in these three zones within a predetermined period of time; and the authority (the Holy Spirit) will be notified. As a result, the Spirit will come to our rescue to protect us from possible "invisible intruders" (in our thoughts) and potential disaster (in our relationship).

Father, help us take the appropriate precautionary measures to secure our marriage from the threat of "intruders." Amen.

March 11 ~ Laugh a Little

A merry heart doeth good like a medicine.

—*Proverbs 17:22 (KJV)*

As newlyweds, I don't think we were aware of the great adventure that we were embarking upon. With a "ready-made" family, there were many challenges that we were about to face. After our honeymoon, we returned, packed a trailer, and immediately relocated to another city. To top off this period of transition, we were surprised to conceive a child just three weeks after our wedding and three years before we planned!

In retrospect, we tackled three of the five major life changes within one month of our wedding day. The honeymoon was quickly over, and we were immediately plunged into an environment that made it difficult to laugh. But, as the months passed, God's grace abounded toward us, and we settled into a routine. For our own physical health and peace of mind, God showed us the need for laughter in our home. Now we always take time to laugh a little.

God, when we become overwhelmed with our daily situations and circumstances, give us the ability to place our problems in your hands and laugh a little. Amen.

Talk It Over: *What prevents you from laughing and enjoying life in abundance? Give it to God and let the laughter begin!*

March 12 ~ Mr. Yuk

Watch out that no bitter root of unbelief rises up among you.

—*Hebrews 12:15*b *(NLT)*

When we were growing up, the poison control center began a program called "Mr. Yuk" to prevent children from ingesting deadly poisons.

Parents were given green stickers with an ugly face on them to put on bottles of cleaners and disinfectant. When children saw these ugly faces, they were discouraged from accidentally drinking deadly poison.

In our marriages, unbelief is a bitter, deadly poison. When we doubt God's ability to heal life's challenges, our unbelief prevents us from pleasing God. So when unbelief shows its ugly face, place Mr. Yuk stickers on your refrigerator to remind yourself of the consequences of unbelief.

Dear Father, help us operate a household based upon the principles of faith. Whenever doubts arise in our hearts, grant us the gift of faith and the ability to believe you at all costs. Amen.

Talk It Over: *What situations in your marriage have caused you to doubt God? Believe God in that situation and watch his glory abound in fullness.*

March 13 ~ Wash Your Hands

Who shall ascend into the hill of the LORD?...He that hath clean hands, and a pure heart.

—Psalm 24:3-4 (KJV)

After a long hard day of work, one of the most important events (after I kiss my wife, of course) is to go to the refrigerator. As soon as I reach for the refrigerator door, my wife barks out, "Did you wash your hands?" Monica knows that in order to maintain a healthy home, clean hands are essential. This greatly reduces the risk of transmitting bacteria and viruses with the potential to cause illness.

And so it is with our spiritual hands as well. We must continually wash them so that the "bacteria and viruses" of the world are not brought into our homes. For example, we must wash our hands of the world's pride in earthly possessions (1 John 2:15-17).

Next time your spouse walks in and heads for the refrigerator, ask, "Did you wash your hands?"

God, help me keep my hands clean from the evil influences of the world. Amen.

Talk It Over: *Discuss with your spouse what worldly influences have entered your home because you have not "washed your hands."*

March 14 ~ Life Insurance

My son, forget not my law; but let thine heart keep my commandments: for length of days, and long life, and peace, shall they add to thee.

—Proverbs 3:1-2 (KJV)

When we contemplate financial health and security, one of the first questions that comes to mind is, Do you have life insurance? Life insurance helps the surviving spouse pay burial and estate expenses should the other spouse die unexpectedly. In an ideal situation, the compensation should be enough to also cover household expenses while the grieving spouse recovers from his or her loss.

Proverbs 3:1-2 informs us of God's biblical life insurance policy. For length of days, long life, and peace, God instructs us not to begin paying monetary premiums but to allow our heart to keep his commandments. Have you purchased a biblical life insurance policy?

Dear God, as I seek to keep your commandments, protect my heart by the power of your Spirit, and bless me and my spouse with length of days, long life, and peace. Amen.

Talk It Over: *Discuss with your spouse ways that you can keep God's commandments as a couple.*

March 15 ~ Healthy Compassion

And Jesus went forth, and saw a great multitude, and was moved with compassion toward them.

—Matthew 14:14 (KJV)

Living with our spouses day in and day out exposes us to all of their faults, their sicknesses, and their diseases. If only our spouse would do a little self-evaluation and work on all of his or her problems, surely our marriage would be a healthy one!

Even though we don't verbalize this attitude, it is a very popular one that arises in many of our marriages. Focusing on our spouses' faults can quickly cause us to lose compassion for them and develop a self-righteous attitude. As Jesus ministered to human beings plagued with sin, quirks, foibles, and idiosyncrasies, he always maintained a high level of compassion toward his creation. This same high level of compassion must exist in our marriages in order to have a healthy, loving, and godly atmosphere.

Father, please help me to always be compassionate toward my spouse. Help me to always address my own sin before attempting to address and correct my spouse's. Amen.

Talk It Over: *Ask your spouse to gently reveal to you when you are being less than compassionate.*

March 16 ~ Spiritual Osteoporosis

"And when ye stand praying, forgive . . . that your Father . . . may forgive you."
—Mark 11:25 (KJV)

As we continue exploring the theme of marital health and wholeness, let me suggest that unforgiveness is like osteoporosis. Osteoporosis is a slow, persistent reduction in the amount of bone mass, which leads to skeletal fractures. Unforgiveness causes a slow, persistent reduction in the amount of God's grace, which leads to spiritual fractures after minimal trauma.

The Bible speaks plainly and clearly about forgiveness. These teachings are especially applicable in our marriages. No marriage will succeed if one of the spouses harbors unforgiveness. Not only will it prevent a couple from achieving intimacy, but it also will prevent the couple from experiencing God's forgiveness in their marriage.

God, you have commanded me to forgive. Please show me my sin and help me remove any unforgiveness that I may have harbored in my heart toward my spouse. Help me free my mate and, in turn, free myself so that our prayers are not hindered. Amen.

Talk It Over: *Are you holding anything in your heart that you need to forgive your spouse for? Talk it over today.*

March 17 ~ The Paradox of Pain

He was nailed to the cross, so that we would stop sinning and start living right. By his cuts and bruises you are healed.
—1 Peter 2:24 (CEV)

One of the body's best defenses is the central nervous system. If a toe is stubbed or a finger jammed, the nervous system immediately responds by sending a signal to the brain that something is painfully wrong.

Imagine the pain that Jesus must have felt as he endured the intense suffering of the cross. Not only was Jesus enduring the physical pain of a brutal execution, Jesus was also enduring the spiritual pain of knowing that something was inherently wrong with the human race he created.

As a couple, the painful realization of our sin should remind us that we are citizens of a fallen human race. Pain should also remind us of our need for a Savior.

Father, as we experience the daily pain of living in a fallen world, we ask you to continue to give us the ability to heal and to be made whole in the midst of our pain. Amen.

Talk It Over: *Are there "pains" in your relationship that will not allow your marriage to be whole?*

March 18 ~ Eyesores

"Your eye is a lamp for your body. A pure eye lets sunshine into your soul."
—Matthew 6:22 (NLT)

Much like a run-down neighborhood with many eyesores, negative images constantly flash in front of our eyes. Our media exalts killing and chaos, crisis and crime, sex and skin. Over a period of time, our eyes and other senses become desensitized and our tolerance level gradually increases. Before we know it, we are not offended in the least by pornography, profanity, murder, injustice, or any other sin that God clearly speaks against.

God instructs us to keep our eyes pure. We can do this by not allowing negative images to pass in front of our eyes. If this means reducing the amount of television that we watch or minimizing our time at the magazine rack, we must make the appropriate steps to keep our eyes healthy. This will allow us to remain sensitive to the needs of our spouse and will promote honest, open, and healthy communication.

Lord, help us keep our eyes from beholding evil. Amen.

Talk It Over: *Talk about how you, as a couple, can reduce the negative images that pass before your eyes.*

March 19 ~ Cardiovascular Health

"A good person produces good words from a good heart."
—Matthew 12:35 (NLT)

One of the main emphases of most health and fitness programs is to promote good cardiovascular health. People are constantly being encouraged to "get your heart rate up." The health benefits of the couple who exercise their hearts on a regular basis are profound to say the least. Exercise conditions the heart and lungs by increasing the oxygen available to the body and by enabling the heart to use oxygen more efficiently.

But how do we exercise our spiritual heart? Our spiritual heart is exercised by having long walks with the Lord, jogging through the pages of the Bible, jumping at every chance to spend time with the Holy Spirit, and running to the Father for his wisdom and guidance. Why not exercise your heart today?

Lord, I desire a healthy heart. Amen.

Talk It Over: *Have you considered exercising your heart today? Start by allowing the Holy Sprit to exercise your heart as you walk through the Word of God.*

March 20 ~ What Kind of Seed Are You Sowing?

Don't be misled. Remember that you can't ignore God and get away with it. You will always reap what you sow! . . . So don't get tired of doing what is good.

Don't get discouraged and give up, for we will reap a harvest of blessing at the appropriate time.

—*Galatians 6:7-9 (NLT)*

The first two years of marriage were difficult for Daon and I. God showed me how the principal of planting and harvesting applied to a healthy marriage. Often I became tired during the intense struggles of the marriage. However, God's Word tells us not to become exhausted in doing well. So, I decided to plant my time into other troubled marriages. I became transparent. I shared our struggles and our victories, and I encouraged other couples to hold on. As a result, I reaped a harvest of strength and healing in my marriage. Planting life and health into others allows you to harvest it within your relationship.

Father, give me the strength to remain strong while doing what is pleasing during difficult times. Amen.

Talk It Over: *If you sow negatively, you shall reap it! If you sow positively, you shall reap it! What kinds of seeds are you sowing?*

March 21 ~ A Healthy Heart

For it is by believing in your heart that you are made right with God, and it is by confessing with your mouth that you are saved.

—*Romans 10:10 (NLT)*

Wholeness begins with accepting Jesus Christ as your Lord and Savior. Before entering into a covenant of marriage, it is vital that you enter into a relationship with the One who ordained marriage. When I accepted Jesus Christ, I became a new creature with a new heart. My old heart would not allow me to be forgiving and loving. Without a new heart, it is impossible to love unconditionally, to forgive daily, or repent for sins. A new heart is a healthy heart!

Lord, I repent of my sins. I confess you as my Lord and Savior. Create in me a new heart. Amen.

Talk It Over: *If you're not hearing God's voice, maybe it's time to make a new confession and ask for a new heart. In marriage, it's imperative to hear God's voice to know how to love yourself and your mate! Repentance is a change of mind about sinning, not saying you're sorry. Repent and make a change. Talk about your commitment with your spouse.*

March 22 ~ Be Fully Persuaded

Abraham's faith did not weaken, even though he knew that he was too old to be a father at the age of one hundred.

—Romans 4:19 (NLT)

In 1996, I endured a traumatic car accident with injuries to my lungs, ribs, colon, spleen, liver, kidneys, pelvis, bladder, and arm. To say the least, I was told I would not be able to experience intimacy with my future mate or bear children. However, years prior to the accident, a prophetic word came to me that I would birth many, both spiritually and physically.

Three years later, I was blessed to consummate my marriage to Daon, and the next year joyfully give birth to our son, Caleb Isaac; and surprisingly enough, I expect the arrival of our daughter this year.

I am fully persuaded that God is able to do all that he has promised. If you believe God for wholeness in your marriage or something that seems even more impossible, be fully persuaded that he can do the impossible.

Father, help my faith so that I don't waver. Amen.

Talk It Over: *Discuss how you can give all your worries and cares to God. He cares.*

March 23 ~ Admit Your Need

Casting all your care upon him; for he careth for you.

—1 Peter 5:7 (KJV)

Life alone can cause us to occasionally worry. Marriage can sometimes cause additional stress. We must learn to admit when we are in need. If we live in denial of our need for God's help, our lives become unhealthy. We can worry about our lack as a husband or wife or our inability to carry out the expectations of our mate instead of trusting God in those areas. It is not God's will for us to please people and constantly battle with the pressures of failure. We must please God by trusting him fully with our cares. Sometimes we think that God doesn't care because we've caused some of the stress in our lives through foolish decisions and acts of selfishness. However, God does care and is able to lift your heavy burdens. God is able to bring balance in your life and in your marriage.

God, I need your help. Amen.

Talk It Over: *Admit to your spouse three areas with which you need help.*

March 24 ~ Mud in the Eye

Again the Pharisees also asked him how he had received his sight. He said unto them, He put clay upon mine eyes, and I washed, and do see.
—John 9:15 (KJV)

John records a very interesting story in which Jesus miraculously heals a man blind from birth. After explaining to his disciples that sin was not the cause of the man's misfortune, Jesus performs a very interesting healing ceremony. Jesus spits on the ground, forms a ball of mud, and places it on the blind man's eyes. Jesus then commands the blind man to wash in Siloam's community pool. The rest is history!

Two points to consider . . .

1. Sometimes a sickness, disease, or marital problem is not a result of sin but so that God may be glorified in its healing.

2. We should not be concerned with the methods God uses to heal our circumstances; instead, focus on thanking him and publicizing his awesome works.

Lord, we welcome your many methods of healing so that you would be glorified in our lives. Amen.

Talk It Over: *Discuss methods God has used to heal the broken areas in your marriage.*

March 25 ~ Rest for the Weary

Live under the protection of God Most High and stay in the shadow of God All-Powerful.

—*Psalm 91:1 (CEV)*

Because our lives have become so busy and hectic, periods of rest and relaxation are practically obsolete. And when there is time to rest, husbands and especially wives feel as if they are being unproductive or wasting valuable time. Scripture informs us, however, that when we live under the protection of the Most High—that is, in constant communion with him—he will provide our lives with much needed rest.

Medically, it has been proved that our bodies need adequate amounts of rest and sleep to recover and rebuild after the trauma of a typical day. Likewise, time in the Lord's presence through prayer and meditation brings us double benefit. It gives us much-needed communion with our Creator, and God, in turn, grants us supernatural rest.

God, remind me to take time to rest in your presence. Amen.

Talk It Over: *Take some time with your mate to relax and lay in the presence of the Almighty God, who desires for us to prosper in body, spirit, and soul. Are you neglecting your need to rest?*

March 26 ~ Soap for Your Spouse

Husbands, love your wives, just as Christ loved the church and gave himself up for her to make her holy, cleansing her by the washing with water through the word.

—*Ephesians 5:25-26 (NIV)*

The fifth chapter of Ephesians explains the close correlation between Christ and the church, and a man and his wife. Paul explains that the husband's responsibility is to continually wash his wife with encouraging words taken directly from the Bible. These words will serve to cleanse her and make her holy so that she may be presented before God without spot or wrinkle.

In the same way, we can also suggest that the wife, too, must wash her husband with encouraging words taken directly from scripture. Frequent baths in the Word of God will cleanse him and make him holy so that he will have an opportunity to appear before God holy and faultless.

Have you washed your spouse lately?

Dear Lord, help us encourage one another with your Word. Remind us to use words that edify and encourage so that we both may appear before you holy and without blemish. Amen.

Talk It Over: *What scriptures can you use to encourage your spouse today?*

March 27 ~ Cognitive Care

We capture people's thoughts and make them obey Christ.
—2 Corinthians 10:5 (CEV)

Our minds often play tricks on us. Especially in marital relationships, it is necessary to constantly evaluate our thought patterns. Many times we make assumptions as to what our spouse may be thinking or feeling and then allow our minds to run rampant with negative thoughts and accusations. It is at these times that an unsuspecting glance or statement can be misinterpreted, resulting in a full-blown argument.

For this reason, Paul commanded the church at Corinth to shut down its imagination and bring all of its thoughts to the obedience of Christ. This was Paul's prescription for cognitive care. So, the next time you are tempted to allow your thoughts to run away with you, give your spouse the benefit of the doubt. Remember that God's Word has commanded us to take these wandering thoughts captive and prevent them from doing more harm than good.

Father, I desire to have a healthy mind. Let your Holy Spirit continue to lead me into all truth. Amen.

Talk It Over: *Discuss with your spouse the thoughts that you have entertained that resulted in division within your marriage.*

70

March 28 ~ Healthy Exposure

Although Adam and his wife were both naked, neither of them felt any shame.
—Genesis 2:25 (NLT)

Shame can be defined as a painful emotion caused by a strong sense of guilt, embarrassment, unworthiness, or disgrace. Unfortunately, since the fall of Adam and Eve, many marital relationships are unhealthy because of the presence of shame. Where excessive amounts of shame exist, neither spouse is able to fully express his or her emotions for fear of exposure, guilt, or embarrassment. Communication breaks down, and intimacy is unattainable.

A healthy marital relationship allows both partners to feel completely at ease and comfortable—naked and unashamed. When this environment exists between God and each spouse, there can be an easy exchange of feelings and confessions. Also, when this environment exists, intimate conversation, unconditional love, and mutual acceptance are available in abundance.

Lord, please allow our relationship to be a safe haven where we can share openly without feeling shame or guilt. Allow us to move closer together in intimate oneness to your glory. Amen.

Talk It Over: *Discuss how the intimacy in your relationship can be improved.*

March 29 ~ Fear Factor

God hath not given us the spirit of fear; but of power, and of love, and of a sound mind.
—2 Timothy 1:7 (KJV)

Our society has developed a hunger for entertainment that elicits fear. Horror, high-speed chases, robberies, explosions, and death-defying jumps have become a way of life. Much like an addiction, with every fear there must be a corresponding increase in the fear factor.

God, however, does not desire his children to live in fear. He desires our marriages to thrive with a spirit of love, power, and a sound mind. Our marriages are designed to have the power to overcome the fears that we may face as individuals and as a team. Whether it is the fear of a possible pink slip or fear surrounding a teen's newly issued driver's license, we are to operate in complete confidence that God is in control.

Heavenly Father, give us the strength to overcome fear. Amen.

Talk It Over: *Are you entertaining thoughts of fear? Take some time to consider what you are putting into your mind and heart.*

March 30 ~ Holding Fast

Hold fast the profession of our faith without wavering; for he is faithful.
—Hebrews 10:23 (KJV)

Gone is the era where one's word was an indelible bond. If someone said something, he or she meant it, and you could count on it. However, things have changed considerably, and if you want to make absolutely sure, you should have everything in writing.

And so it is with many of our marriages. Many couples have chosen to completely override their vows based upon a difficult situation or circumstance. Although the writer of Hebrews was referring to a believer's profession of faith, our profession of marriage should be no different. We must hold on to our profession without wavering.

We have chosen to adopt a "no entertainment" clause. In the midst of difficult situations, we have vowed not to "entertain" thoughts of divorce. For us, divorce is not an option. We have chosen to hold fast to our profession.

God, remind us of our vows when we enter difficult situations. Give us the strength to remain steadfast in our marriage and to hold fast to our profession. Amen.

Talk It Over: *Discuss a "no entertainment" clause in your marriage!*

March 31 ~ Struggle Makes Us Stronger

"Salt is good, but if it loses its saltiness, how can you make it salty again? Have salt in yourselves, and be at peace with each other."
—Mark 9:50 (NIV)

As a fitness trainer, I strive to be an example for my clients by lifting weights and staying fit. In order to increase muscle mass, I must lift weights beyond my comfort. I get the greatest results when I lift to the point of struggling as my spotter assists me in accomplishing the task. Likewise, when we struggle in our marriage beyond comfort, it makes us stronger and builds our character. The results are extraordinary, giving us an opportunity to show the love of Christ toward our mate. Although we struggle, the spotter (Christ Jesus) will never leave us alone to endanger ourselves. Without the struggles, we would not grow to become salt for the world. Without struggles, we can never expect to achieve a healthy, balanced marriage.

Father, help us appreciate struggle and not avoid it. Remind us of the stories in the Bible where others overcame through their struggles; then, give us strength to be overcomers. Amen.

Talk It Over: *Discuss with your mate how your struggles have made you stronger and more like Christ.*

April

A DAILY DOSE OF LOVE

Lloyd and Clare Doyle

April 1 ~ A Work in Progress

The LORD God said, "It isn't good for the man to live alone. I need to make a suitable partner for him."

—Genesis 2:18 (CEV)

*O*n our wedding day, we start a journey of commitment. Today most people know each other before they marry, some longer than others. But the wedding day is the official beginning of new life together as a married couple. Suddenly your relationship changes because you have deeply and profoundly committed to another person.

However, your wedding day is not the ultimate level of your commitment. A wedding is the start of the marriage relationship. Just because you've said, "I do" does not mean that's all you have to do. Marriage is a continually ongoing commitment. It is a work in progress. This month we'll be exploring many different ways of nurturing our marriages—how we can have fun and grow closer together all the days of our lives.

Lord, help us daily to commit to our relationship with each other. Amen.

Talk It Over: *Think back to your wedding day. First, talk about something funny that happened that day. Then, talk about the covenant of commitment you made on that special day.*

75

April 2 ~ Wedding Joy

In your presence there is fullness of joy; in your right hand are pleasures forevermore.

—Psalm 16:11

We had written our own marriage service. And so many friends and family had come. It was truly a joyous event. But what was most important was that it was a worship service. It expressed both our love for each other and our Christian love for God in which we were grounding our future. It was a day of great joy.

The days right after our wedding were also filled with excitement. Even though life goes on and the honeymoon can't last forever, the joy of being together not only can continue, but also can grow! If we keep our commitment to our marriage and make it stronger by intentionally nurturing it, then joy can grow ever deeper. Even in hard or trying times, God can supply a joy that transcends and makes life good.

Lord, thank you for all the joy you bring to life. Amen.

Talk It Over: Think back to your honeymoon (or early days of marriage). Talk about the new or fun things you did together. Then do something as a couple that brings you both great joy now.

April 3 ~ Get Going

Therefore a man leaves his father and his mother and clings to his wife, and they become one flesh.

—Genesis 2:24

Two weeks after our wedding, we went hiking. To reach the summit of one peak, we had to scale vertical granite. The climb was exhilarating, exciting, and terrifying. Once at the top, Clare (like a cat) looked down and froze. Petrified with fear, she kept saying, "I can't move." Several hikers came to help. No avail. Then I assured her that I was afraid too, but that together *we* could do it.

76

In a sense, that's what we all have to do in marriage: face our fears, let go, and get going together. No longer are things just *me*. Instead, they become *we*. This does not mean we lose our individual identities. It means the two are helpmates for each other. We let go and get going together.

Lord, help us let go of fear and move forward in our marriage. Amen.

Talk It Over: *Think of a positive accomplishment that you as a couple have made. Talk about ways you would like to grow as a couple.*

April 4 ~ Time for Marriage

For everything there is a season, and a time for every matter under heaven.
—Ecclesiastes 3:1

The passage in Ecclesiastes goes on and on about there being a time for everything. Ecclesiastes also concludes that the problem is we do not always know what time it is.

Indeed, there is a time for everything. And there must be time for yourself and time for your marriage. No matter what stage of marriage you are in, you must make time to nurture it. It will not happen on its own. Whether you are newly wedding, career building, parenting, empty nesting, retiring—whatever stage you are in—you must take time to nurture your relationship.

Lord, help us each and every day to let each other know how special we are to each other. Lord, even when life is hard and stressful, help us remember our love for each other. Amen.

Talk It Over: *Talk about times when it has been easy to nurture your relationship. Talk about times when it has been difficult. Make time today to be especially attentive to each other.*

April 5 ~ Re-Creating Together

Create in me a clean heart, O God, and put a new and right spirit within me.
—Psalm 51:10

77

Watching movies. Oh, we love to watch movies. Our favorites are comedies because they help us laugh and have a good time. Not only do we laugh at the time we're watching them, but when we recall watching them together, we also laugh all over again. We have fun together.

In the beginning, you created your marriage. You created it by committing to each other. But you have to daily re-create your marriage. What better way than through recreation together. It is so important to have fun together and to laugh together, to learn together and to grow together.

Lord, help us re-create our marriage today and every day we have together. Amen.

Talk It Over: *Think of one thing you can do today to re-create your marriage. Do it!*

April 6 ~ Each Day's Gift

I know that there is nothing better for them than to be happy and enjoy themselves as long as they live; moreover, it is God's gift that all should eat and drink and take pleasure in all their toil.

—Ecclesiastes 3:12-13

Two families worked hard all their lives. Money had been scarce, but they always made it through. They relied on their faith and one another. Years later, as things eased up financially, they began to plan for the future. Both couples retired. They set up housekeeping in new homes. They found things they enjoyed doing together. Both couples love tending to their plants. They love helping their children and grandchildren. Life has not ended with their retirement; instead, it has begun anew. Life is different, but these couples are happy and enjoying their new life-style.

Truly, each day is a gift from God. It is a gift to be happy and to enjoy life.

Lord, help us find happiness in every stage of our lives. Amen.

Talk It Over: *List three things you enjoy doing together. Do at least one of them this week and have fun.*

April 7 ~ If You Snooze, You Lose

Sleep a little. Doze a little. Fold your hands and twiddle your thumbs. Suddenly, everything is gone, as though it had been taken by an armed robber.

—Proverbs 6:10-11 (CEV)

She wants chocolate and flowers every so often. He wants time in his lounge chair to watch sports. She wants to drive to the mountains, and he wants to hit the beach. As individuals, we all have our wants, needs, and expectations. We have different ways of relaxing and different ways of wanting to nurture ourselves and our relationship.

That is the key. We must nurture our relationship. It will not just happen. We have to take time and be together and continue to rekindle the fire of our love. If we don't, it can go out, and we'll wonder what happened.

Dear God, help us not to ignore our relationship so that suddenly it is gone. Help us daily rekindle the flame of love. Amen.

Talk It Over: *Think of one thing you know your spouse would enjoy doing to relax. Tell each other what you've thought of, and make plans to do something each of you would enjoy.*

April 8 ~ Physical Attraction

My darling, I am yours, and you desire me.

—Song of Songs 7:10 (CEV)

It was attraction and desire that brought them together in the first place. She noticed his deep blue eyes; he noticed her long brown hair. He liked the way she laughed, and she liked the sweet, deep tones of his voice. They were drawn to each other. They wanted to be together, holding hands, being close. Then they moved from attraction to love and marriage.

You know, we need to keep that type of early attraction alive and going in our marriages. It can die if it is not nurtured. Remember the things that attracted you to each other. Think about those things that drew you to your spouse. Look for them now, and look for new "attractions" to nurture in whatever stage of marriage you may be in now.

Lord, thank you for giving us desire for one another. Amen.

Talk It Over: *Look closely at your spouse. Tell your spouse how desirable he or she is to you.*

April 9 ~ Sex Is a Gift

Kiss me tenderly! Your love is better than wine, and you smell so sweet.
—Song of Songs 1:2 (CEV)

Part of being together as a couple includes physical intimacy. It is a precious gift given to us by God. God created us male and female and gave us to each other. It is vitally important that we make time in our life for this precious gift of being together.

In some stages of life, we have time to be physically intimate with very little effort. At other stages it may be more difficult. Children, aging parents, physical ailments, career stresses, and various other responsibilities can push us away from each other. But it is so important to take time to kiss each other tenderly, to be physically intimate, and to love each other, body and soul.

Lord, thank you for the gift of our love for each other. Amen.

Talk It Over: *Make time to be physically intimate. It is a precious gift, not to be wasted.*

April 10 ~ Crying Together

When Jesus came closer and could see Jerusalem, he cried.
—Luke 19:41 (CEV)

It had been a particularly bad time. Stress was eating away at their lives. Good job after good job was passing them by. They were trying to conceive and nothing was working. One suffered from anxiety, the other from depression. They had both been suffering alone until one night they decided to pray together. They headed for the church. The lights were on low. They prayed individually, they prayed together, and they cried together. They left feeling stronger, united, and able to deal with life.

Jesus cried. Jesus was human, and he experienced all the emotions that we as human beings feel. Knowing that he cried frees us to accept and express our own emotions. Being truly committed to each other also means sharing our feelings and nurturing each other—sometimes by crying.

Lord, help us share our emotions with each other and, most important, with you. Amen.

Talk It Over: *Talk about times that have been difficult and how you've gotten through. Commit to crying and praying together next time things are tough.*

April 11 ~ Deep, Abiding Love

Now make me completely happy! Live in harmony by showing love for each other. Be united in what you think, as if you were only one person.
—*Philippians 2:2 (CEV)*

She lay in a hospital bed hooked up to so many wires and tubes. Oh, how they had loved each other for their fifty years of marriage. Family responsibilities had taxed most of their early marriage. Then cancer cruelly entered into their lives, requiring a radical mastectomy and treatments.

Since the beginning, their love was harmonious. It showed in all the little things they did. She would try to cook his favorite foods, and he faithfully drove her to her hair appointments (though she could drive, she didn't like to).

As she lay in that bed dying, he held her hand, looked in her eyes, and said, "If only I could put my arms around you and hold you tight. I don't care what the years and cancer have done to your body. I just want to hold you close."

81

They had a deep, abiding love—a love that made them completely happy; a love that they lived out in every way. If we can show love to each other in large and small ways, no matter what life hands us, then we can live happily together.

Lord, help us live so harmoniously that we always want to hold each other tight. Amen.

Talk It Over: *Hold hands and tell your spouse what little things mean so much to you.*

April 12 ~ Life Is Short

Dress up, comb your hair, and look your best. Life is short, and you love your wife, so enjoy being with her. This is what you are supposed to do as you struggle through life on this earth.

—Ecclesiastes 9:8-9 (CEV)

Recently we have known many people who have lost their spouses. Some faced grave illness, and the couples were able to face death together. Others lost their spouse unexpectedly in an instant. These people had no time to prepare, no time for a farewell expression of love.

None of us has any guarantee about our time on this earth. Therefore, each day is a precious gift from God. As the scripture reminds us, one sign of our love is our attention to "grooming." It's a subtle way we can live each day to its fullest and let our spouse know how much we care. There are other ways, of course, such as being affectionate, holding hands, giving a gentle caress or a kind gesture, writing a love note—the list could go on and on. Remember, each day is a day to enjoy each other.

Lord, help us treasure the precious gift of being together today. Amen.

Talk It Over: *If you knew this were your last day together, what would you do or say to let your spouse know how much you love him or her? Why not do or say some of these things today?*

April 13 ~ "Just Because"

Even if you live to a ripe old age, you should try to enjoy each day, because darkness will come and will last a long time. Nothing makes sense. . . . Be cheerful and enjoy life.

—Ecclesiastes 11:8-9a (CEV)

He was gone with no warning or hint. They had done everything together. Birthdays, Christmas, anniversaries—all the special times they had celebrated together. Now, she was alone, but she had so much good to remember.

There was the way he supported her when the children were born; the trips to the mountains, to the beach, to nowhere; and the "just because" gifts he brought her. Theses were the small gifts that let her know how much he loved her. They treasured each other, and they treasured being together.

Ecclesiastes reminds us to enjoy each day. Life is difficult. But if we can enjoy each other, our togetherness is a gift that, along with the comfort and grace of God, will see us through even the dark times.

Lord, help us enjoy this day together and express our love for each other. Amen.

Talk It Over: *What "just because" expressions of your spouse's love for you have meant the most to you? Find a way to make your spouse feel special today—"just because."*

April 14 ~ Gathered in Christ

"For where two or three are gathered in my name, I am there among them."
—Matthew 18:20

Being together is so important to our Christian faith. It helps us grow stronger and learn. It provides us with strength and comfort. We need to be together as a couple, and we need to be with others as a couple.

In several towns where we have lived, we have arranged dinner groups with other clergy families. We would gather once a month for eating and fellowship. Sometimes we met in a home, and sometimes in a restaurant.

Some churches have Supper Clubs; Sunday school classes have dinners. And sometimes friends just get together. But gathering together in friendly fellowship with other Christian couples can help us grow—as individuals and as couples.

Lord, thank you that when we are together and when others join us, you are there. Amen.

Talk It Over: *Make a list of other Christian couples with whom you enjoy or would enjoy spending time together. Arrange a time for you all to eat and fellowship together soon.*

April 15 ~ Traditions

"And no one puts new wine into old wineskins; otherwise, the wine will burst the skins, and the wine is lost, and so are the skins; but one puts new wine into fresh wineskins."

—Mark 2:22

The families we grew up in had many similarities and yet many differences. When we married, we couldn't do everything the way the Golsons did or the way the Doyles did. We had to find a new way. Some traditions we could keep, others had to be blended, and new ones needed to be created.

That's the way it is with marriage. We become a new family, and we have to begin afresh. We have to begin our own traditions. We have to form our own way of doing things. This is a process that continues throughout marriage. We can always add and change and find new ways to build tradition.

Dear God, help us build traditions that will strengthen our marriage. Amen.

Talk it Over: *Talk about traditions you celebrated as a child and traditions that began after you married. How are these traditions alike and different?*

April 16 ~ Oysters and Coconut Cake

About this time some Pharisees and teachers of the Law of Moses came from

Jerusalem. They asked Jesus, "Why don't your disciples obey what our ancestors taught us to do?"

—Matthew 15:1-2a (CEV)

It's tradition. We've done it for generations. We're not sure why we do it, except that Doyles before us have done it. The tradition is having coconut cake and fried oysters for breakfast on Christmas morning. Yuk! Sometimes we fudge and have ours with Christmas lunch or dinner. We do it because it is family tradition, and we like to be connected with those who have gone before us. Do we always do it just as they did? No. We have to do what works for us. Traditions can help us build family relationships; but if we become too dogmatic—too rigid and unyielding in the observance of the tradition—the tradition can hinder rather than nurture. Let your traditions nurture your family.

Lord, help our traditions build up our relationship. Amen.

Talk It Over: *Talk about traditions you have as a couple/family. What works best and nurtures your relationship(s)? What changes might make some of your traditions better? Do you need a new tradition?*

April 17 ~ Christmas Pajamas

Treat others as you want them to treat you. This is what the Law and the Prophets are all about.

—Matthew 7:12 (CEV)

When I was a child, we had the tradition of getting new pajamas on Christmas Eve. It was something to count on every year. Each Christmas Eve we would come home from Communion, open our pajamas, and prepare for bed. When Lloyd and I married, he continued this tradition for me. As we had children, we began the tradition for them. It is a special family time.

Then one year we noticed Daddy did not have Christmas pajamas. We had left him out of the cycle. He never was upset or disgruntled. Our tradition changed the very next year. Now everyone gets new sleepwear to celebrate the night of Jesus' birth.

85

In marriage, it is often easy to see what you get. What's more important is how you treat your spouse. How do you wish to be treated? Do so to your spouse.

Lord, help us treat one another with love and respect. Amen.

Talk It Over: *Thank your spouse for something special she or he does for you. Do something special for your spouse today.*

April 18 ~ Growing Roots

"And when the sun rose, it was scorched; and since it had no root, it withered away."
—Mark 4:6

In marriage, there is a lot of give and take. There is a lot of compromise. Mary likes to flip the television button; Allen likes to watch the weather. But they want to spend time together, and late night is often the only time they have together each day. So they compromise. She flips through the news stations, and around and back, and he catches both the news and weather in bits and pieces.

The plant without roots will be scorched and die. Likewise, if we don't nurture our marriage, it, too, will wither and die. If we become so focused on what *I* want or how *I* want to spend time, we draw further and further apart.

Think about your marriage. How can you compromise so that you can grow stronger roots together?

Lord, help us strengthen the roots of our marriage. Amen.

Talk It Over: *Make a list of things you know your spouse enjoys that you do not necessarily enjoy. Share your lists with each other; then work out a way to compromise so that you may enjoy doing something together from each of your lists.*

April 19 ~ Musical Joy

Make a joyful noise to the LORD, all the earth. Worship the LORD with gladness; come into his presence with singing.

—Psalm 100:1-2

Music, music, music. We have it in our home. We started with a drum set. We've added an electric piano, an upright piano, chicken shakes, harmonicas, recorders, and even toy instruments. We also have all variety of CDs and tapes. Gospel, classical, rap, rock—you name it, and we have it. Music is such a wonderful way to worship God and to nurture the soul. Music draws us in, and it can draw us closer together. When the drums beat, everyone in the house moves. When hymns are playing, everyone hums along. We are drawn together.

What a gift we've been given. As we make joyful noises together, we can become closer to each other and closer to God.

O Lord, help us make a joyful noise together. Amen.

Talk It Over: *Praise God together with music today!*

April 20 ~ Courage

"Be strong and courageous; do not be frightened or dismayed, for the LORD your God is with you wherever you go."

—Joshua 1:9

He loved the outdoors—doing fun and exciting things. She liked reading books or doing needlework. One day he suggested white-water rafting. She thought he was nuts, but she reluctantly agreed. It was a fun day, filled with excitement and newness, and a little fear. Afterward, she was more receptive, yet still afraid.

One day an opportunity came along for her to take a canoeing and kayaking class. She signed up, hoping to overcome her fears. She learned a lot and became excited about going canoeing someday with her husband. They made plans and soon went together.

Sometimes we have to be strong and courageous. We have to step out of our "comfort zones" and explore new and different activities. Yet we never have to be frightened, for wherever we go, God is always with us.

Lord, help us have enough courage to try new things together. Amen.

Talk It Over: *Tell your spouse about some things you would like to try together as a couple. Do at least one thing each of you wants to try. Have fun!*

April 21 ~ Golfing Together

Remember this saying, "A few seeds make a small harvest, but a lot of seeds make a big harvest."

—2 Corinthians 9:6 (CEV)

He used to get so frustrated. She was always playing golf with her friends. He was always left behind. One day, he decided that she loved golf so much that he would try to learn so that, occasionally, they could play together. He learned to play the game, and he really enjoyed it. They would play together every now and then. Soon, they played more and more. Now, they travel the country playing golf. But more important, they are together, enjoying each other. He is no longer frustrated, and she enjoys doing one of her favorite things with the man she loves.

It was a big step. He had to try something new. He had to commit a lot of time to learning and practicing, but, oh, the harvest was certainly worth it.

Lord, help us plant a lot of seeds for our marriage so that we will have a big harvest. Amen.

Talk It Over: *What are the hobbies or activities your spouse most enjoys? Which of these would you be willing to try so that you might be able to spend more time together? Discuss these questions and put together a "plan of action."*

April 22 ~ Blessing Break

I will make them and the region around my hill a blessing; and I will send down the showers in their season; they shall be showers of blessing.

—Ezekiel 34:26

Early in our ministry together we were assigned to a church that sang a selection of songs we were unfamiliar with. Two of these songs, "Showers of Blessings" and "Count Your Blessings," became favorites of ours. In the beginning, we wondered why these songs were so special to the congregation, but they became important to us as well.

In daily living, we often get bogged down with our responsibilities, forgetting the many blessing in our lives. Sometimes we just need to slow down, examine our lives, and look for the blessings we experience. When we focus on our blessings, we have renewed energy to focus on each other and on those around us.

God, help us remember you have blessed our lives in so many ways. Amen.

Talk It Over: *Work together to list the blessings you have had in your life together this week, this month, this year, this decade, this lifetime. Give God thanks together.*

April 23 ~ Date Night

Anyone who hears and obeys these teachings of mine is like a wise person who built a house on solid rock. Rain poured down, rivers flooded, and winds beat against that house. But it did not fall, because it was built on solid rock.
—Matthew 7:24-25 (CEV)

Date night may sound extravagant and impossible to some couples—especially to busy parents. Regardless, it is an excellent and necessary way to stay in touch as a couple. Think about the time you spent together before you were married—how exciting and wonderful it was simply to be together. You might say, "We're together anyway; why bother?" But it's not the same. No matter how long you've been married, you still need to plan for regular "special times" together—times when you may focus only on each other. It takes intentional effort to keep your relationship strong.

Just as Jesus said you are to build your life on his teaching, so also you are to build your marriage on the solid rock of commitment—commitment to Jesus Christ and to each other. That's a foundation that will never fail.

Lord, help us build a solid rock foundation for our marriage. Amen.

Talk It Over: *Talk about favorite dates you've had together. Arrange to do something special just the two of you this week.*

April 24 ~ Mini-Vacationing

He said to them, "Come away to a deserted place all by yourselves and rest a while." For many were coming and going, and they had no leisure even to eat. And they went away in the boat to a deserted place by themselves.
—Mark 6:31-32

Once it seemed impossible to go on with the day-to-day routine, yet there was no time for a vacation, even a short one. Realistically, even if there had been time, there was no money. But something had to be done. One night we took off and drove to a nearby state park. We walked around the lodge, pretending that we were there for a stay. After eating dinner in the lodge dining room, we drove back to town, saw a late movie, and then went home. We were refreshed and ready to move on.

Even Jesus and the disciples grew weary and needed a chance to rest and regroup and reenergize. Do you ever reach a point when everything just seems too overwhelming? Take a mini-vacation.

Lord, help us find ways to rest awhile so that we can keep going. Amen.

Talk It Over: *Make plans for a mini-break, and then take it.*

April 25 ~ Stormy Vacation

After Jesus left in a boat with his disciples, a terrible storm suddenly struck the lake, and waves started splashing into their boat. Jesus was sound asleep.
—Matthew 8:23-24 (CEV)

For months we had planned to attend a conference. We'd worked out schedules, arranged childcare, done the finances, made special train travel arrangements. That's when it happened. One child got sick, and the caregiver got sick. We made other arrangements. We were ready. Then the weather struck. We called to confirm our train departure. Delay. Hour after hour the train's frozen tracks were reported. Soon it became apparent we would miss the conference. Everything was canceled. But we still needed time away. Finally, we checked into a nearby hotel. We spent two days resting and enjoying each other's company. The last night we had a picnic in the hotel because of an ice storm. In the midst of storms, we found a way to relax and rest.

Jesus knew the importance of resting, even in the midst of storms.

Lord, help us find rest together in the midst of the storms of our life. Amen.

Talk It Over: *List ways you could be together and rest. Choose one and do it today, if possible, or another day this week.*

April 26 ~ Salt

You are like salt for everyone on earth. But if salt no longer tastes like salt, how can it make food salty? All it is good for is to be thrown out and walked on.
—Matthew 5:13 (CEV)

Jesus was talking about the effectiveness of the disciples, but the same principal can apply to marriage. How can we have a marriage if the love is gone? We have to work on keeping love and our relationship alive. It is so important to keep the love in marriage. And let's face it: Sometimes it is hard, for all of us have quirks. Some like to flip television channels, some don't clean up after themselves, some snore, and others overeat. We all have quirks, but we can overlook these because of our love for each other. But sometimes we have to work hard at staying "salty."

Lord, help us keep the "salt" in our marriage. Amen.

Talk It Over: *Think back to when you first met your spouse and remember one thing you loved about her or him then. Then talk about it.*

April 27 ~ Dealing with Anger

You can see the speck in your friend's eye, but you don't notice the log in your own eye. How can you say, "My friend, let me take the speck out of your eye," when you don't see the log in your own eye? You're nothing but show-offs! First, take the log out of your own eye. Then you can see how to take the speck out of your friend's eye.
—Matthew 7:3-5 (CEV)

91

Angry words were welling up inside. Harsh feelings were what I felt. I wanted to lash out, scream, and say angry words. But was that right? Instead of acting on my angry impulses, I began to look at myself. *Oh, how much he has to put up with!* I thought.

We need to regularly examine ourselves and honestly admit the annoying things about us that might be hard for our spouses to tolerate. Then perhaps we can be more tolerant when our spouses annoy us!

Lord, when we are angry, help us remember that we are not perfect. Amen.

Talk It Over: *Look closely at yourself and think about the things you do that might bother your spouse. Commit to change at least one thing because you love your spouse, and pray for God's help.*

April 28 ~ Future of Hope

I will bless you with a future filled with hope—a future of success, not of suffering.

—Jeremiah 29:11 (CEV)

What a wonderful promise. God wants us to have a good and successful future. God cares about every last hair on our head. God cares about us. Of course, we do live in a broken world where there is suffering and pain. But with God's help, we can get through the suffering.

If we take time to have fun together and build memories together, then we will have the staying power to get through the more difficult times. What a wonderful promise we have that God wants us to have a future of hope.

Lord, help us remember that with you we have a future filled with hope. Amen.

Talk It Over: *Each of you take six squares of different colored construction paper. On each square list one experience or time in your marriage that was difficult. Then tear up your squares. Next, hand your torn pieces to your spouse. With glue and a piece of white construction paper, make a picture of hope for your spouse out of the torn pieces of paper. As you give each other your pictures, talk about some of the difficult times in your marriage and how you got through* *those difficulties. Then thank God together for being with you in the past and for giving you hope for your future together.*

April 29 ~ Nature

I lift up my eyes to the hills—from where will my help come? My help comes from the LORD, who made heaven and earth.
—Psalm 121:1-2

This psalm often brings people comfort in times of distress. It also reminds us that God created this world—and what a glorious place it is! As a couple, we can experience the glory of God's creation by enjoying it together.

One couple goes camping and enjoys seeing many different places. One couple travels the globe. One couple likes to sip coffee each morning on their patio. Another likes to enjoy their houseplants. But all experience God's presence in their lives as they share spectacular and ordinary moments in nature with their spouse.

Let us always remember to keep our focus on God and God's wonderful creation, which includes us.

Lord, thank you for the gift of nature. Help us enjoy this gift today. Amen.

Talk It Over: *Go outside today with your spouse and enjoy God's creation together.*

April 30 ~ Go Now in Peace

I pray that God the Father and the Lord Jesus Christ will give peace, love, and faith to every follower!
—Ephesians 6:23 (CEV)

You can live happily ever after, not as the fairy tales say, but as a real couple journeying through life under God's grace. There is no foolproof guarantee for a successful marriage. But if you unconditionally love each other, nurture your marriage, and seek Christ's guidance, you have a solid foundation for God-given happiness together.

Marriage takes time, effort, and energy. That's what you promised in your vows—not just for that day, or just on your anniversary. The vows you took are for each and every day of your life. Keep on nurturing your marriage, and may the peace of God-in-Christ be yours!

Lord, thank you for the gift of our marriage. Help us nurture it daily so that it may always continue to blossom and grow until we are parted by death. Amen.

Talk It Over: May these devotions be an impetus for greater love. What are your dreams and goals for nurturing your marriage during the next six months? the next two years?

May

ALL IN A DAY'S WORK

Kwasi Kena and Safiyah Fosua

May 1 ~ Work

"But seek his kingdom, and these things will be given to you as well."
—Luke 12:31 (NIV)

Work! Though work is a small word, it is great in potential to stir deep emotions. Consider the typical workday. Morning routines are geared toward preparing for work. We fight time and traffic as we commute to work. The workday is often filled with stressful demands and troubling problems. If we're not careful, these work-related issues can follow us home and intrude upon our private lives. Work rarely remains inside an eight-hour time constraint. It is invasive. It can even set up a throne and attempt to rule us. But, is work all there is to life? Work is necessary, but our purpose as Christians is to seek the kingdom of God.

How might we function at work if we see it as a place to demonstrate our love for God? This month, let us consider the workplace to be an arena in which we can both mature as Christians and reflect God's glory.

Dear Lord, this month help us reexamine the ways in which we think about and function in the workplace.

Talk It Over: *Discuss the extent to which you focus your attention on work—emotionally, spiritually, financially, and so forth.*

May 2 ~ Re-creation

"And no one pours new wine into old wineskins. If he does, the new wine will burst the skins, the wine will run out and the wineskins will be ruined. No, new wine must be poured into new wineskins."

—Luke 5:37-38 (NIV)

"What are you going to do now?" Roberta asked. Her husband, Mike, stared hopelessly at the classified section of the paper. The company Mike used to work for went bankrupt, leaving him jobless at thirty-five years of age. "They don't need people to work machinery anymore; robotics and computers have taken over," bemoaned Mike. Originally, Mike had gotten the job because he had "connections." Now, he found himself unemployed and feeling obsolete. "Maybe this is your chance to try something new," Roberta said encouragingly. "There are some courses you could take at the vocational college in high-demand areas." Mike mulled over her suggestion and imagined what it would require to "re-create" himself.

Lord Jesus, give us the courage to try new things, learn new skills, and face the future confidently through faith in you.

Talk It Over: *Complete the following sentence. "If I suddenly lost my job and felt obsolete, I would _____." Share any concerns raised by your answers and pray about them together.*

May 3 ~ Your Talent

"Again, it will be like a man going on a journey, who called his servants and entrusted his property to them. . . . But the man who had received the one talent went off, dug a hole in the ground and hid his master's money."

—Matthew 25:14, 18 (NIV)

No one knew security software better than Jerry did. Coworkers called him "the genius who sat on his potential." When asked whether the company's network security system was adequate, Jerry mumbled a perfunctory, "Yeah, sure." *They don't pay me enough to respond every time this company gets*

96

worried, Jerry thought to himself. Without a financial reward, Jerry was content to do only what he was asked to do. *This is just a job; no need to waste my talent,* he reasoned.

One year later . . .

After months of litigation with a rival firm, the legal expenses and bad press surrounding the case forced Jerry's employers into bankruptcy. A computer hacker had stolen plans for a new product design. Jerry's security software failed to protect the company. The news media vilified his reputation, and the company fired Jerry from a job that he thought was not worthy of his talent.

Dear Lord, help us work because of the inspiration that comes from working up to our God-given potential.

Talk It Over: *Discuss the following: Which is the greater source of inspiration for your present job—financial reward or satisfaction of a good day's work?*

May 4 ~ No Turning Back

Jesus replied, "No one who puts his hand to the plow and looks back is fit for service in the kingdom of God."

—Luke 9:62 (NIV)

Marilyn had never felt so alive! She had joined a Bible study class that was studying the words of Jesus. This week's Bible verse remained etched in her mind, "Jesus replied, 'No one who puts his hand to the plow and looks back is fit for service in the kingdom of God.'" For the first time in Marilyn's life, she felt she wanted to serve Christ. At the end of class, Marilyn joined others in the class who touched the backs of their wooden chairs to symbolically express their desire to *put their hands to the plow* and follow Jesus.

The next morning . . .

Marilyn was a dispatcher for a cab company. Usually, Marilyn was the main instigator of the bawdy "shop talk" that took place. Now, she wanted to put that behind her. As usual, the drivers heckled Marilyn with lewd comments. *How am I going to make it?* she wondered. Just then her hand touched the back of her wooden chair and she remembered her vow—no turning back.

Dear Lord, help us turn toward you and away from old offensive behaviors.

Talk It Over: *As a couple, agree to exhibit Christian behavior at work; then, carry some material object with you to remind you of your agreement.*

May 5 ~ Restoration

Brothers, if someone is caught in a sin, you who are spiritual should restore him gently. But watch yourself, or you also may be tempted.
—Galatians 6:1 (NIV)

"She's a liar!" Angie said, bursting through the door in frustration. "Who's a liar?" asked her husband Burt. Angie spewed for the next thirty minutes, retelling the day's events at work. Her friend and coworker, Helena, insisted on taking credit for work that Angie had produced. Angie was fantasizing about every possible way to embarrass Helena when Burt asked a question that she wasn't ready for: "Can you forgive her?"

Why? Why should I forgive her? Angie fumed silently. "Well," Burt continued, "what Helena did was terrible. I've never seen you so angry. But I'm wondering what would happen if you forgave her. What if you explained to her how much you value your friendship and how she hurt you by taking credit for your work? If your friendship means anything to Helena, maybe she will admit her mistake. In the process, you two may be able to restore your friendship."

Dear Lord, help us find ways to restore relationships when we are tempted to destroy them.

Talk It Over: *Discuss any work-related relationships that may need restoration. End with prayer for insights about restoring those relationships.*

May 6 ~ Loving Unlovable People

"But I tell you who hear me: Love your enemies, do good to those who hate you, bless those who curse you, pray for those who mistreat you."

—Luke 6:27-28 (NIV)

"I boiled inwardly until I blew hot air into the sky." As Marjorie read those words from her journal, a satisfying smile spread across her face. She had written those words three months ago after an argument with her supervisor. Marjorie was so enraged that she had wanted to change jobs. While considering her options, a few unsolicited questions had interrupted her thoughts: *So you're going to run away from another situation? Why not try to improve your department?*

Where did those questions come from? Marjorie had wondered. Regardless of the origin of those questions, they had gotten Marjorie's attention. Over time, her prayers had evolved from wanting her supervisor to move to wishing that her supervisor would just leave her alone. Finally, Marjorie began to pray for patience and understanding when she learned that her supervisor's wife was diagnosed with cancer. As Marjorie continued to pray for her supervisor, she noticed a greater capacity to love others.

Dear Lord, help us realize that our capacity to love is increased when we are challenged to love the unlovable.

Talk It Over: *As a couple, identify people you have trouble loving. Choose one or two people you have identified, and begin to pray that God will bless them.*

May 7 ~ Follow Me

Then he said to them all: "If anyone would come after me, he must deny himself and take up his cross daily and follow me."

—Luke 9:23 (NIV)

"He'll do anything for a promotion," Sydney complained. One of Sydney's coworkers spent an excessive amount of energy promoting himself in front of upper management. To Sydney's dismay, he learned that his coworker actually received a promotion after only six months on the job. Now Sydney faced a dilemma: should he also play office politics or continue to depend on his work record?

Sydney shared his frustration with his wife, Carol. "But if you start promoting yourself and forcing your way into the private circles of upper management, what will happen to you?" Carol replied. "What does your 'self' really need?" Carol's words drove Sydney into silent reflection.

Dear Lord, help us sort out what is best for our inner "selves."

Talk It Over: *Discuss the importance of maintaining your "self" in ways that exhibit Christian character.*

May 8 ~ Important Work

But Martha was distracted by all the preparations that had to be made. She came to him and asked, "LORD, don't you care that my sister has left me to do the work by myself? Tell her to help me!"
—Luke 10:40 (NIV)

Adrienne shuffled through the paperwork on her desk, barely noticing the next person in line. It was nearing the end of the day, and Adrienne knew that she wouldn't be able to clock out until all of her paperwork was finished. The woman standing in front of her desk cleared her throat, announcing her arrival. Adrienne glanced at her and put her index finger in the air without saying a word. That simple gesture was all it took to unleash an unholy tirade from the woman. She had been bounced from one line to the other all afternoon.

Instinctively, Adrienne bristled and prepared to respond with unequaled fury when "something" stopped her. As if time were standing still, she replayed the scenario in her mind in a split second. The woman had a baby in her arms and two toddlers holding her skirt. Her face showed signs of fatigue and frustration. *Is my paperwork more important than this lady?* Adrienne thought.

Dear Lord, help us remember how important it is to care about people first.

Talk It Over: *Consider ways in which you can put people first at your workplace.*

May 9 ~ Subtle Temptations

Then he said to them, "Watch out! Be on your guard against all kinds of greed; a man's life does not consist in the abundance of his possessions."

—*Luke 12:15 (NIV)*

Fred rested his head in his hands. Mounting debt had taken its toll on him. No one had prepared him for the subtle temptations of middle management. *You've got to look the part,* Fred had thought. After landing the job, Fred had bought several expensive suits and had leased an impressive luxury car. Before long, the leather luggage and designer fountain pens had followed. *If you're going to go after the big fish, you've got to have the right equipment,* Fred had reasoned.

Everything seemed to be going well until the economy took a nosedive. Suddenly, no one was interested in making big purchases. The "big fish" weren't biting, and Fred's commission-based income plummeted. The bills continued to roll in, but Fred only had his possessions that made him "look good." No one had prepared him for the subtle temptations of middle management.

Dear Lord, help us recognize the subtle temptations that lead to greed.

Talk It Over: *Consider the following questions: What role does image play in your job? What do you really need in order to perform well at work?*

May 10 ~ "Push"

Masters, provide your slaves with what is right and fair, because you know that you also have a Master in heaven.

—*Colossians 4:1 (NIV)*

Greg prided himself on getting the most production out of his department. No one ran a "tighter ship" than he did. Over time, Greg's sense of identity became tied to his reputation to compel people to perform beyond industry standards. This ability to drive people gave Greg a sense of power and authority that he had never experienced before. Eventually, pushing people beyond their limit became a source of entertainment for him. At lunch, Greg often joked about how his workers whined when he pushed them to meet his quota. People had become like things, like possessions, to him. He lost sight of their faces and chose to see their ability to produce products. For that he earned the nickname "Push."

One day, Greg was surprised to see the assembly line stopped. He was even more amazed when his boss called him into the conference room to discuss why twenty-seven workers refused to work until someone listened to their complaints about working for "Push."

Dear Lord, we choose to see people as precious human beings rather than as cogs in machinery.

Talk It Over: *Think of special ways to acknowledge the importance of the people with whom you work.*

May 11 ~ Persevere

Not only so, but we also rejoice in our sufferings, because we know that suffering produces perseverance; perseverance, character; and character, hope.
—Romans 5:3 (NIV)

"How can you keep working for Mr. Jacobs?" Sam's friend asked. Sam just smiled in response to the question. Mr. Jacobs was a surly manager with an irritating disposition. No one could stay composed when Jacobs went on a tirade—except Sam. Sam's uncanny ability to withstand Mr. Jacobs's strident personality was due to a friendly relationship that he established a year earlier.

A year ago, Sam met Mr. Miller, a friend of Sam's late father. Sam's father had worked for Mr. Jacobs as well. On many occasions, Mr. Miller ate lunch with Sam and retold vivid stories about how Sam's father survived in this same workplace. "Your father was a joy to work with," Mr. Miller said reminiscing. "He wore Mr. Jacobs down with quiet consistency and job performance. Your father had such an even disposition that Mr. Jacobs never got the satisfaction of seeing him upset. You're made of that same stock, so don't let Mr. Jacobs get to you." When tempted to lose his temper, Sam remembered that he, too, could persevere as his father did.

Dear Lord, we choose to rejoice in the midst of sufferings, knowing that we can persevere.

Talk It Over: *Decide to turn a situation around at work through unflustered perseverance. Share your progress with each other periodically.*

May 12 ~ Is It "Good" Enough?

Do not allow what you consider good to be spoken of as evil.
—Romans 14:16 (NIV)

"I told her that she needed to be more careful about who she went out with. You can't be too careful these days." Cassandra recalled the unsolicited advice she had given her coworker. Cassandra had just broken up with an unfaithful boyfriend. She still smarted from the emotional wounds suffered from that shattered relationship. Now, she spoke with impassioned conviction about the dangers of not "checking out" a potential dating partner thoroughly enough. Anyone who made eye contact with Cassandra was fair game. Her advice was sound but often unwelcome by her captive audience. People accused her of being "preachy."

At lunch, Cassandra sat alone wondering why her coworkers were "too busy" to eat with her. People failed to appreciate the "good advice" that Cassandra was offering.

Dear Lord, help us know the difference between giving good advice and imposing unwanted personal opinions.

Talk It Over: *Talk about the perception that you believe others have about you when you share advice with them.*

May 13 ~ Keep the Faith

Therefore, since we have a great high priest who has gone through the heavens, Jesus the Son of God, let us hold firmly to the faith we profess.
—Hebrews 4:14 (NIV)

Melvin looked up at the ceiling for a few seconds in disgust. He had just noticed that Stan, his supervisor, had a sexually explicit calendar lying on his desk. "Hey, Melvin, how's it going?" Stan said, startled by Melvin's presence. Trying to regroup, Stan invited Melvin to join him in "appreciating" the beauty of the month. "She's really easy on the eyes, huh Mel?" Stan showed no embarrassment at having the calendar or inviting Melvin to look at it. Meanwhile, Melvin struggled to deal with the uninvited image in his mind.

That single incident disturbed Melvin tremendously. As a new Christian, he wanted to hold firm to the faith that he had professed. He was bothered by the temptation and upset that he could not clear his mind. Somehow, he found the strength to take the first step in keeping the faith—he turned and walked out the door.

Dear Lord, help us deal with unexpected temptations in ways that please you.

Talk It Over: *If you experienced a disturbing encounter as Melvin did, how would you deal with your feelings about it afterward?*

May 14 ~ At the Close of the Workday

Give thanks in all circumstances, for this is God's will for you in Christ Jesus.
                                                    —1 Thessalonians 5:18 (NIV)

One evening, we had the rare privilege of having dinner with a great Civil Rights leader and his wife after a program at the university. "Ah! That's good coffee!" the man said.

"Yes, dear, it is good coffee, isn't it?" his wife added. He took another sip. "My, that coffee tastes good!" he repeated. This time, she only smiled in response as she relished his enjoyment of one last cup before they retired for the evening.

The years had taken their toll on this well-respected man, and now he was a mere shadow of the man I remembered from my youth. From what I understood from his wife, it was a miracle that he was there with her, with us, enjoying a cup of coffee. Though his moves were slow and deliberate, nothing had altered his spirit—or hers. I went home that evening with a new sense of purpose. From that day forward, I made it my business to look for ways to enjoy whatever moments I could with my partner for life—particularly at the close of the workday.

Dear Lord, today we are reminded that there is more to life than work. Help us enjoy life's simple pleasures with each other.

Talk It Over: *Discuss some simple pleasures that the two of you may enjoy at the close of the workday.*

May 15 ~ Love Bends

In this same way, husbands ought to love their wives as their own bodies. He who loves his wife loves himself.
                                                         —*Ephesians 5:28 (NIV)*

"Are you sure you are all right with this?" Marissa asked.

"Yes, of course I am!" John answered

Marissa was accustomed to the woman making adjustments when career moves were considered. This time, the tables were turned; Marissa was next in line for a big promotion in a branch office on the other side of the United States. After talking it over with John, they agreed that she should take the job and that their family would relocate. Though she never doubted John's sincerity, all this role-reversal business made Marissa uncomfortable. What would his parents say? What if it didn't work? She almost wanted John to veto the project to let her off the hook. She made one last plea: "What about your job?"

"But what about *yours?*" John countered. "You have worked hard for this promotion, and you deserve to give it a try. You have bent over backward for my career more times than I can count; can't I at least bend a little for yours?"

Dear Lord, prepare us to "bend" out of love when opportunities for career changes arise.

Talk It Over: *Discuss your readiness to relocate, learn new job skills, and so forth, if one of you were offered a terrific job in another location.*

May 16 ~ Encouraged to Do Good Deeds

And let us consider how we may spur one another on toward love and good deeds.
—Hebrews 10:24 (NIV)

"Way to go, Bobby! All right, Maria!" Wilbur was making his morning rounds around the plant. People loved Wilbur. He was "Mr. Encouragement." Few people would have imagined that Wilbur was the owner of this business. He wasn't cooped behind glass in some boardroom. Wilbur was a hands-on type of guy. He believed that the most important people in his company were his frontline people—the receptionist, the clerical help, the assembly workers. Every morning, Wilbur gave them an unofficial pep talk. He knew everyone's first name and invited their suggestions for improving production and quality by simply asking, "How's it going?" If anyone had learned the art of motivation, it was Wilbur. By word and action, Wilbur demonstrated what it means to spur people on toward love and good deeds.

Dear Lord, we recognize that we have the capacity to encourage people every day. We pray that we will never forget our potential to inspire others to do good deeds.

Talk It Over: *Brainstorm simple things you can do to encourage others to do good deeds. Commit to trying at least one of your ideas today.*

May 17 ~ Changes

Don't let anyone look down on you because you are young, but set an example for the believers in speech, in life, in love, in faith and in purity.
—1 Timothy 4:12 (NIV)

"He works second shift now so they won't have to get a babysitter."
It felt like the tenth time that I was overhearing my mother's telephone conversations with friends about her visit to see her grandson, my son, after the birth of his first child. My oldest son and his wife were making earnest efforts to take joint responsibility for parenting our grandson. "Gertie," she continued, "times have certainly changed since we raised our children. Now fathers are in the delivery room, and a whole lot of the

106

mommas are working! I never thought I'd see that grandson of mine changing diapers, but I think he's doing just fine. . . . You are right, girl; times are certainly changing. . . . Yeah, they looked happy to me."

About then I forgot about eavesdropping and began to daydream about the kind of changes I might be describing to my telephone friends when I reach my mother's age.

Dear Lord, our children need us. Help us make whatever changes we need to make in order to bless our family.

Talk It Over: *Consider your present family needs. Are there any changes that could or should be made in your work schedule?*

May 18 ~ Perspective

The brother in humble circumstances ought to take pride in his high position. But the one who is rich should take pride in his low position, because he will pass away like a wild flower.

—James 1:9-10 (NIV)

"This is where I work!" Melissa said with pride. She worked for a large produce distribution center. "What do you do?" asked her friend Barbara. For the next few minutes, Melissa described her role in the business and the importance of what they did. Although Melissa had an entry-level job, she took pride in her work because she recognized that what she did was a vital part of the success of the business. With joy, Ms. Sanford, the owner of the business, put different pictures of smiling children on the walls each month. Each month this company donated enough produce to feed three hundred children in their city. "When all of us work well, we make a better profit. When that happens, we have more to donate to people who need food. I am proud to be a part of this company—even if I do just mop the floors," said Melissa in triumphant tones.

Dear Lord, help us take pride in the role that we play at work.

Talk It Over: *Describe the role that you play at your place of employment. Consider working with renewed vigor today as an offering to your employer— and to God.*

May 19 ~ Little Things

Catch for us the foxes, the little foxes that ruin the vineyards, our vineyards that are in bloom.

—Song of Songs 2:15 (NIV)

Barry worked as a quality control inspector for a major industrial company. He prided himself on being highly disciplined and precise. This penchant for perfection played itself out in other areas of Barry's life as well. At the dinner table, Barry's wife, Maureen, routinely responded to comments like these: "Honey, this popcorn needs a little more salt. Sweetie, get me another fork, please; this one's a little dirty. Darling, would you cook this steak a few more minutes? It's a little rare."

For years, Maureen tried to make Barry's life a "little" better, until one morning . . .

Barry took one sip of his coffee and said, "This could use a little more sugar; would you bring me some?"

"No!" replied Maureen. "I'm a little tired." Barry looked in disbelief. Maureen had never responded like that toward him before. *"Catch for us the foxes, the little foxes that ruin the vineyards."*

Dear Lord, guide us toward conversations that encourage and strengthen our relationship.

Talk It Over: *Share with each other your responses to the following question: What affect do work-related habits have on our conversations?*

May 20 ~ Humility

Humble yourselves, therefore, under God's mighty hand, that he may lift you up in due time.

—1 Peter 5:6

"They keep promoting everybody but me!" Jason said in exasperation. "I do all the work around here. . . . I've been here longer than anybody else. . . . I never get the respect I deserve."

Jason's harangue never ceased. Everyone knew how highly Jason regarded himself. In reality, Jason was good at what he did. He was a valuable worker, but he demanded so much credit that management found it difficult to get others to work with him. Jason's negative work attitude often followed him home. Instead of seeing his home as a safe place to let off steam, he often held his family hostage with his self-pity.

Dear Lord, today I choose to humble myself before you prior to entering the workplace.

Talk It Over: *Discuss the following: According to your experience, is work only about job performance or is our ability to relate to others equally important? What benefits result when you choose to be humble?*

May 21 ~ When You Least Expect It

Do not forget to entertain strangers, for by so doing some people have entertained angels without knowing it.
—Hebrews 13:2 (NIV)

There was no nice way to say it: Jennifer's job was dull. Sure, the pay was good, but the daily routine was too predictable. Jennifer feared that monotony would dull her sense of creativity and adventure. In the midst of her doldrums, an interesting elderly woman wandered in from outside and made her way to Jennifer's desk. She looked out of place; this was an industrial plant. Immediately, the woman asked Jennifer if she knew where Mr. Donald Smith worked. Jennifer looked on her employee roster but found no Don Smith. For the next ten minutes, the woman politely asked a series of innocent questions that Jennifer patiently answered. Finally, the woman thanked Jennifer for being so kind and walked outside.

Initially, Jennifer thought the woman would be another worrisome interruption. Instead, the conversation actually lifted Jennifer's spirits. She seemed to connect with the woman as they chased after each question. In retrospect, the encounter was a blessing because the woman was so friendly and loving in her speech. You never know when you may be entertaining angels.

Dear Lord, help us see encounters with strangers as great opportunities to share your love and grace.

Talk It Over: *Discuss possible ways to respond to nonthreatening strangers.*

May 22 ~ You're Not Lost

Trust in the LORD with all your heart and lean not on your own understanding; in all your ways acknowledge him, and he will make your paths straight.
—Proverbs 3:5-6 (NIV)

"After all I've done for this company, this is what I get—a pink slip." George looked at his termination notice in disbelief. For ten years he had worked as the director of airport security. After terrorism put the country on alert, George got nervous—he was from the Middle East. His accent had not been an issue before; now it identified him as "other." His superiors decided to step up company security practices and ordered more thorough background checks on all employees working in "sensitive" areas. George was one of those employees. Working was a source of pride for George. Without a job, he felt like less than a man.

At home, George could only mutter repeatedly, "We're lost; we're lost." George's wife, Monica, consoled him, saying, "People are nervous now. They are doing strange things, but God knows what we need. We just have to trust God. We're not lost because God's not lost."

Dear Lord, help us remind each other to trust in you when we face our greatest challenges.

Talk It Over: *Discuss the role that you think employment should play in determining your self-worth. Then, discuss the role that a relationship with Jesus Christ plays in determining your self-worth.*

May 23 ~ What Do You Expect?

Be self-controlled and alert. Your enemy the devil prowls around like a roaring lion looking for someone to devour. Resist him, standing firm in the faith.
—1 Peter 5:8-9a (NIV)

"I can't believe the way people treat each other around here," Belinda said in hushed tones. She had only been on the job a few weeks and was a little leery of sharing her opinions with anyone. Fortunately, Belinda was able to find a prayer partner at work with whom she could discuss her feelings. There was a tremendous level of distrust throughout the workplace. Belinda's supervisor had a "no nonsense" leadership style—authoritative, full of threats, and intolerant of rebuttal.

Cindy, Belinda's prayer partner, listened to Belinda's concerns with sincere interest. "It is disturbing when we're confronted with challenging behaviors. I shared the same disgust that you do when I was hired here. After my first day here, I talked to my husband about it, and he said something that made rethink my attitude. He said, 'What do you expect? Do you think everyone at work is a Christian?'"

Dear Lord, help us understand what it means to work "in the world."

Talk It Over: *Discuss how to cope with ungodly behaviors that you may encounter in the workplace.*

May 24 ~ Day-Tight Compartments

"Therefore do not worry about tomorrow, for tomorrow will worry about itself. Each day has enough trouble of its own."
—*Matthew 6:34 (NIV)*

How often do we worry about things that have not happened yet? How would you respond if you learned that your job description was expanded to include an unanticipated responsibility? How do you respond to deadlines? What about the thought of a "possible" problem with your report? Too often, our natural response is to worry about what tomorrow may bring.

Worry can fuel the imagination to drive us into tomorrow before tomorrow ever arrives. If we tally the number of times that tomorrow's problems became actual problems, we may be surprised at the results. How can we combat premature entry into tomorrow? Why not deal with life in "day-tight compartments"—"each day has enough trouble of its own."

Dear Lord, we recognize there is no need to borrow trouble from the future. Help us live in "day-tight compartments."

Talk It Over: *Write down the things that worry you. Discuss how living in "day-tight compartments" could help limit the amount of worry that concerns you.*

May 25 ~ What to Do About Time?

Be very careful, then, how you live—not as unwise but as wise, making the most of every opportunity, because the days are evil.

—Ephesians 5:15-16 (NIV)

"All I want you to do is sit at this desk and answer the phone if it rings. You might want to bring a book; it can get pretty boring around here."

Angela couldn't believe her ears. This was her first day on the job, and her supervisor told her to bring a book to work! Angela struggled with the idea of reading on the job because she believed that you were supposed to "work" at work. She grew up in a household that never enjoyed much idle time. Now, Angela held a job that confounded her with plenty of idle time and the opportunity to take advantage of it. This was a moral issue that troubled Angela. In her estimation, there was no room in the workday for any activities outside of work.

What should happen at work? Who should decide how to spend idle time at work? Given the opportunity, what would you do?

Dear Lord, we face opportunities to fill time every day; show us how to respond when faced with the luxury of extra time.

Talk It Over: *What kinds of things do you believe are all right to do during idle moments at work?*

May 26 ~ Who Is the Master?

"Everything is permissible for me"—but not everything is beneficial. "Everything is permissible for me"—but I will not be mastered by anything.

—1 Corinthians 6:12 (NIV)

"Honey, I'm home." Silvia's words hung in the air awaiting a response. Her husband, Ben, stared at the computer monitor unmoved by her announcement. After checking in three other rooms, Silvia finally found Ben in the basement, reworking his spreadsheet.

"Sweetie, didn't you hear me calling you?" Silvia asked with a perturbed tone.

112

"Oh, hi, sugar; how was your day?" Ben answered, oblivious to her exasperated voice.

"Ben, why aren't you ready? You know Mom invited us to dinner tonight," Silvia retorted.

The demands of Ben's job consumed his attention. Work had blurred the line between job responsibilities and family life. Silvia began to wonder why work held Ben's attention so intently. Ben's work ethic was admirable, but could it be that work had become Ben's master?

Dear Lord, whenever we need it, remind us to keep our family priorities in proper perspective.

Talk It Over: *How do you know when it is time to stop working at home?*

May 27 ~ Above Board

Rather, we have renounced secret and shameful ways; we do not use deception, nor do we distort the word of God. On the contrary, by setting forth the truth plainly we commend ourselves to every man's conscience in the sight of God.
—2 Corinthians 4:2 (NIV)

"I need you to sign these work orders, Roger."

Everything seemed innocent enough until Roger began to read the work orders more closely. The orders were to dispose of the computer hardware on the second floor.

"How are we disposing of these computers?" Roger asked.

"Oh, I don't know, the way we always have," came the reply.

Roger had just heard about "e-trash," which referred to the toxins in computer hardware. "E-trash" requires a special type of disposal. The work order would have combined their old hardware with that of several other companies. No one seemed to be interested in the final destination of this refuse.

Roger declined to sign the work orders until he got some questions answered. Upon further investigation, Roger learned that the disposal company was sidestepping environmental laws by shipping e-trash to other countries. Following a television exposé, this disposal company and all of its clients were facing an international class action lawsuit. Roger was glad that he had decided to act above board.

Dear Lord, teach us to ask the right questions about unclear issues.

Talk It Over: *Discuss the way that you might respond if you learned that your employer was engaged in questionable practices.*

May 28 ~ Knowing When to Leave

"And if any place will not welcome you or listen to you, shake the dust off your feet when you leave, as a testimony against them."
—*Mark 6:11 (NIV)*

Jobs are sometimes difficult to come by. But, what happens when you discover that people on your new job do not welcome you?

Cindy walked into her first staff meeting with a knot in her stomach. She was the first woman to be promoted to middle management in ten years. Cindy was a systems analyst who was well versed in her field. Unfortunately, her superiors were computer illiterates. They insisted on running the second-generation family business using "traditional principles."

At work, Cindy's suggestions were frequently overlooked or tabled and sent to committee for further study. Her instincts were to stay and fight the subtle discrimination that she was facing. She felt a sense of duty to represent all women everywhere facing similar challenges. Still, nagging questions concerned her. What would she gain if she stayed and fought? What would she gain if she found a different job? Cindy struggled to know when it is right to leave a job.

Dear Lord, help us determine when to "shake the dust" off our feet and leave a troubling situation.

Talk It Over: *What helps you determine when it is best to leave a disturbing work situation?*

May 29 ~ Labor Division

A kindhearted woman gains respect, but ruthless men gain only wealth. A kind man benefits himself, but a cruel man brings himself harm.
—*Proverbs 11:16-17 (NIV)*

114

Frank looked around the house in dismay. Dirty dishes were piled here, toddler's toys were scattered there, and the air betrayed no hint that dinner had been started.

"Patience! Where are you?" Frank yelled throughout the house.

"Shhh, you'll wake the baby," Patience replied in hushed tones.

"What happened? It looks like a war zone around here," Frank said, trying to control his consternation.

"We need to talk," Patience responded softly.

Frank and Patience both worked full-time jobs. Patience arrived home an hour before Frank did. Normally, Patience rushed in the door to put the house back together and start dinner. Tonight, she had to stay at work an extra half hour. She got home ten minutes before Frank did. Patience walked in, took one look at the dirty breakfast dishes and the toys strewn about, and decided it was time to talk. Both Frank and Patience loved each other and were very kindhearted, but neither of them had ever taken time to talk about the division of labor around the house.

Dear Lord, help us share honestly and kindly our expectations of labor division around the house.

Talk It Over: *Discuss the following. Do you believe Patience should have spoken up sooner? Does being kind mean avoiding touchy conversations with each other? What issues regarding labor division around the house do you need to discuss?*

May 30 ~ Adjustments

"Lord, if it's you," Peter replied, "tell me to come to you on the water." "Come," he said. Then Peter got down out of the boat and walked on the water to Jesus.
—Matthew 14:28-29 (NIV)

Imagine the adjustment in thinking Peter had to make in order to climb out of a secure boat and begin to walk on water. The ability to adjust to new things is something that Ed and Laura needed. Ed and Laura were highly successful in their professions. Both earned six-figure salaries. For the first few years of their marriage, they traveled in the fast lane of the corporate world. Laura was rumored to be the next vice president of operations. Then, without warning, Laura discovered that she was pregnant.

This unexpected turn of events thrust Laura and Ed into the valley of decision. Once her firm learned that she was pregnant, what would her chances be of becoming vice president of operations? After the child was born, what would happen to Laura's career? This was a road that Ed and Laura had never walked down before. Like Peter, they needed to adjust their thinking and learn to walk on water.

Dear Lord, when the unexpected arises, give us the courage to adjust our thinking and face the situation head on.

Talk It Over: *When the unexpected happens, what role do you allow God to play in your decision making?*

May 31 ~ Breaking Bread

When he was at the table with them, he took bread, gave thanks, broke it and began to give it to them. Then their eyes were opened and they recognized him.
—Luke 24:30-31a (NIV)

Work has an innate ability to overrun the boundaries of nine to five. Without warning, work concerns can pile into the backseat of our cars and follow us home. Thankfully, there is a way to redeem each day. The resurrected Jesus spoke with the travelers to Emmaus without them recognizing him. Only when he broke bread did they understand that they were in the presence of Jesus the Christ. Mealtimes can be times of revelation for us. The relaxing atmosphere created by enjoying a good meal may be enough to help us see the beauty of our children's artwork or the joy of our spouse's laughter.

At mealtime we can pray before eating and continue the blessing through our conversations with each other. "Breaking bread" affords us the opportunity to learn more about each other by being attentive to what has affected us. After a long day at work, consider the benefits of breaking bread with your family.

Dear Lord, mealtimes can become a collection of sacred moments for our family. May our mealtimes be holy times of fellowship.

Talk It Over: *In what ways are mealtimes sacred moments for your family?*

June

ALL IN THE FAMILY

Ulrike and Clifton Guthrie

June 1 ~ Family Stories

This is the story of the family of Jacob.

—Genesis 37:2a

A shocking number of stories in the Bible are about broken families: parents abusing children, and children revenging themselves on parents or hurting each other. Think about Cain and Abel (Genesis 4:1-16); Abraham's near sacrifice of Isaac (Genesis 22); Amnon's rape of his sister, Tamar, and Absalom's revenge (2 Samuel 13).

Our wager is that most of our families, in some way, are like these families in the Bible. They are complicated stories of deep love and terrible pain. We are children who have somehow grown up to have children. We are like a young woman who looks in a mirror one day and suddenly sees her mother staring back. But scripture tells of a God whose own divine story runs like a thread through the very hearts of our families, a thread that may draw us all together in the end.

We begin our month's journey with the family story of Jacob. Telling some of his family story over the next several days will be no cakewalk. We will encounter pettiness, jealousy, kidnapping, and deception. But before it is over, we will also encounter forgiveness, blessing, and reconciliation.

God, you know us as we really are. Sew your thread of grace through the heart of our family.

Talk It Over: *What stands out when you tell family stories? Bitterness and bickering, or acts of kindness and generosity?*

June 2 ~ Family Gossip

Joseph, being seventeen years old, was shepherding the flock with his brothers; he was a helper to the sons of Bilhah and Zilpah, his father's wives; and Joseph brought a bad report of them to their father.

—*Genesis 37:2*b

Gossip is like electricity that runs through the lines of a family, and it can be especially destructive in large or blended families. Jacob had such a family. He had many children (Exodus 1:4 says it was eventually seventy!), with at least four different women: his wives Rachel and Leah, and two of their servants, Bilhah and Zilpah. Of all these children, Genesis mentions by name the twelve sons, including Joseph, who became leaders of the twelve tribes of Israel, but only a single daughter, Dinah, who was raped (see Genesis 34). Women in that culture were the most vulnerable members of the family, making young Joseph's gossip about Bilhah and Zilpah particularly reprehensible.

We admire Joseph as the fast-talking dream interpreter for the pharaoh. But Joseph's gifted tongue could be a blessing or a curse, depending on how he chose to use it.

Forgive us, God, for tongues that gossip and ears that are too eager to hear bad things about others. Let our words build up others rather than tear them down.

Talk It Over: *How do you talk about one another in your family? Do the stories you tell about each other build one another up, or tear each other down?*

June 3 ~ Daddy's Favorite

Now Israel loved Joseph more than any other of his children, because he was the son of his old age; and he had made him a long robe with sleeves. But when his brothers saw that their father loved him more than all his brothers, they hated him, and could not speak peaceably to him.

—Genesis 37:3-4

We only have two children, and everything seems like a balancing act. Are the household chores distributed fairly? Are their allowances fair for their ages? Do we take care that they are both fully secure in the knowledge that they are loved by both of us?

One of the most destructive things that can happen to a family is for parents to play favorites between their children. In Jacob's family, the central family tragedy was that he loved his youngest son, Joseph, more than his other sons. Jacob should have scolded Joseph for his gossiping tongue and defended his wives when Joseph brought a bad report about them. Instead, he gave him a valuable and beautiful robe. The other brothers, who also wanted their father's attention and approval, naturally resented their favored brother, Joseph. From the moment it was given, this robe was trouble.

You accept us unconditionally, O God. Help us as parents to love our children in ways that encourage them to love others, too.

Talk It Over: *Think about the different relationships between members of your family. Do any of them exclude others, or cause jealousy and stress in your family? As a couple, find a way to pay more attention to a person who feels neglected.*

June 4 ~ Being Consistent

Once Joseph had a dream, and when he told it to his brothers, they hated him even more. He said to them, "Listen to this dream that I dreamed. There we were, binding sheaves in the field. Suddenly my sheaf rose and stood upright; then your sheaves gathered around it, and bowed down to my sheaf."

—Genesis 37:5-7

Joseph was Daddy's favorite, and everybody knew it. He rubbed salt in his family's wound, not by having a dream about his success, but by reporting it.

Children have different gifts and abilities. Some will be successful, and others will struggle in life. Joseph *did* turn out to be something like a prodigy at dreaming and dream interpretation. But, in keeping with his tendency to gossip, it was his tongue that caused the trouble. However true the dream was, his brothers "hated him even more" for his boasting (Genesis 37:8). In a second, even more grandiose dream, Joseph envisioned "the sun, the moon, and eleven stars" bowing down before him (Genesis 37:9)—a dream so immodest that even Jacob finally had to rebuke him. But the family tragedy had already been set into motion. Jacob's correction of Joseph is a day late and a dollar short, as they used to say.

Lord, teach us to be wise and consistent as we raise our children, guiding them to share their talents graciously with others. Amen.

Talk It Over: *What gifts or strengths do you see in your children—or children in your extended family? How might you encourage them to use those gifts with generosity, kindheartedness, and patience?*

June 5 ~ When Parents Aren't Looking

Then Judah said to his brothers, "What profit is it if we kill our brother and conceal his blood? Come, let us sell him to the Ishmaelites, and not lay our hands on him, for he is our brother, our own flesh." And his brothers agreed. When some Midianite traders passed by, they drew Joseph up, lifting him out of the pit, and sold him to the Ishmaelites for twenty pieces of silver. And they took Joseph to Egypt.

—Genesis 37:26-28

This all happened behind Jacob's back, of course. It is probably good that we don't know about all the dramas that unfold between our children when we aren't looking. We both grew up as middle children and became adept at child politics—negotiating positions within the shifting alignments of our siblings. It wasn't unusual for one child to be "ganged up on" by the others, realizing that tattling to the parents would only make them more unpopular.

Our two kids love each other, but there are also times when they can barely stand to be under the same roof. As they grow into teenagers, how will they treat each other? What will happen when they leave home? Will they stay close or drift apart? As parents, we set the tone in the family; but in the end, the love our children share must find its own way.

God, help us model good relationships with our brothers and sisters for the sake of our own children. Amen.

Talk It Over: *Think together about the relationships you have with your brothers and sisters. Resolve today to send them an e-mail, give them a call, or make a visit.*

June 6 ~ Love and Grief

Then Jacob tore his garments, and put sackcloth on his loins, and mourned for his son many days. All his sons and all his daughters sought to comfort him; but he refused to be comforted, and said, "No, I shall go down to Sheol to my son, mourning." Thus his father bewailed him.

—Genesis 37:34-35

For years, the widower Dazell kept the lighthouse at North Head on Grand Manan Island, off the coast of New Brunswick. On those barren rocks he raised a family of twelve children. Despite the danger of the tides and the steep cliffs, the children grew up happily and without incident. The day came when one of the sons moved away from the lighthouse to live on the mainland. Soon after that, a friend asked the father how he was getting along. "I'm feeling lonesome," he replied. Mr. Dazell explained that now he had only eleven children in the lighthouse to keep him company. (Story source: Edwin Mitchell, *It's an Old State of Maine Custom* [New York: Vanguard Press, 1949], 50.)

Such is the intense love we have for each of our children that we truly may not know how to live without them when they leave the nest, or if we become separated from them by divorce or death. It can be cruel to offer advice to parents who have lost or been separated from their children. Better to quietly remember that our God experienced such grief when Jesus died, and understands.

God, be with those who grieve, and teach us how to cherish the days we are given to spend with those we love. Amen.

121

Talk It Over: *What grief or loss do you carry as a couple? What fears do you have about children of your own or children in your community? How has faith helped you cope with your grief, loss, or fear?*

June 7 ~ Using Our Children

Before the years of famine came, Joseph had two sons, whom Asenath daughter of Potiphera, priest of On, bore to him. Joseph named the firstborn Manasseh, "For," he said, "God has made me forget all my hardship and all my father's house." The second he named Ephraim, "For God has made me fruitful in the land of my misfortunes."

—Genesis 41:50-52

Joseph's sudden success in a foreign land fooled him into thinking that he had started a new life. He had risen to the top, married, and had two sons of his own. But inside his heart, whether he admitted it or not, he was still the lost boy who missed his father and had been betrayed by his brothers. Written into the very names of Joseph's two sons was the family's unresolved grief: Manasseh means "making to forget" and Ephraim means "to be fruitful." Like many parents, Joseph seemed to think that the purpose of having children is to bring healing and purpose to their own lives. But "forgetfulness" and "fruitfulness" wouldn't come to Joseph until he sought reconciliation with his father. On that day, Jacob would bless his two grandsons and adopt them as his own (see Genesis 48).

God, help us remember that our children are not here for our sake, but that they belong to you and are entrusted to us as a gift. Amen.

Talk It Over: *What personal hopes or needs from your childhood do you lay upon your own children? How does this complicate their lives? If you do not now have children but hope to someday, discuss your own childhoods in light of your hopes and dreams for your future children.*

June 8 ~ A Suitable Blessing

All these are the twelve tribes of Israel, and this is what their father said to them when he blessed them, blessing each one of them with a suitable blessing.

—Genesis 49:28

After Jacob discovered that Joseph was not only alive, but was the ruler of Egypt, he moved to be near him again. There they all lived united as a family at last, enjoying seventeen good years—years so good that they took the bitterness of separation out of their mouths. But Jacob was old (147 years! See Genesis 47:28), and his life started to draw away from him.

Laying on his deathbed, he gathered his twelve sons around him. Once they had been divided by their father's favoritism, but now he took time to lay his hands on each one and bless them. He blessed them each with a "suitable blessing," a strong and true word about the character of each son (though some of these blessings seem like curses!). But by doing so, he affirmed them. Jacob had finally grown up as a parent. He had learned to love his children for who they were.

Lord, let our children, and all children, be blessed through us as a couple. Amen.

Talk It Over: *Name aloud the ways that your children—or special children in your lives—are a blessing to you, to others, and to God. Find a way to speak a word of blessing to each of them today.*

June 9 ~ The Family Plot

They carried him [Jacob] to the land of Canaan and buried him in the cave of the field at Machpelah, the field near Mamre, which Abraham bought as a burial site from Ephron the Hittite. After he had buried his father, Joseph returned to Egypt with his brothers and all who had gone up with him to bury his father.
—Genesis 50:13-14

Jacob died in his old age with his reunited family at his bedside. But how would he keep them knit together as a family after he was gone? He did it by making it his dying wish for them to carry his body back to Canaan and bury him in the family plot (see Genesis 49:29-33). This was no easy request. It would have taken months to walk those several hundred hard miles by foot from Egypt to Mamre. But they did it. It must have changed them forever to make that journey together and then stand looking at each other over their father's burial mound. There they could see the burial plots of their great-grandparents, Abraham and Sarah; their grandparents, Isaac and Rebekah; and Leah, the mother of six of them.

Bound by a common heritage, they buried their differences and became brothers once again.

God, keep us connected to the rich soil of our family's past, and help us make that past a gift for our own children to cherish. Amen.

Talk It Over: *Do you regularly visit the graves of family members? Or show family photographs? How best can you connect your children—or children in your extended family—with their family heritage?*

June 10 ~ God's Goodness

Joseph wept when they spoke to him. Then his brothers also wept, fell down before him, and said, "We are here as your slaves." But Joseph said to them, "Do not be afraid! Am I in the place of God? Even though you intended to do harm to me, God intended it for good, in order to preserve a numerous people, as he is doing today. So have no fear; I myself will provide for you and your little ones." In this way he reassured them, speaking kindly to them.

—Genesis 50:17b-21

Genesis begins with the story of creation, and ends with the story of a family. After God created the world, God looked over all that had been made and pronounced it very good. Here at the end of Jacob's story, Joseph looked over all that had come to pass in their family, both brokenness and healing, sin and forgiveness, and traced the line of God's work in it all: "God intended it for good," he said.

More important than Joseph's insight of faith is the way that Joseph forgave his brothers. A man of great power, he could have lorded it over them. He could have exacted revenge for the way they had sold him into slavery long ago by accepting their offer to be slaves to him now. Instead, he vowed to provide for them and their families and reassured them with his words. Joseph treated his brothers with the same goodness that he recognized in God.

Creator God, help us treat our families with the goodness we see in your creation.

Talk It Over: *How is God creating good in and through your family? Vow to speak to others with kind words today.*

June 11 ~ Setting Limits

There were many lamps in the room upstairs where we were meeting. A young man named Eutychus, who was sitting in the window, began to sink off into a deep sleep while Paul talked still longer. Overcome by sleep, he fell to the ground three floors below and was picked up dead. But Paul went down, and bending over him took him in his arms, and said, "Do not be alarmed, for his life is in him."

—Acts 20:8-10

We were visiting some friends we hadn't seen in years, and enjoying the chance to introduce our children to one another. It was a school night for them, and we had an early flight to catch. After dinner, we washed the dishes and let the children play. At nine, we tucked our children in bed.

At ten o'clock, their children were still going full tilt and making a game of keeping our kids awake. Mature cable television shows blared in the living room. Same story at eleven, despite our repeated requests that our kids be allowed to sleep. It was sometime after midnight when their children finally collapsed in a heap of exhaustion and tears. The parents shuffled off to bed and our chance for adult conversation was over.

Eutychus's parents must have been relieved that he was all right after falling out of a window. But it sure makes you wonder what he was doing up after midnight in a crowded room full of adults!

God, help us respect the needs of our marriage and our children by setting appropriate limits. Amen.

Talk It Over: *How can you keep a healthy balance in your family life between time alone as adults and time with children? If you do not have children, how can you keep a healthy balance between time spent apart or focused on other things and time spent focused on each other?*

June 12 ~ Staying Connected

By the rivers of Babylon—there we sat down and there we wept when we remembered Zion. . . . How could we sing the LORD's song in a foreign land?

—Psalm 137:1-4

125

When the people of Israel were exiled to Babylon, they were heartsick for their homes. They wondered whether the God they had worshiped there was still with them in this new place. Could they find the courage to live and worship in an alien culture?

In our mobile and global society, today's couples make many compromises to be together. When we decided we wanted to be married, Uli moved from England to live in America and has lived here ever since. Even though we practice many British customs in our home and visit her parents whenever we can afford to, there are times when she feels like she is in exile from her memories. We work hard to stay connected with her roots, but we sometimes wonder whether our children will grow up feeling close to Uli's family or remember that part of where they come from.

God, you are present with all exiles—whether our childhood home is across the ocean or in another state. Help us honor each other's families and memories as we raise our children. Amen.

Talk It Over: *Make a list of the ways you can keep your childhood memories alive for your own children—or children in your extended family. How can you help them feel connected with their roots?*

June 13 ~ Become Like Children

At that time the disciples came to Jesus and asked, "Who is the greatest in the kingdom of heaven?" He called a child, whom he put among them, and said, "Truly I tell you, unless you change and become like children, you will never enter the kingdom of heaven."

—Matthew 18:1-3

Dr. Robert Coles, author of *The Spiritual Life of Children*, wrote about a conversation he had with a young girl from the slums of Rio de Janeiro. Her neighborhood was at the foot of Corcovado Mountain on which stands the famous ninety-eight-foot-tall statue of Jesus, arms spread wide as if trying to embrace the city. She had no father, and her mother had to work as a maid in a rich tourist hotel, despite being terminally ill with tuberculosis.

"When I look at Jesus up there," she said, "I wonder what He is thinking. He can see all of us, and he must have an opinion. . . . I hope Jesus

126

sees everything that goes on here. I hope he doesn't just stare into the ocean, like that statue!" (Robert Coles, *The Spiritual Life of Children* [Boston: Houghton Mifflin Co., 1990], pp. 90, 93.)

Children see the world the way it is. Their clarity of vision can help remove the scales from our eyes and the calluses from our hearts.

Jesus, we lift our suffering world into the strong embrace of your love, and pray for the coming of your kingdom for all. Amen.

Talk It Over: *Think of some hard questions your children—or other children in your lives—have asked you about God, the meaning of life, or the world around them. How do you answer those questions by how you live and pray?*

June 14 ~ From Weakness to Strength

I will pour out my spirit on all flesh; yours sons and your daughters shall prophesy, your old men shall dream dreams, and your young men shall see visions.
—*Joel 2:28*

We asked our daughter, Emelia, if she wanted to go for a walk in the woods after church. Our normally feisty and dramatic five-year-old said she couldn't—because she was too weak. Taken aback by this sudden change of character, we asked her why she was feeling weak. She said it was because during Sunday school she had been taught that "I am weak but he is strong," from the song "Jesus Loves Me, This I Know."

This prophecy from Joel tells a very different story than that familiar tune. It promises that our sons and daughters will be empowered with God's Spirit. This isn't only for their sakes, but also for the sake of the church. It is the children in our midst who may have the deepest dreams and the clearest visions.

Spirit of God, Spirit of strength, open our hearts to hear the words of grace our children speak. Amen.

Talk It Over: *Name some ways that you have experienced God through your children—or other children you know. How do they talk about God? When do you as a couple feel strong in your faith?*

June 15 ~ At the Pace of the Children

Then Esau said, "Let us journey on our way, and I will go alongside you." But Jacob said to him, "My lord knows that the children are frail and that the flocks and herds, which are nursing, are a care to me; and if they are overdriven for one day, all the flocks will die. Let my lord pass on ahead of his servant, and I will lead on slowly, according to the pace of the cattle that are before me and according to the pace of the children."

—Genesis 33:12-14b

We have made a decision as a couple not to let our children enroll in more than two after-school activities at a time. Life becomes too crazy for everyone if we try to do more. We all seem to be happier if the children have plenty of time to play in the tree house, swing from the maple tree, and kick the soccer ball around the yard.

In this story, Jacob proves to be a thoughtful father. He knows full well that it's no good pushing children or nursing animals faster than they can go. Without the flocks and the children, the family has no food and no future. Wisely, he decides not to try to keep up with the rest of the world, or let others determine how fast the family chooses to go. He lets the youngest and most vulnerable members set the pace for the whole family. In our frantic world, slowing down and simplifying our lives may be one of the most important gifts we give to our children.

Jesus, friend of the small and the frail, teach us to be content to set a reasonable pace for our family. Amen.

Talk It Over: *Do you ever feel like you and/or your children are being pushed too fast? When or how? How can you ensure that your family has plenty of time to relax and play?*

June 16 ~ Welcoming Children

Whoever welcomes one such child in my name welcomes me.

—Matthew 18:5

Nick is blending families after a divorce. He goes to great lengths to make his children and stepchildren feel settled: He moved to another state to be only minutes away from his children. He has kept the rhythm of spending family summer vacations at the coast close to their grandparents. He focuses on giving them the important comforts of home, not impressive treats. He juggles making his new preschool stepdaughters feel welcome while making his own two biological children feel they're still part of his heart. He takes his kids' typical regressions in stride. This is hard work for all, but it's eased by the love in which it's bathed.

Jesus' words about how we welcome him by welcoming a child remind us that children need our special attention. Whether we ourselves are divorced or not, we know too well the trauma it causes children. How we extend ourselves for the children around us shapes our society at large, child by child. Such caring for children is an incredibly important vocation.

Lord, may this priority for children become rooted deep in our hearts. Amen.

Talk It Over: *Consider caring for children—your own and others—as a call from Jesus. How can you "welcome" the children in your lives?*

June 17 ~ Keeping the Feast

Now every year his parents went to Jerusalem for the festival of the Passover. And when he was twelve years old, they went up as usual for the festival.
—Luke 2:41-42

Some Sundays our children invent creative excuses why they shouldn't go to church: not feeling well or lovely weather for hiking are typical. But they know that despite their moaning and groaning, we will always insist that they go. Persistent about searching for a loophole, they then ask why we have to go, and we remind them that we need each other there in our community of faith. We go to worship God and to learn the story of our faith. Reminding them about their friends there and the all-important snack after worship gets us out the door.

As with family rituals such as preparing for bedtime or welcoming guests, we help our children form habits of going to worship. True, they don't always get it; they don't always enjoy all of it. But we trust that, one day, like Jesus at age twelve, they will understand for themselves why they

129

have been brought there, and they will choose to engage their faith tradition at a deeper and more personal level.

God, we long for all children to grow in their understanding of you. Amen.

Talk It Over: *Which religious rituals do you keep with your children? If you do not have children of your own, how can you help pass on the rituals of your faith to future generations?*

June 18 ~ Among Friends and Relatives

When the festival was ended and they started to return, the boy Jesus stayed behind in Jerusalem, but his parents did not know it. Assuming that he was in the group of travelers, they went a day's journey. Then they started to look for him among their relatives and friends.

—Luke 2:43-44

Since Cliff is a theological seminary professor and Uli is a theological books editor, we often have to attend the same professional conferences. We've moved frequently, and our friends and families are far-flung. Consequently, sometimes we've taken our children, Tom and Emelia, with us to conferences—at some cost, particularly in how to juggle jobs while caring for them. Sometimes we've hired babysitters at the hotel, sometimes we've split the hours, and sometimes we've benefited from the goodness of grandparents who've taken the kids in.

Jesus' parents were not negligent in going a whole day without realizing Jesus was not with them. Their society depended on one another for help. And just imagine how much more fun it must have been for kids to be able to go from family to family on a long trip rather than be cooped up in a car with Mom and Dad! A society of people who are interdependent and can rely on one another's help has a great strength.

God, thanks for the friends and relatives who help us raise our children. Amen.

Talk It Over: *How do you rely on others to raise your children? And how do you reciprocate? If you do not have children of your own, how can you be of help to family and friends who do?*

June 19 ~ The Bumpy Road to Independence

His mother said to him, "Child, why have you treated us like this? Look, your father and I have been searching for you in great anxiety." He said to them, "Why were you searching for me? Did you not know that I must be in my Father's house?"

—Luke 2:48b-49

The first time I brought a boyfriend home was a day when we had a day off (from school) but the rest of my family didn't. My parents were most perturbed: *What would the neighbors think?* Meanwhile, I was wondering: *Don't you think that after bringing me up decently for seventeen years, I've learned anything? Will you ever stop treating me like a little girl? Can't you trust me to do the right thing?*

Like Mary and Joseph, my parents were showing parental concern. Like them, we were having a necessary tug-of-war. Letting go and being let go takes trust. Whether it's a five-year-old learning to ride a two-wheeler or a daughter starting to date, both the parent and the child have to trust that they're ready for the next big step of maturity. It will be a step on the path they've been taught.

God, help us trust that our children will opt to be in your house when we worry about them. Amen.

Talk It Over: *How do you as a couple typically handle transitions that your children make? Who is the one to push them to the next "level," and who is more likely to protest? If you do not have children of your own, how can you help prepare the children in your lives for increasing independence and responsibility?*

June 20 ~ Fulfilling Need

"Is there anyone among you who, if your child asks for a fish, will give a snake instead of a fish? Or if the child asks for an egg, will give a scorpion? If you then, who are evil, know how to give good gifts to your children, how much more will the heavenly Father give the Holy Spirit to those who ask him!"

—Luke 11:11-13

One summer we spent two weeks on the road exploring Canada. We were together 24/7 in the car, hiking, or sightseeing. Short-temperedness set in. Tom wanted the CD player, but Emelia insisted it was her turn. Emelia wanted us to play twenty questions; Tom preferred reading. Wanting some time to herself, Uli became irritated at both of them. Cliff turned on the radio. We all needed some space.

The kids' requests weren't unreasonable. More often our irritated responses were. We decided we'd enforce a regular hour-long family quiet time after lunch for napping, sleeping, or reading. We decided the CD player would be offered to the other sibling after each CD. We played twenty questions *ad nauseam,* and Emelia was thrilled.

We are our children's first "God" figures. If they can trust us and be sure of our attentive love, then they'll trust God and be sure of God's attentive love for them. Frustrating our children because of our own impatience leads only to distance. In this passage from Luke, God generously supplies our needs and doesn't trick us.

God, by remembering your kindness to me, help me not to frustrate my child. Amen.

Talk It Over: *How do you frustrate your children—or other children in your lives? What would help you cope better?*

June 21 ~ Praying with Our Children

[Jesus] was praying in a certain place, and after he had finished, one of his disciples said to him, "Lord, teach us to pray, as John taught his disciples." He said to them, "When you pray, say: Father, hallowed be your name."
—Luke 11:1-2

Every so often, our children ask us, "Can we find a different prayer?" Though we also *ad lib* prayers, the core of our night and mealtime prayers are ones we learn by rote, usually Celtic ones because they have such good rhythm, balance, and imagery. They're particularly memorable and rich, and so they don't grow stale quickly. It's their brevity and evocative images the kids like. The prayers give them a vocabulary to use with God—just as Jesus, with the Our Father prayer, gives his disciples a language for praying to God.

132

Our children look to us to teach them how to pray, as the disciples looked to Jesus. We're creating and practicing an important habit and relationship with them, without which they quickly feel their day is as incomplete as if a good-night kiss or bedtime story were missing.

In the love of the Father, in the light of Christ, in the leading of the Spirit, we place ourselves today. Amen.

Talk It Over: *How do you sustain interest and vitality in your prayer life with your children? If you do not have children of your own, how can you help to "teach" other children to pray?*

June 22 ~ Leave-taking

"Be strong and courageous; do not be frightened or dismayed, for the LORD your God is with you wherever you go."

—*Joshua 1:9*

At age fourteen, I traveled alone from my parents' home in northern England by bus, train, cross-Channel ferry, train again, Paris Metro, train again, to an unfamiliar French family. I remember: the creepy guy looking for prostitute recruits on the train to Paris; being scared silly when I missed my connecting train; and seeing two people jump to their deaths from a bridge.

A few years later when my friend Joan and I spent a year studying at different German universities, we developed a leave-taking ritual of saying together: "Be strong and courageous; do not be frightened or dismayed, for the LORD your God is with you wherever you go." It gave us a quiet confidence that I didn't quite have years earlier in France.

Whether our children are leaving for their first overnight camp or for their dad's home in another city, going to college or out on their first date, such rituals give them courage to venture away from us remembering they are never alone.

Even if I settle on the far side of the sea, your right hand holds me fast. Amen. (Psalm 139:9-10, paraphrase)

133

June 23 ~ Looking Beyond Ourselves

"Give, and it will be given to you. A good measure, pressed down, shaken together, running over, will be put into your lap; for the measure you give will be the measure you get back."

—Luke 6:38

Around our house, the words "Be generous!" have become a kind of mantra. Like many families today, we live far from our relatives. Cliff's are scattered across the United States, and Uli's in Europe. Since our children are growing up so far from their grandparents, we visit a few elderly folk roundabout. Sometimes we just pass the time of day with them; other times we bring Easter or Valentine treats so they won't be overlooked on special days.

We want our children to grow up thinking of themselves not only as the recipients of kindness and generosity, but also as providers of it. It's ok if they're a bit bored visiting a neighbor, or making coleslaw and setting the table at the soup kitchen in town. They are learning to be generous. And they know the other part of the mantra is "and others will be generous to you." A good measure, shaken together, and running over.

God, give us willing hearts to find opportunities with our children to be kind to our neighbors. Amen.

Talk It Over: In what ways do you encourage your children—or children in your extended family—to be generous to others?

June 24 ~ Financially Stressed

So [Elijah] . . . went to Zarephath. When he came to the gate of the town, a widow was there gathering sticks; he called to her and said, "Bring me a little water in a vessel, so that I may drink." As she was going to bring it, he called to her and said, "Bring me a morsel of bread in your hand." But she said, "As the LORD your God

134

lives, I have nothing baked, only a handful of meal in a jar, and a little oil in a jug; I am now gathering a couple of sticks, so that I may go home and prepare it for myself and my son, that we may eat it, and die." Elijah said to her, "Do not be afraid; go and do as you have said; but first make me a little cake of it and bring it to me, and afterwards make something for yourself and your son."
—1 Kings 17:10-13

We're already completely stressed about how to pay our taxes or buy the week's groceries, just the necessities, the widow's flour and oil. Then along comes a letter about our church's capital campaign, or perhaps the car transmission goes out. The widow of Zarephath is so depressed about her situation that she's preparing their final meal before they starve to death. Then here comes this man of God who brazenly asks for even the little she has. Not only is she going to have nothing for their final meal, now her religious community is going to know about her desperate situation and why she can't contribute to that capital campaign.

Despite her despair, and despite ours in tight times, she and we do have a scrap of faith left in this God of ours, the one who tells her, "The jar of meal will not be emptied and the jug of oil will not fail until the day that the LORD sends rain on the earth" (1 Kings 17:14). She and we will have enough till circumstances change again. We won't perish, even though it might be stomach-churningly tight for a while.

Lord, give us this day our daily bread. Amen.

Talk It Over: *How do you cope, as a couple, with financially tight times?*

June 25 ~ Needing a Break

In the morning, while it was still very dark, he got up and went out to a deserted place, and there he prayed. And Simon and his companions hunted for him. When they found him, they said to him, "Everyone is searching for you."
—Mark 1:35-37

Children seem to gravitate to us parents. Whether Cliff stays up late to finish class preparations or go see a movie alone, or Uli gets up at dawn to edit or work in the garden, our children must think we're having a secret

135

party or playing games on the computer judging by the way their parent-antennae seek us out. Especially when we're under work pressure, or when we've already spent long periods of time together, it seems almost impossible not to be needed by our children.

This story snippet about Jesus almost makes his disciples appear like such needy children. Even when times of rejuvenation are planned—whether for spiritual nourishment, exercise, or simply some time apart from one's usual demands—those times are often at the brink of being sabotaged. In our family, we help each other keep those much-needed times alone by waylaying the children or agreeing without resentment to the other's plans for some solo time with friends or at the movies.

Jesus, help me withdraw to a solitary place sometime today. Amen.

Talk It Over: *How do you support each other's need for a break—whether from children or other daily demands?*

June 26 ~ Two by Two

Then [Jesus] went about among the villages teaching. He called the twelve and began to send them out two by two, and gave them authority over the unclean spirits.

—*Mark 6:6b-7*

Our daughter often says, "Mom and I are a team. Daddy and Tom are a team." Since Cliff stayed home with Tom when Tom was little, and Uli has spent the last few years home with Emelia, those are the most familiar pairings to her. Yet precisely because of this, we make a point of shaking up those predictable pairings now and then. Sometimes it's for something as banal as Cliff and Emelia running to the hardware store, or Uli and Tom picking fresh peas together; other times we take the kids on separate treats: a movie, ice cream, or shooting baskets at the park. And we go on dates ourselves, too!

As we imagine the disciples also found by pairing up, we return to the family fold with bonds strengthened, confidences shared, and new stories to contribute to our common life. Breaking out of the usual patterns of family pairings and allegiances prevents stagnation: We hear new things, experience new things, and keep in touch with one another.

God, help us make opportunities to foster our relationship with each member of our family. Amen.

Talk It Over: *Consider whether you gravitate to or avoid certain family members. How can you nurture relationships with all family members?*

June 27 ~ Christ's Own Forever

Not that I have already obtained this or have already reached the goal; but I press on to make it my own, because Christ Jesus has made me his own.
—Philippians 3:12

Among the photos of the hours following Tom's birth, a favorite shows Uli propped up in bed, surrounded by a handful of our closest friends, a huge bag of potato chips, champagne, and beautiful flowers. After years of hoping, months of vomiting, and hours of pushing, our friends joined us to thank God for the birth of our child. We broke bread and sang, "All things bright and beautiful, all creatures great and small, all things wise and wonderful, the Lord God made them all."

The custom at the church we attended those years in Atlanta was to present each baptized person with a banner including the poignant words *Christ's Own Forever.* If the long years of trying to conceive weren't enough to remind us of the fragility of our efforts, then these words said by the priest while marking our children with the sign of the cross surely were: "Thomas, Emelia, you are sealed by the Holy Spirit in Baptism and marked as Christ's own forever. Amen."

Our children, like we ourselves, are yours, O God. Amen.

Talk It Over: *How does it change your way of relating to your children—or special children in your lives—to know they are Christ's own forever?*

June 28 ~ Living with Wolves

I am sending you like lambs into a pack of wolves. So be wise as snakes and as innocent as doves.
—Matthew 10:16 (CEV)

137

A mother recently told us that she had received an unexpected phone call the other day. It was the voice of the school secretary saying, "There's something the matter with your son, Jared." Like any parent who heard these words, immediately her body tensed and her mind raced to the corners of her darkest fears. The voice continued—all that had happened was that Jared had somehow managed to get a small plastic bead caught between his teeth, and they thought she should know.

Fortunately, many of our fears for our children don't come to pass, but that doesn't mean those fears are foolish. Jesus sends us out into the world knowing full well that there really are wolves out there. But Jesus' advice is that we do better to exercise a little wisdom and innocence than to hide our families behind fences.

Giver of Wisdom, help us know how to live as your people amid the dangers of life without cutting ourselves off from the world. Amen.

Talk It Over: *Tell each other a fear you tend to have for your children—or special children in your life. Name one thing you could do in response to that fear that would be overprotective and one thing that would be wise.*

June 29 ~ Not on Our Schedules

Both of them were righteous before God, living blamelessly according to all the commandments and regulations of the Lord. But they had no children, because Elizabeth was barren, and both were getting on in years.

—Luke 1:6-7

Several years after we were married, we finally made an appointment with the fertility specialist. We had been trying to have children for a while and were starting to wonder whether there was a medical reason. It turned out happily in our case: we found out three days later that Uli was already pregnant.

But it is common in the Bible for couples to have difficulty conceiving or be unable to have children. The stories of Sarah, Rachel, and Elizabeth come to mind. It is a common theme in real life, too. But not all adults choose to be married, of course, and not all couples choose to or are able to have children. Zechariah and Elizabeth's story reminds us that having or not having children is not about how much God loves us or how much we love God. However or whenever children come into our lives, they come not on our schedules or on our terms, but as sheer gifts.

Giver of All Life, with profound gratitude we thank you for all of your children who bless us in our lives. Amen.

Talk It Over: *What are some ways that couples you know honor the conceiving and raising of children as a gift from God, and not as something in their control?*

June 30 ~ Blessing Our Children

[Jesus] grew and became strong, filled with wisdom; and the favor of God was upon him.—Luke 2:40 (after Jesus is presented at the Temple as an infant)

Jesus increased in wisdom and in years, and in divine and human favor. —Luke 2:52 (after Jesus is found in the Temple as a twelve-year-old boy)

"The Lord be with you," our pastor greets us, and we respond "And also with you." In one way or another, we find ways to bless one another. A friend is sick: we tell them we're praying for them. A baby is born: we tell the parents how happy we are for them. Even on a daily basis, as our children leave home, we say, "Have a good day. We love you," offering them our blessing, wishing them our best.

In these verses from Luke's Gospel, which round out the Temple stories about Jesus that we recalled earlier this month, we get a summary that tells us things are going well with Jesus. What more can we hope for our own children than that they grow up, they become wiser, and they grow in divine and human favor?

We give thanks for our children. May God's arm be about them, may Christ's love guide them, may the power of the Spirit keep them, now and forever. Amen.

Talk It Over: *Reflect on how you talk as a couple about your children. What do you most want for them? If you do not have children, what are your hopes and desires for the special children in your lives?*

July

FACING CHALLENGES

John and Ginny Underwood

July 1 ~ Love Involves Challenges

Live a life of love, just as Christ loved us and gave himself up for us as a fragrant offering and sacrifice to God.

—*Ephesians 5:2 (NIV)*

My husband (John) and I (Ginny) first met when we were barely teenagers. We were at summer camp. I still remember the first time I ever laid eyes on him. We are very blessed to say that we've known each other for the better part of our lives. We've known each other fourteen years and have been married for eight years. We've grown together into adulthood, as working professionals and now as parents. Through the years, we've learned how to love each other beyond our faults and to forgive each other's shortcomings. We've also learned to put each other first and not let worldly challenges interfere with our partnership. Living a life of love is learning to face the challenges of life together.

This month we will share God's words about some of the challenges we have faced in our marriage, particularly those that have been influenced by the culture in which we live. It is our hope that in these devotions you will find inspiration for facing your own challenges, as well as insights for guiding each other and, if you have children, your family, in today's culture.

Father, help us love each other unconditionally, as you love us, and give us the wisdom to face the challenges of our culture. Amen.

July 2 ~ The Challenge of Finding Strength

One who is slow to anger is better than the mighty, and one whose temper is controlled than one who captures a city.

—Proverbs 16:32

Strength is perceived in many different ways in our culture. Many times it's a physical show of power, whether in the bodybuilding gym or the company boardroom where big mergers take place. It can be measured in an earthly sense with size and material value. The scripture, however, refers to a different kind of strength—the kind of strength a mother sacrificing for her children understands; the kind of strength a missionary worker knows when leaving home to take care of those less fortunate. True strength is to humble yourself before God. It's to take control of your emotions and allow your faith to lead you. It's finding the patience to listen for the answers in God's time, not our own.

God, help us rely on our spiritual strength rather than our physical strength, in order to do the things that please you. Amen.

Talk It Over: *Discuss with your spouse areas where each of you could use spiritual strength rather than physical strength.*

July 3 ~ The Challenge of Pulling Your Load

Finally, be ye all of one mind, having compassion one of another; love as brethren, be pitiful, be courteous.

—1 Peter 3:8 (KJV)

Pulling your load in a family unit is more than taking out the trash on Thursday nights or making sure the baby has shoes on her feet and her hair brushed. It's about emotionally supporting the values and ideology of

142

each other. At times your load, or your responsibilities to the family, may seem larger and heavier than your spouse's. It may mean covering for each other while one goes on a weeklong business trip or deals with all-consuming projects for a period of time. You always need to remember your base, your center: God and family. Let's not forget the reason that we work is to provide for the family. Providing means more than just bringing home a paycheck.

Lord, help us provide for the people we love not only financially but also emotionally and spiritually. Amen.

Talk It Over: *Discuss what areas each of you feel overwhelmed in at times. Name at least three ways to help support each other.*

July 4 ~ The Challenge of Taking Time for Important Things

To every thing there is a season, and a time to every purpose under the heaven.
—Ecclesiastes 3:1 (KJV)

After a long, stressful drive home from work, our eighteen-month-old daughter and I (Ginny) stormed into the house. An unexpected downpour left us drenched, and I had an armful of wet groceries. We were later than usual, both tired and fussy. As I went to put away the food, I barely noticed the crying baby tugging at my pants. I dropped a bag, and as I knelt down to pick it up, my daughter threw her arms around me as though I rescued her from a raging sea. We stopped everything and just held each other. Those were the most important minutes of my day. She taught me how important it is to take the time to become centered with God and to keep everything else in a proper perspective.

God, thank you for the little reminders in life that help us refocus and prioritize those things that are truly important. Amen.

Talk It Over: *In what ways have you let the routines of life overshadow moments for spiritual and emotional growth?*

July 5 ~ The Challenge of Overcoming Barriers

A good name is more desirable than great riches; to be esteemed is better than silver or gold.

—Proverbs 22:1 (NIV)

Some Native American tribes believe a child isn't born until you give it a name. We spent many hours during the pregnancy of our first child debating names. We both felt it should be strong and unique—the very attributes we hoped for our child. We went through the normal lists of baby books. We settled on a name that we felt was gender neutral: Avery. In our evolution to married people having a child, we decided we didn't want our baby coming into this world with set parameters. Our culture is very good about boxing people into roles with limited expectations. Whether boy or girl, we wanted our child to choose its own path.

Likewise, the "names" *husband* and *wife* should be defined by the individuals rather than our culture. Every couple must apply their own characteristics to give the names meaning in their family.

Father, please help us guide each other and our family in your loving light. Help us empower one another to think for ourselves and become everything we can be for your glory. Amen.

Talk It Over: *List barriers you have faced during your lifetime, as well as barriers you may be facing now. Talk about how you overcame and/or can overcome these barriers, and what you can do to make sure these same barriers do not hold back other family members.*

July 6 ~ The Challenge of Showing Your Love

"In your anger do not sin": Do not let the sun go down while you are still angry.
—Ephesians 4:26 (NIV)

One of the most tragic events in the history of our families happened during the childhoods of our grandparents. As Native peoples, they were forced to attend boarding school away from their families. It was a harsh environment. As a result, most of the men we knew growing up were not affectionate. They never openly shared emotions or hugged.

We have seen that as people grow older, even the harshest tend to soften. They are now left with regret about not allowing themselves to show love sooner. Don't wait. Express your love for the people who are meaningful to you today. Don't allow circumstances beyond your control to be a barrier.

Lord, thank you for your healing grace. Thank you for allowing us to learn to love each other and to cherish life. Help us spread your love openly and freely. Amen.

Talk It Over: *Think about people you love. Evaluate if you are expressing your love to them. If not, why and how can you make a change?*

July 7 ~ The Challenge of Communicating Hopes and Dreams

Do not let any unwholesome talk come out of your mouths, but only what is helpful for building others up according to their needs, that it may benefit those who listen.

—Ephesians 4:29 (NIV)

Early in our marriage we shared with each other our hopes and dreams. Those conversations have served as a map to where we are today. We learned the hard way how important it is to check in with each other about those dreams. At some point along the way, our focus shifted. Our careers and aspirations began to change, but we didn't discuss it. We found ourselves floating on separate paths without a real direction. We had to get back to the basics, evaluate our dreams, and plan again—together—the direction we wanted to go. It meant refocusing, defining, and communicating our hopes and dreams—those things that make life meaningful and fulfilling.

You have to remember the reasons why you are where you are and why you are doing the things you are doing. Each decision you make guides the future of your marriage.

Dear God, thank you for the hopes and dreams you give us. Please help us communicate and make choices together that will bring growth. Guide us in your path. Amen.

Talk It Over: *Ask yourselves where you see yourselves/your family in the next five to ten years. What are your current dreams and aspirations?*

145

July 8 ~ The Challenge of Learning from Mistakes

The LORD detests the way of the wicked but he loves those who pursue righteousness.
—Proverbs 15:9 (NIV)

We all gain perspective about relationships and marriage from our parents. The two of us are children of divorce. From our complex childhoods, we've taken a few lessons to heart: communication, affection, trust, compromise, and sacrifice are all necessary ingredients for a successful marriage. It's important as a couple to evaluate perceived mistakes, looking at the cause and effects in order to gain a true understanding of the situation. If you are able to obtain that understanding, then you are less likely to repeat the mistake. A mistake is only destructive when it is repeated and nothing is gained or learned. Handled appropriately, a mistake is actually an opportunity for growth.

Lord, help us open our eyes to our own actions and shortcomings. Help us openly evaluate ways that we can become better servants for you. Amen.

Talk It Over: *Take stock of mistakes that have had a negative impact on you and/or your family. Look for patterns. List ways to correct actions and to learn from the mistakes.*

July 9 ~ The Challenge of Being a Filter

"No good tree bears bad fruit, nor does a bad tree bear good fruit."
—Luke 6:43 (NIV)

When walking through the mall, our daughter, Avery, asks at least a hundred questions from end to end. "Mommy, what's her name?" "Daddy, what are they doing?" The questions seem asked out of habit rather than true interest. However, we make a concerted effort to answer her questions to the best of our ability. As she grows, we want her to always feel comfortable asking us about things she doesn't understand. While she's young, we are Avery's filter for the world. We want her to have a good understanding of the world around her—an understanding that incorporates our influences and core values—just as Jesus, our "filter," gave us a good understanding of God. As we take time now to build basic values into her life, we open the door and keep it open for more important questions that will inevitably come later.

Each of us seeks understanding every day. We filter input from our friends, family, spouses, news outlets, and so forth. It's important for us to use God as the lens through which we view the world and share perspective.

O God, please guide me and give me wisdom to see the life lessons in everything. Help me point out those lessons to my loved ones so I may guide them and help them grow in your grace. Amen.

Talk It Over: *Discuss with your partner your thoughts and beliefs on important issues. Find a common ground and, if you have children, discuss how to relay your shared beliefs and thoughts to them.*

July 10 ~ The Challenge of Being a True Winner

How much better to get wisdom than gold, to choose understanding rather than silver!

—Proverbs 16:16 (NIV)

Our culture is very competitive. There's always a winner and a loser. You see it in sports, business, and even within families. In some cultures, it is dishonorable to win and beat down the opponent. In some Native American tribes, winning meant doing no harm to your opponent. It's called "counting coupe." The object is to get close enough to touch your opponent and get away without getting hurt. That lets your opponent know that you had an opportunity to harm him or her but you did not. It's about mercy and respect. We must teach the people we love that life is about the journey and how you play the game.

Father, remind us that every new day brings new experiences, new lessons. Help us recognize that even when we are not successful in the world's eyes, there are still opportunities to grow. Amen.

Talk It Over: *Look at the role competition plays in your life. Assess your beliefs on competition, on winning and losing. How much value do you place on the end result?*

July 11 ~ The Challenge of Setting a Loving Example

My son, give me thine heart, and let thine eyes observe my ways.
—Proverbs 23:26 (KJV)

Loving is being an example. Children base their future relationships on how their parents react to each other. It's important to be affectionate, to touch, and to verbally tell your spouse that you love them in front of your children. They need to see a healthy relationship. It has been proved that children who grow up in violent homes tend to look for relationships with the same characteristics, the familiar. Boys are likely to grow up to be abusers and girls are likely to migrate toward abusive men. If bad has such an influence, why can't good? Be the example of love and partnership you wish for your children. Also, remember that many eyes watch you every day—perhaps those of your nieces, nephews, young church members, or even neighbors. Express the love you would like to see in the world, and you will influence others to imitate that love.

Lord, I give you thanks for giving us the love we share with others—for our hopes, dreams, smiles, laughter, and joy. Please help us express these things to each other and to the young people in our lives, sharing the love you give us every day. Amen.

Talk It Over: *Discuss with your spouse how you view a healthy relationship. Compare your view to the views of your own parents.*

July 12 ~ The Challenge of Having a Good Work Ethic

From the place of his habitation he looketh upon all the inhabitants of the earth. He fashioneth their hearts alike; he considereth all their works.
—Psalm 33:14-15 (KJV)

When I (John) was growing up, my grandfather was the mark by which I measured myself: strong, honest, straightforward, stern, faithful, and hardworking. He had an unfaltering dedication in his work ethic. He got up every day at 3:00 A.M. and never stopped working until he went to bed at night. He never complained, moaned, or cried about his role. For him, it was a matter of pride. He looked at the hurdles and obstacles of his work as challenges. He believed that you should always do your best, because it doesn't matter if anyone is watching or not; God sees you, your heart sees you, and others see you. Today, give your best not because of money or prestige but because you love yourself and God.

God, please give us strength to deal with the obstacles that lie before us. Help us to take pride in providing the things we need and to appreciate a job well done. Amen.

Talk It Over: *List tasks that have to be done but you don't like to do. Discuss ways you can refocus and find a blessing in each.*

July 13 ~ The Challenge of "Living a Little"

Set your minds on things above, not on earthly things.
                                                    —*Colossians 3:2 (NIV)*

It amazes me that I (Ginny) often allow my work to be all-consuming. It seems I spend Sunday nights making sure we're ready for the week, and the next minute I look up and it's Friday afternoon. Where does the time go? We often operate on autopilot, going through the motions without actually experiencing the moment. If you don't make time to live a little in between the monotony, you may wake up and find that your life has passed you by. We do have to just get by sometimes, but it's not enough to just merely exist. God has created this beautiful world for us to enjoy. There's a lot more to life than what's between point A and point B. Make every minute count this week. Try not to give in to daily rituals. Appreciate the time you have together to experience this beautiful world God created for us.

Father, please help us have the courage to break out of our daily routines and find new ways to experience your blessings. Amen.

Talk It Over: *Look for ways to change your weekly routines. Make conscious decisions to try and experience new things.*

July 14 ~ The Challenge of Being Responsible

For the grace of God that brings salvation has appeared to all men. It teaches us to say "No" to ungodliness and worldly passions, and to live self-controlled, upright and godly lives in this present age.

—Titus 2:11-12 (NIV)

We live in a culture that blames. It's a huge money-making industry for psychiatrists and therapists. People are seeking out reasons for why they are where they are in their life.

Everybody has contributing factors: family history, economics, culture, spiritual influences, and so forth. At what point do you stop blaming outside influences for your own actions? Contributing factors play a role but are not solely responsible for where you are in life. You are responsible for your own path. Realizing that you have ultimate control over your own actions places control of your life where God intended it: within you.

Lord, help me take ownership of my actions so I can make better decisions for myself and for others. Amen.

Talk It Over: *Talk about situations that appear to be out of your control. Discuss ways you might change your actions to influence the outcome of the situation.*

July 15 ~ The Challenge of Earning Trust

Love does not delight in evil but rejoices with the truth. It always protects, always trusts, always hopes, always perseveres.

—1 Corinthians 13:6-7 (NIV)

When our daughter was born, I kept waiting for my maternal instincts to kick in. I was like a fish out of water. The first six weeks of Avery's life were a huge learning experience for me on the virtue of trust. Trust is the pillar of everything: love, marriage, and our relationship with God. It is a precious gift that takes a lot of commitment and hard work. I had to earn my daughter's trust. I did that by feeding her and nurturing her from day

150

one. I had to commit to her—not unlike my commitment to my husband. I had to open myself up. I had to risk rejection and disappointment in order to earn trust and find the love that I was seeking.

Trust between partners takes as much effort as building trust with children. It is something that has to be nurtured and valued every day.

Father, please give us the strength to commit to each other and to be faithful and trustworthy. Amen.

Talk It Over: *Discuss your problem areas with trust. Determine what areas you need to work on in order to give and receive trust.*

July 16 ~ The Challenge of Remaining Spiritually Centered

Through him all things were made; without him nothing was made that has been made. In him was life, and that life was the light of men.
—John 1:3-4 (NIV)

When I was a kid, I (John) was told that every creature and organism that God created is alive. Everything has a life force, a spiritualness that is given by God. By being spiritually centered, you realize that God is all around you. It's not found just in people, but in all of God's creations. By realizing you are a spiritual being, and not only a physical being, you open your eyes, your heart, and your mind to God. You allow yourself to touch, feel, and sense his presence everywhere. Whether it is in a city skyscraper or on a secluded mountaintop, you are connected to God.

God is always there reaching out to us, yet we often don't take the time to respond to his call. Look for ways God is reaching out to you today.

Father, help me take the time daily to close my eyes and to feel your presence, to open my eyes and to see the abundance of life in all your creations. Amen.

Talk It Over: *Every day for a week, go out and inspect the life around you, thanking God for making you a part of his creation. Today, enjoy some time together outdoors in God's creation.*

July 17 ~ The Challenge of Being Honest

But that on the good ground are they, which is an honest and good heart, having heard the word, keep it, and bring it forth fruit with patience.
—Luke 8:15 (KJV)

When we think about honesty, the boy who cried wolf comes to mind. In this story, we see the need for an outward expression of honesty—specifically, for the boy to tell the townspeople the truth. Yet all outward expressions of honesty are the result of an inward reality—the reality of who we are before God.

People often tell lies because they are afraid of the consequences of telling the truth. We are very good at masking ourselves outwardly and lying to ourselves inwardly. Yet God sees through the deception. We need to understand that being honest allows us to lay our burdens down. Honesty has the ability to free our spirits. Honesty is the key to all our relationships. Look for opportunities to build and grow through honest conversations.

Lord, give us the strength to accept the responsibility of our shortcomings. Help us take ownership of our actions so that we may be able to control our behavior. Amen.

Talk It Over: *Think silently about things you have lied about and how you carry those things with you today. How would honesty have made a difference? How can honesty—with God and those involved—make a difference now? Discuss with your partner how to build trust, understanding, and a truthful relationship.*

July 18 ~ The Challenge of Being Compassionate

"For I was hungry and you gave me something to eat, I was thirsty and you gave me something to drink, I was a stranger and you invited me in."
—Matthew 25:35 (NIV)

The most compassionate person I (Ginny) ever knew was my grandmother. She was a wonderful Comanche woman, small in stature but filled with an abundance of love. As one of the younger grandchildren, I always knew I had a special place in her heart. It wasn't until her death that I realized how far-reaching her compassion was. For three days, our home was filled with visitors. We heard countless stories of her generosity, her giving heart, and her loving nature. She freely gave gifts of the spirit: time, kindness, and patience. She loved everyone she encountered unconditionally.

As you walk together in marriage, remember the people that inspire you. Draw from their examples to help your love flourish and grow. Remember how wonderful those people made you feel, and try to honor them by exhibiting the same love.

God, thank you for blessing us with hearts that feel compassion. Help us hear the call when others are in need, especially those closest to us. Amen.

Talk It Over: *Talk about situations in your life when someone showed compassion to you. Look for opportunities to share compassion with people around you. Think silently: How can you show compassion to your spouse?*

July 19 ~ The Challenge of Continually Seeking God

Jesus said, "Let the little children come to me, and do not hinder them, for the kingdom of heaven belongs to such as these."

—*Matthew 19:14 (NIV)*

"Even before reason there is an inward movement which reaches out towards its own," writes Plotinus (III 4.6). I (John) can't remember a time when I didn't know God. When I was born, my father lifted me to the sky, giving me back to God to watch over and raise me. God has been in my life since that time.

In the Christian faith, people often equate the beginning of their relationship with God to their baptism. I feel, however, that an individual's relationship with God begins when we are born. God is already in us; the important thing is how we choose to nurture that connection—how we choose to continually seek God. In the beginning and the end, we come to God. We need to learn to seek him day by day along the journey, individually and as a family. Find ways to center your family spiritually every day.

153

Father, help me continually seek you day by day. Amen.

Talk It Over: When was the first time you acknowledged God's presence in your life? Discuss your individual relationships with God.

July 20 ~ The Challenge of Trusting God

For we walk by faith, not by sight.

—2 Corinthians 5:7 (KJV)

You've heard of Jesus turning water into wine. What about making potatoes appear out of thin air? An old Seminole woman, who faithfully attends church, once debated whether or not to go to church because she had nothing to take. Being an elder, she felt ashamed to go empty-handed. As she talked in front of the house with her children about not going to church that evening, a truck passed by and they heard a loud thud. A sack of potatoes lay in the road. God sent her a message and answered her prayers.

God is the great provider. All he asks is that we believe in him. The more we believe and trust that he will provide for us, the surer those things will come to pass. In your marriage, you might find yourself waiting for a sign—an answer to prayer. It may not be as obvious as a sack of potatoes dropping on your doorstep, but listen and wait and know that God will fulfill your needs.

God, thank you for answered prayers and for all that you provide. Help us always to be faithful and trust you. Amen.

Talk It Over: Discuss times when your trust in God has been tested. Did God answer your prayers?

July 21 ~ The Challenge of Being a Good Leader

Let no man despise thy youth; but be thou an example of the believers, in word, in conversation, in charity, in spirit, in faith, in purity.

—1 Timothy 4:12 (KJV)

An NBA player who was criticized for his behavior on the court once answered the media by saying he wasn't a role model. He shunned the responsibility of leadership as easily as tossing in a towel. Each of us is a leader at some point in time, whether we want to be or not. Whether you're a high-paid athlete, a rock star, or an average person, someone is watching you. You are influencing someone's life. It's how you choose to lead that makes the difference. You can choose to be an example of good or an example of bad. Your spouse, family members, coworkers, and even strangers will be influenced by your actions. It's only when we accept the challenge and the opportunity of being a leader that we have control over our actions, and the essence of control is thinking before we act.

Father, help me accept the challenge of being a good leader, and give me the strength to glorify you with my actions. Amen.

Talk It Over: *Discuss people you have an influence on and determine if you are sending the right messages.*

July 22 ~ The Challenge of Forgiving

"For if you forgive men when they sin against you, your heavenly Father will also forgive you."
—*Matthew 6:14 (NIV)*

If you ever need lessons on how to forgive, watch young children playing together. My three-year-old daughter does not have the capability to hold grudges—yet. She plays with the same children every day. She sometimes tells me that another child has pushed her or hit her. However, the next day she's back playing and interacting with each child, as if nothing ever happened. I don't know how much of it is the inability to remember the incident or the innate knowledge that it doesn't really matter. Either way, I wish it were a character trait I still possessed. Grudges are the burdens of our soul. They prevent us from fully experiencing God's love.

Father, give us strength to forgive each other. Help us be Christlike in our relationships. Amen.

Talk It Over: Individually, list hurtful incidents and burdens that you carry with you every day. Share and discuss your lists as you feel able to do so. Together or individually, pray and ask God to lift your burdens, to give you the strength to get rid of your pain. Then, symbolically destroy your burdens.

July 23 ~ The Challenge of Accepting Diversity

There are different kinds of gifts, but the same Spirit.
—1 Corinthians 12:4 (NIV)

Diversity is the understanding that we are all God's children. We come from the same place. We all have unique gifts that we can share with one another. Like-minded people tend to migrate toward one another, but we should be gathering with people different from us to get a wide range of ideas. True diversity is having the ability to open your mind up to all options, from all people.

Lord, help us realize that we are all your children and that these bodies we occupy are merely shells for our spirits. Help us see the inner spirit in one another rather than the outer shell. Amen.

Talk It Over: Research two cultures different from your own. Look for similarities between cultures and note differences in practices and beliefs. Discuss the value of these differences. Also, discuss how diverse experiences have enriched your life.

July 24 ~ The Challenge of Supporting Each Other

And let us consider how we may spur one another on toward love and good deeds.
—Hebrews 10:24 (NIV)

During our first year of marriage, we moved to a new city and I started a new job. It was a rocky time. We were away from family, and the challenges in the new position were difficult. I remember coming home from

156

work one day to find that John had baked me a cake and had bought me flowers. I was so moved. I realized that no matter how terrible the outside world may be, I can always come home to someone who will always love me and will always be on my side.

Supporting each other is utilizing each other's strengths in areas where we tend to have weaknesses.

Father, help us open up and vocalize to each other when we need help. Help us also recognize when our strengths are needed. Amen.

Talk It Over: *Individually, list your strengths and weaknesses. Exchange lists and compare. Discuss ways you can strengthen or support your spouse's weaknesses.*

July 25 ~ The Challenge of Not Judging

Therefore let us stop passing judgment on one another. Instead, make up your mind not to put any stumbling block or obstacle in your brother's way.
—Romans 14:13 (NIV)

"Don't judge a book by its cover" is so cliché but worth repeating. My husband looks like a Native American. He has dark eyes, dark hair, and dark skin. It's amazing how often people judge him at first glance. From coworkers to new acquaintances, they treat him with caution. It's too bad. They don't know that he's the kindest spirit they may ever meet. They don't know that there's nothing he wouldn't do to help them if they asked. They don't know that he has a natural ability to love unconditionally.

We know our spouses better than anyone else. Remember it took time to reach the understanding we have for each other. Try to give others the same chance when building new friendships. Many times you will find it's well worth the effort.

Father, help us have open and loving hearts. Open our eyes to all people, and help us experience deeper meaningful relationships. Amen.

Talk It Over: *Have you passed judgment on someone you have never really talked to? Talk about how you might get to know that person on a deeper level.*

In what ways do you pass judgment on each other? How can you keep from putting stumbling blocks in each other's way?

July 26 ~ The Challenge of Finding a Place to Belong

Now we know that if our earthly tent we live in is destroyed, we have a building from God, an eternal house in heaven, not built by human hands.
—2 Corinthians 5:1 (NIV)

We both grew up attending Native American churches. The songs and prayers were often in Native languages. All the church members either were somehow related to us or had lived in our community for generations. When we decided to move to another city, attending a new church was a culture shock for us. We longed to feel the connectedness to people that we had experienced in our home churches.

We came to realize that God's Spirit is everywhere. The church service may be different, but the reason we go never changes. So, we asked God to open our hearts to hear his words, and we were able to build a new family away from home.

Many others face the same struggle and challenges in finding a place. It may not be about language or culture but about being accepted and fitting in. Reach out to those who you know need help finding God.

God, help us remember that home is where the heart is. If our heart is with you, then we are at home anywhere because you are constantly with us. Amen.

Talk It Over: *Discuss ways that your "comfort zone" restricts you from experiencing God in different places, people, and things.*

July 27 ~ The Challenge of Surrounding Yourself with People You Want to Be Like

Do not be yoked together with unbelievers. For what do righteousness and wickedness have in common? Or what fellowship can light have with darkness?
—2 Corinthians 6:14 (NIV)

Today's scripture refers to marriage, but we want to expand it to include all relationships. Having grown up in broken families, we both have seen what happens when couples hang around with people who don't value marriage. It presents opportunities for behaving in ways that married couples should not behave. That's why John and I have focused our energy on finding couple friends who share the same family values we have. You have to have an inner circle of people who feed off one another for spiritual nourishment. This inner circle helps you gain strength to go out into the world and share your Christian values.

Lord God, please guide us and help us find brothers and sisters who are good examples so that we may gain strength to become good examples ourselves. Amen.

Talk It Over: *List morals and characteristics you value. Do you have couple friends who complement these values? If not, discuss ways to seek out such friends.*

July 28 ~ The Challenge of Being Patient

Knowing this, that the trying of your faith worketh patience.
—James 1:3 (KJV)

We live in such a "now" culture. We have technology that allows us to use our time more efficiently, yet we still don't have enough time to do everything we want to in any given day. We tend to live our lives competing with man's time clock and having disdain for God's clock. God would not have us sit idle, but we must have faith that he will open doors for us so that we may influence the people around us and perhaps have an impact on a larger scale.

Patience is kind and nurturing; it listens, it teaches, it guides, it leads by example, and it waits for direction.

Father, help us listen to your voice and be comforted by our faith as we walk patiently on the path you lay before us. Amen.

Talk It Over: *Think and talk about the past week. Were you overstressed at certain times? Worried? Where or how could patience and prayer have played a role in changing the outcome?*

July 29 ~ The Challenge of Being Thankful

Giving thanks always for all things unto God and the Father in the name of our Lord Jesus Christ.

—Ephesians 5:20 (KJV)

For every breath we take, for every kiss we give, for every hug we offer or receive, for every meal we eat, we have our heavenly Father to thank. God gives us so many blessings and gifts that every day should be like a birthday party! When people are spoiled, they don't look at the wrapping or read the writing on their gifts. They just want to know if they got what they asked for. Being thankful helps you appreciate all your gifts. The more thankful you become about everything, the more blessings you are able to see. Thankfulness enriches your life!

Lord, forgive us for being blind to the gifts you give us every day. Please open our eyes and our hearts to appreciate the fullness of your love. Amen.

Talk It Over: *Thank God quietly today for ten things that you appreciate but never express gratitude for. See if those blessings are not magnified by your thankfulness. Share together as you choose.*

July 30 ~ The Challenge of Not Being Worrisome

He replied, "You of little faith, why are you so afraid?" Then he got up and rebuked the winds and the waves, and it was completely calm.

—Matthew 8:26 (NIV)

The scripture tells us that Peter began to sink when he took his eyes off of Jesus. He allowed the troubles around him to take his focus off of God. We face troubled waters every day—sometimes raging, sometimes merely uncomfortable. What we have to realize is that, like Peter, if we want to wade through the water successfully, we have to keep our focus on Jesus. If we do, all the troubles will take care of themselves. To be worrisome only brings more suffering and strife. It could even become a self-fulfilling prophecy. You may not be able to control the situation or the outcome, but you *can* control how you react.

160

God, help me realize that you are always there for me each and every day. Help me realize that together we can make it through anything life tosses our way. Amen.

Talk It Over: *Make a list of things that worry you. Discuss your lists and pray together, asking God to lift your burdens and to help keep you focused.*

July 31 ~ The Challenge of Keeping God First

But rather seek ye the kingdom of God; and all these things shall be added unto you.

—Luke 12:31 (KJV)

Everything in life has an order. Many Native American tribes believe that all things natural work in circles. Why should it be any different for God's love? There's an order in which the things in your life should be placed for balance. That order is God first, then family, and then self. When we put God first in our lives, he protects, guides, and blesses our family.

If you don't have God as the center, you're on the wrong path. God is the glue that will hold your family together. The love that you give God, he multiplies a thousand times and gives back to you and your loved ones.

It is God's love alone that enables you to face all the challenges of life.

Father, help us see that by placing you first we are actually lifting up ourselves and our loved ones. When we put you first, you empower us to face every challenge that comes our way. Amen.

Talk It Over: *Evaluate your priorities in life and determine if you have the proper balance or order. From this day forward, how can you ensure that God remains in the center of your lives?*

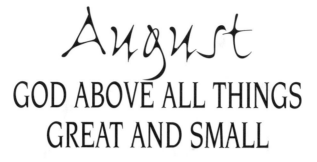

August

GOD ABOVE ALL THINGS GREAT AND SMALL

Amy Valdez Barker and Richard Barker II

August 1 ~ Come, Buy, Eat!

"Come, all you who are thirsty, come to the waters; . . . Why spend money on what is not bread, and your labor on what does not satisfy?"
—*Isaiah 55:1-2 (NIV)*

*I*f only life were truly as simple as "buying without money and without cost." Sometimes our focus is on where the next paycheck is coming from, how many bills we have to pay, and what we deem "valuable." We argue about who makes more money, why we think we don't have enough money, and why we need to give to this or that cause.

In today's verses, God reminds us that it isn't *what* we have or *what* we do that will delight our souls. God asks, "Why spend money on what is not bread?" That's a good question. Why *do* we get caught up in the pursuit of material things? Will this enhance our relationship?

What kind of "bread" do you seek to fill your needs? Is it the bread of life, which is Jesus Christ? This month you'll have opportunity to seriously ponder this question as we consider the value of the "things" we encounter in our lives.

Jesus, our Bread of Life, help us focus on you and figure out, together, what is the good stuff that satisfies our souls. Amen.

163

August 2 ~ Guilt Offering

The LORD said to Moses: "When a person commits a violation and sins unintentionally in regard to any of the LORD's holy things, he is to bring to the LORD as a penalty a ram. . . . It is a guilt offering."

—Leviticus 5:14-15 (NIV)

Today's verse talks of "unintentional" sin. Though sometimes I sin unintentionally, when it comes to money, more often I sin *intentionally*.

One time when my husband was planning to visit his friends in Iowa, I said that we didn't have much money to last us until the next paycheck and his road trip would eat into our funds (I knew that we had enough money in our savings to fall back on). So, we got into a long argument over whether or not his commitment to his friends was more important than our financial situation.

I later realized that it was unfair of me to use our finances to change his mind. I knew I had used money as a means of manipulation in our relationship, so I offered my apologies as my "guilt offering."

Great and Gracious God, thank you for accepting our "guilt offerings." Keep us from using money to manipulate each other. Amen.

Talk It Over: *Do you or your spouse ever use money to control each other? If so, talk about how this affects your relationship.*

August 3 ~ Paper and Metal

Their silver and gold will not be able to save them in the day of the LORD's wrath. . . . For it has made them stumble into sin.

—Ezekiel 7:19b (NIV)

164

For centuries, a common goal in life has been to accumulate as much silver and gold as possible. We spend a lot of time trying to get to the "next level" by improving our earning potential. Every time we think we've got plenty, we soon find ourselves wondering where it all has gone. We're always striving to have more.

John Wesley said, "Earn all you can; save all you can; give all you can." When he began to "earn all he could," he didn't change his life-style to obtain a better house, more clothes, or a new and improved life. He used only the amount of money he needed to live, and he gave the rest of it away. What would it take for us to live like Wesley?

Our God, we tend to let the silver and gold in our lives control us. Help us learn to be content with the gifts you have given us. Amen.

Talk It Over: *Do you work to get to the "next level" only to become dissatisfied with what you've accumulated?*

August 4 ~ Letting Go!

"Remember that in your lifetime you received your good things, while Lazarus received bad things, but now he is comforted here and you are in agony."
—*Luke 16:25 (NIV)*

Jesus told this story to illustrate our love for money. The rich man had everything, and then there was Lazarus, the poor man who only wanted a mere morsel to fill his belly. When their lives on earth ended, Lazarus found himself living in the luxuries of heaven, and the rich man found himself in agony. Whether he liked it or not, he had to let go of all his possessions.

Have we, too, become so blinded by our possessions that we don't see others who are in need? Jesus didn't tell us why Lazarus was living on the streets. The story simply tells us that Lazarus was in need and that the rich man should have had compassion on him and shared his blessings.

Jesus, help me to see those who are in need and to use the blessings you have given me to bless others. Amen.

Talk It Over: *Have you or your family been blinded by your possessions? Is there a Lazarus in your lives?*

August 5 ~ An Economic Worldview

"In one hour such great wealth has been brought to ruin!"
—Revelation 18:17a (NIV)

In September of 2001, the world came to a halt in the period of one morning. The world watched the fall of a great United States city whose economic security was symbolized in two buildings.

The greatest tragedy of that dreadful day was the tremendous loss of innocent lives. To some, the next greatest tragedy of that day was that the world economy and markets came to an abrupt stop.

My husband showed no fear in those days after September 11. He seemed to have a great faith in knowing that God would take care of us no matter where the economic world would end up. He continued to believe that, in the end, God would prevail and justice would win.

God reminds us that the treasures of our hearts should have nothing to do with the economic status of the world.

Great God, who has always taken care of us, help us have faith in you and stop storing our treasures in an economy that can be wiped away in one moment. Amen.

Talk It Over: *How does the economic worldview shape your lives? Where do you store your "treasures"?*

August 6 ~ Security Under God's Wings

"May you be richly rewarded by the LORD, the God of Israel, under whose wings you have come to take refuge."
—Ruth 2:12 (NIV)

I love the story of Ruth because she radiates a sense of dedication to a life that was unfamiliar and insecure. She lost everything in her married life after ten years. But Ruth was willing to give up her family, her gods, and her security to follow her mother-in-law back to her own home country.

Ruth's example shows us how God provides for us even in hard times. I can't imagine losing my husband and then giving up the life I know today to stay with my mother-in-law in her world. When life seems empty and broken, I believe God pulls us back under God's wing.

166

Great and Glorious God, thank you for the security of your everlasting love. Help me turn to you and continue to follow you when life feels insecure. Amen.

Talk It Over: *How would your life change if you felt completely secure in God's love? What is holding you back from feeling the security of God's love?*

August 7 ~ It's a Deal!

Do not take advantage of each other, but fear your God.

—Leviticus 25:17a

In Leviticus, the writer goes on to tell us that we should not take advantage of our "countrymen." When there is plenty, raise the price; but when there is little, lower the price. Our economic market has taught us the opposite. If there is very little of something, then it is considered to be in "high demand," and the price skyrockets. But, if there is plenty of it, then it is considered "overstocked," and the price is cheap.

The contradiction seems strange to me, but, at the same time, I see both points of view. God was asking us to be fair to one another and honor one another's lives. When there is plenty, then all should benefit. When there is little, then all should work together to help one another.

God, help us be mindful of the transactions in our lives. We realize that those who sell are only trying to make a living, too. Keep us honest and helpful to one another in the world. Amen.

Talk It Over: *Have you or your spouse ever taken advantage of a bargaining situation? How did you feel after it? How do you think the vendor felt?*

August 8 ~ Dividing the Spoils

The Lord said to Moses, "Divide the spoils between the soldiers who took part in the battle and the rest of the community."

—Numbers 31:25-27 (NIV)

167

At one time I thought that all we needed to do to solve all the world's problems was to take all the wealth in the world and divide it among all the people. Give everyone a fair start in life and an equal part of the world's riches. Wouldn't it be simple? But my husband pointed out that it wouldn't be that easy. Some people would be smart with their money while others would spend it foolishly. Then, in a few years, there would be the rich and the poor again.

Part of me believes that God grants us wealth and treasures to continue to test us. Where are our priorities? How would we divide the spoils?

OK, God. We know that the idea of wealth and riches sometimes goes to our head. Help us to remember the blessings you've given us and to share our blessings with others. Amen.

Talk It Over: *What would you do with ten million dollars? How would you divide the spoils?*

August 9 ~ True Riches

"Whoever can be trusted with very little can also be trusted with much, and whoever is dishonest with very little will also be dishonest with much."
—*Luke 16:10 (NIV)*

Our integrity and honesty are tested by different situations. I remember a time when I found a cell phone that was much nicer than ours. For a moment, it would have been much easier to keep it. But, the whole idea that God was watching and that it wasn't our property kept nagging at us. Eventually, we looked through the cell phone for a home number. We called the owners, told them we had their cell phone, and mailed it back to them. They were very thankful and sent us twenty dollars.

We weren't looking for the twenty dollars, nor were we looking for the recognition. What we were looking for was the value of integrity and honesty in our own lives. Even if no one else was watching, our God was watching.

Thank you God for the gift of integrity. Help us when we are weak and tempted by our greed. Keep us strong and faithful for you so that we might enjoy the riches of heaven. Amen.

August 10 ~ Soft Hearts, Great Rewards

Jesus answered, "If you want to be perfect, go, sell your possessions and give to the poor, and you will have treasure in heaven. Then come, follow me."
—Matthew 19:21 (NIV)

Matthew 19 gives us the basic treasures of heaven on earth. In this chapter, Jesus helps us remember the value of marriage and the rewards that come with the union of a couple's soft, caring hearts. He also tells us to remember the value of little children, for the kingdom of heaven is theirs. And, last, he tells the story of the rich young man who has trouble letting go of earthly possessions in order to recognize true treasures on earth.

It reminds me of the story of the man who asked for gold. But when a sack of gold fell in his path, his heart was hardened and his eyes were closed and he mistook it for an annoying rock that was in his way. He simply kicked it aside and kept on asking to find his treasure of gold.

Hi, God! It's us, again. We confess that there are times in our lives when our hearts have been hardened and our eyes have been closed. Help us appreciate the treasures of each other and of the special people you've put in our lives. Amen.

Talk It Over: What has your heart been hardened to lately? Where have your eyes been closed? Do you value your marriage as treasure from God?

August 11 ~ The Simple Life

Better a little with the fear of the LORD than great wealth with turmoil.
—Proverbs 15:16 (NIV)

The Rockefellers, Bill Gates, Donald Trump, and many more have been ranked through the years as the wealthiest people in the world. Some say that such persons are so wealthy that they have more money than 10 percent of the poorest nations in the world.

At a recent Academy Awards ceremony, one actress wore jewelry on her neck, ears, and feet that came to a net worth of more than twenty-one million dollars. The jewelry alone needed five bodyguards. Without the jewelry, however, she would have come unaccompanied.

Many times we envy those who have so much wealth. They seem to have so much glitz, glamour, and glory. But, if it came down to it, would that wealth give us all that we are searching for in life?

For the simple, we give you thanks. For the humble, we give you praise. May we never join the ranks of those who are only looking for their next raise. Amen.

Talk It Over: *Make a list of what you would do if you had great wealth. Make a list of what you would do if you had great happiness. How do they compare?*

August 12 ~ The Greed Monster

A greedy man brings trouble to his family, but he who hates bribes will live.
—Proverbs 15:27 (NIV)

Las Vegas is the "signature city" of the big greed monster. People who come to gamble their lives away in the casinos in Vegas are always looking for more.

A slot machine is a bribing machine that calls to you and says, "Come on, just one little coin and I can give you many more; just try me, it can't hurt one bit." Every now and then, somebody hits the jackpot and becomes instantly rich. But eventually the greed monster gets to them, too, bribing them with just a little bit more and then leaving them with nothing.

God invites us to an all-inclusive resort spa where we'll feel like a million dollars without having to be bribed into trouble. The jackpot is eternal life. This should give us a sense of satisfaction to help us squash that little greed monster!

Lord God, help us find in our hearts the jackpot that you have to offer us. We know that in you we will find an all-encompassing satisfaction that will give us the richness we are searching for. Amen.

Talk It Over: *How has greed brought trouble to your family? How have you been "bribed" in your life?*

August 13 ~ Treasures of a Parent

But his mother treasured all these things in her heart.

—*Luke 2:51b (NIV)*

Last Christmas at my parents' home, my husband stumbled across baby books my mother had kept for me. I was the firstborn child, and the records of my birth and growth were great.

When my husband asked his mother about his baby books and his childhood memorabilia, her comment was that she ran out of time with him. He was the third child, and she was raising two others when he was born. But that didn't keep her from treasuring in her mind and heart every moment of his life.

Now, with us expecting our first child, I know that we will be storing every moment, every memory we have with our baby. I don't think you can ask for many more treasures than the treasures of being a parent.

Gracious Creator God, thank you for the mysteries of life. Thank you for the gifts that you give each parent. Thank you for the glorious relationships you give your own children. You will always be the loving parent who treasures us all. Amen.

Talk It Over: *What were some of the things your parents treasured from your childhood?*

August 14 ~ A Precious Gift

Then Leah said, "God has presented me with a precious gift. This time my husband will treat me with honor, because I have borne him six sons."

—*Genesis 30:20 (NIV)*

In the thirtieth chapter of Genesis, Jacob's wives are having a reproduction competition. In those times, women were valued by the amount

171

of sons they could give their husbands. Rachel and Leah took God's command to be fruitful and multiply seriously.

What draws us to this verse is the value of the precious gifts that both Leah and Rachel held so dearly. The precious gift of their children was what they thanked God for.

But the competition between them almost put the "gift" on the back burner. They were no longer focused on the value of the gift, but on their obsession to outreproduce each other. They were no longer focused on God's gifts, but on who had the most gifts.

Many times we, too, overlook our precious gifts from God because we are obsessed with obtaining more.

God, thank you for all the blessings you have given us. Help us appreciate your blessings even in times of need. Amen.

Talk It Over: *What is the "precious gift" you may have overlooked in your life?*

August 15 ~ Cleverly Fashioned Images

Now they sin more and more; they make idols for themselves from their silver, cleverly fashioned images, all of them the work of craftsmen.
—*Hosea 13:2a (NIV)*

The "cleverly fashioned images" of our time are so incredible. We walk into store after store of jewelry, clothing, toys, and so much more. Yet, we continue to say that we aren't idolizing the possessions we own. I am as guilty as the Israelites. I obsess over the position I am seeking in life. I need to know that my life-style is secure. I overly value the opinion of my colleagues and friends. And, God knows, I love my clothes.

Whether or not we obsess over our possessions or idolize our positions in life, God is looking only for recognition. God has blessed us with all the possibilities in our lives; the least we can do is give God the recognition and love God's looking for.

Great God, from you all things are created and made. Help us never forget the Maker of life, the Creator, the Parent. Thank you, God. Amen.

Talk It Over: *What is the sum of what you hold dear in your life?*

August 16 ~ Recording Treasures

Joab son of Zeruiah began to count.

—1 Chronicles 27:24 (NIV)

Joab was one of the treasurers of the land. The treasurers divided up the treasures of the land and were the stewards of the resources.

Like Joab, we all are stewards of the resources God has given us. In most families, however, one spouse tends to be the primary steward of the family resources—and this person often has a "thankless" job. No one ever complains when there is money to spend, but once the word gets out that we have to cut back, there is nothing but groans and moans! Many times the primary "family banker" feels that he or she is to blame, and animosity begins to develop among family members.

When times are good, do we say, "Thank you!" to the primary "family banker" for watching our resources and giving us the opportunity to live comfortable lives?

Great God, thank you for the gifts and talents you have bestowed upon each of us. Help us learn to appreciate each other for the talents we possess. Amen.

Talk It Over: *When was the last time you said thank you to the primary "financial officer" in your house? Did you complain the last time she or he reported that money was low? How can you show your appreciation for all she or he does?*

August 17 ~ Setting Aside for God

On the first day of every week, each one of you should set aside a sum of money in keeping with his income.

—1 Corinthians 16:2 (NIV)

For the first few years of our marriage, Richard and I sometimes begrudged giving to the church because we could barely afford the little "extras" we enjoyed. I often felt guilty that I worked for the church and yet didn't tithe. Richard, however, who didn't grow up in the church, didn't even understand the concept of tithing.

The apostle Paul told the Corinthians that giving should become a part of daily living. Setting aside a gift for God's people each week should be done in gratitude and joy. He was reminding the Corinthians—and us—that because Jesus joyfully gave us the great gift of life, we, too, should give out of the joy of our hearts.

Richard and I began to realize that out of giving, we receive a great deal of "wealth" in life—wealth that cannot be earned or spent. By setting aside for God first, all the rest seems to fall into place. It's not always easy, but God loves a cheerful giver.

God, help us find a way in our hearts to set aside our resources for you. We know that sometimes it may seem that we don't have enough to live on, but we know that in you we will always be blessed. Amen.

Talk It Over: *Do you set aside your resources for God? Do you tithe?*

August 18 ~ Wellspring of Life

Above all else, guard your heart, for it is the wellspring of life.
—Proverbs 4:23 (NIV)

We humans value success. By our measurements, a person is successful if they gain wisdom, authority, power, and prestige. The author of Proverbs says, however, that there is another kind of success: succeeding God's way.

I have had the opportunity on several occasions to visit developing countries. By my standards, I pitied the people whose homes were nothing more than a few pieces of tin put together. But my father pointed out to me that they have a great deal more than I could ever imagine. Despite the conditions they may live in, they have succeeded in life. They have one another. They have joy and laughter. They have happiness and contentment. They have faith and, above all, love. These are the things they value and guard in their hearts. This is success God's way.

God, may you help us succeed in your way. Amen.

Talk It Over: *How do you measure success?*

174

August 19 ~ Forgetfulness

He said to them, "Do you still not understand?"
—Mark 8:21 (NIV)

I remember lamenting over not having enough money. We had just moved and were in a new city. One of us had a job and the other was looking. The credit card bills were coming in, the rent was due soon, and it seemed as if we weren't going to have enough for our car payments or groceries. Through prayer, we managed. We lived through those hard times, and God always provided for us.

The disciples were lamenting, too. They had given up their careers and lives to follow Jesus. They were in a boat, and they had only one loaf of bread among them all.

The funny part is that Jesus had just fed four thousand people with seven loaves of bread, and still the disciples were complaining about not being able to feed a dozen people with one loaf of bread. How quickly we forget Jesus' ability to provide for our needs!

Thank you, Jesus, for feeding us when we are hungry, quenching our thirst when we are thirsty, and clothing us when we are naked. Amen.

Talk It Over: *When and how has God provided for you when you were in need?*

August 20 ~ Lists

Be joyful always; pray continually; give thanks in all circumstances, for this is God's will for you in Christ Jesus.
—1 Thessalonians 5:16-18 (NIV)

I am a list maker. In our house, we have lists of things to do, things to buy, and people to call. Sometimes our lists are helpful, and sometimes they are not. Sometimes they hinder my spirit because just when I think I'm getting close to the bottom of my list, I always need to add more.

Lists are a symbol of the demands and priorities that are in our lives. The apostle Paul was giving a list of priorities to the Thessalonians. It was a directive to help them order their lives. Paul called them to live

175

in unity and peace and, above all, to put God, through Jesus Christ, as the priority of their lives. Now that's an appropriate "to do" list for each of us.

God, lists are great for organizing life as long as you're always on top. Help us make you our priority. Amen.

Talk It Over: *Are you a list maker? What demands do you place on each other? What are some ways you can ensure that God is always at the top of your list? What are some ways to make your family a priority on your list?*

August 21 ~ Crooked Road

"Prepare the way for the Lord, make straight paths for him. . . . The crooked roads shall become straight, and the rough ways smooth."
—Luke 3:4-5 (NIV)

Being married has helped me with the concept of doing what is right (making paths straight) instead of doing what is easy (taking the crooked road). At times I have wanted to just give up my honest values and, like many people today, take the easy, crooked road filled with false accusations, anger, and being discontented with the things I have. It's so easy to get caught up in trying to get this or that and forget to live a life of sharing and sympathy. Thankfully, I have a wife who both encourages and enables me to make my paths straight. I often look to her when making decisions because she has qualities and perspectives I don't have. Her advice helps me weigh my own ideas and, most of the time, take the right path.

It's not always easy to make paths straight, but with the help of God and each other, we can do it.

Jesus, our straight path in life, help us share our strengths and our weaknesses with each other.

Talk It Over: *Talk about how you can use each other's strengths and weaknesses to help make your paths straight.*

August 22 ~ Are You Worthy?

"So if you have not been trustworthy in handling worldly wealth, who will trust you with true riches?"

—Luke 16:11 (NIV)

Trust is a major part of any relationship, especially a marriage. Always telling the truth is a very hard thing for some people to get used to. Often people are too scared to suffer the consequences of something they have done, so they lie.

This verse from the book of Luke reminds us that we have to be trustworthy partners in our relationship. This allows us to take advantage of the true riches that trust can give. I can honestly look my wife in the face and tell her the truth about everything in my life. We have accepted each other for who we truthfully are.

Jesus, our giver of worldly wealth and riches, help us be strong and brave when it comes to honesty and trust. Guide us in learning to trust and be trustworthy in all aspects of our lives so that we may see the happiness and riches it brings. Amen.

Talk It Over: *What kind of things do you feel uncomfortable telling your spouse? Tell each other why you feel uncomfortable when talking about these things.*

August 23 ~ Change for the Better

You are my refuge and my shield; I have put my hope in your word.
—Psalm 119:114 (NIV)

This is one of the verses I turn to, along with my wife, when things are not going so well—such as when a big project is due or we're short on money and don't know what to do to make ends meet. Oftentimes we are the ones who have created the situation that is causing all of this tension.

When God is our refuge and shield, we have the resources we need to battle our daily problems. And when we live according to God's Word, we have the hope that a better day will come our way.

Rather than discourage us, may the hard times encourage us to analyze our life-style and habits in light of God's Word.

Jesus, the provider of refuge and bearer of our shield, supply us with the courage to tackle the big projects in life and stay patient through the hard times. Amen.

Talk It Over: *What are the bad habits and challenges that are pulling you down in life?*

August 24 ~ Where Are They Now?

I lift up my eyes to the hills—where does my help come from? The LORD will watch over your coming and going both now and forevermore.
—Psalm 121:1, 8 (NIV)

This psalm provides me with an explanation of how God watches over us during our life on earth and forevermore. It allows me to realize that God is watching over my deceased father—and everyone else. Even though we can't see or touch a person to know that they are OK, we can be sure that God is watching over that person always.

Jesus, we know of your love and parental instincts for your children, and we appreciate the things you do for all of us as we come into this world and go on to the next. Amen.

Talk It Over: *Have you or your spouse lost a loved one? Talk about how it affected your lives.*

August 25 ~ The Prize Bride

Bring before him Queen Vashti, wearing her royal crown, in order to display her beauty to the people and nobles, for she was lovely to look at.
—Esther 1:11 (NIV)

King Xerxes was bringing out everything he could to justify his bragging rights. You can only imagine how Queen Vashti felt when her husband told his servants to get her so that he could put her on display. She probably felt cheap. Can you blame her for refusing? King Xerxes wasn't at all interested in having her by his side as a partner or companion to help rule his kingdom. She was just another one of his "royal toys."

We are privileged to be a part of a culture and a time when men and women are considered to be created equal and, therefore, worthy of being treated equally. Most of us didn't enter into marriage strictly for the "bragging rights." Most of us, we hope, have entered into a partnership for the long haul.

Thank you, God, for the opportunity to be in a partnership with someone you created so wonderfully beautiful in my eyes and in yours. Amen.

Talk It Over: *What were the characteristics that first attracted you to your spouse? What has helped you and your spouse see each other as equals?*

August 26 ~ Don't You Care?

Jesus was in the stern, sleeping on a cushion. The disciples woke him and said to him, "Teacher, don't you care if we drown?"

—*Mark 4:38 (NIV)*

How many times do we wonder why life seems to hand us all the bad apples at the same time? The number one question we want to ask God is, "Teacher, don't you care?"

It was like that for us early in our marriage. We had a lot of hopes and dreams and were living in a very expensive, tiny, one-bedroom apartment. We wondered how we would pay all the bills we accumulated. The job I had prayed for was nowhere in sight. My husband wanted to finish school, and we kept wondering if things would get better.

At times we wondered whether or not God even cared. But, in that time of trials, God was always by our side. Then one day, God made himself known to us and helped us make some decisions that cleared the path for a bright new future. All along, Jesus was just waiting to say, "Why are you so afraid? Do you still have no faith?" (Mark 4:40 NIV).

Jesus, we know you care. We apologize for the times when our faith seems to be dim. Remind us that no matter what, you will always be by our side, through the darkness and through the light. Amen.

179

Talk It Over: When has God seemed far away? Have there been times when you felt you didn't have the faith you should have had?

August 27 ~ Meaningless

"Meaningless! Meaningless!" says the Teacher. "Utterly meaningless! Everything is meaningless."

—Ecclesiastes 1:2 (NIV)

OK, let's face it. There are days when we feel like ranting and raving these very words. But, without meaning in life, where would we be? The "teacher" in Ecclesiastes goes on to echo his frustration about seeking knowledge and wisdom. He seems to feel that the more knowledge and wisdom he obtains, the more meaningless life becomes.

I feel like that occasionally. It seems that the more we strive to be productive, competent contributors to society, the more we see how greedy, angry, and selfish the world really is.

No matter how dreary the world may seem, we know that God still calls us to serve. God asks us to give up our lives so that we may serve others. If nothing else adds meaning to my life, I'm glad that God is there to do it for me.

Great and Glorious God, thank you for bringing the simple meaning of life to those of us who seem to have forgotten it. Help us focus on the humility and generosity of the ultimate leader in our life, Jesus Christ. Amen.

Talk It Over: When have things seemed meaningless to you? What has added meaning to your life?

August 28 ~ Cornerstone

So this is what the Sovereign LORD says: "See, I lay a stone in Zion, a tested stone, a precious cornerstone for a sure foundation; the one who trusts will never be dismayed."

—Isaiah 28:16 (NIV)

This verse makes me think of an old tire commercial. A baby in a tire is cruising down a wet, slippery street. At the end of the commercial a voice says, "You can trust us with your precious package." This commercial comes to mind because today's verse says that the stone being laid for the foundation is a "tested" stone, one that has been able to survive rigorous testing and precarious situations. God has given us the full-proof money-back guarantee. This cornerstone will be there for an eternity.

So often we entrust our lives to the most economical, easy-way-out things. We give into temptation, put ourselves before others, and buy a lot of stuff to fill the holes in our lives. In reality, the only thing we need is the Cornerstone that will hold us together forever, the Cornerstone that has been tested for centuries and has endured all things, the Cornerstone that never fails. That Cornerstone is Jesus.

Jesus, our great rock and redeemer, thank you for the secure foundation you give us in life. Amen.

Talk It Over: *What is your cornerstone? Have you invested in the economical life, or have you made a deposit on the top-quality investment of life?*

August 29 ~ Chosen

But you are a chosen people, a royal priesthood, a holy nation, a people belonging to God, that you may declare the praises of him who called you out of darkness into his wonderful light.

—1 Peter 2:9 (NIV)

John Grisham's book *The Testament* tells the story of a very wealthy man who has suddenly changed the last will and testament of his life before his untimely death. His greedy children are eagerly awaiting his death, certain that they are deserving of the riches that their father has left them.

It seems that he has chosen his illegitimate daughter who knows nothing of his existence or his wealth as her benefactor. The daughter has chosen a life of service and has given herself to the people in Brazil. She has nothing, wants nothing, and wishes only to serve others. She is the "chosen one."

181

This book taught me a lot about people and life. When we want so badly to be considered the "chosen one," we would do anything to get it, even if it means caring more about ourselves than about the one who gave us life. But when we humbly seek to serve God and further others before ourselves, unaware of the precious "prize" that awaits us, God smiles upon us.

God, help us not to expect anything in return. Help us to be thankful for the gifts we have and to be certain that we always serve others first. Amen.

Talk It Over: *What "inheritance" are you waiting for? What have you done to deserve it?*

August 30 ~ The House

By wisdom a house is built, and through understanding it is established; through knowledge its rooms are filled with rare and beautiful treasures.
—Proverbs 24:3-4 (NIV)

The house is the ultimate metaphor for life and treasure. Many people spend their lives trying to obtain a bigger and better house than their last. I think the author of Proverbs says it all in this verse.

A large family wisely builds a house that can comfortably accommodate them. But a small family who builds a huge house with no one to fill it is unwise in their thinking. For one thing, they have a lot of house to heat and cool. And if they are ever lonely, that loneliness will only be heightened by the emptiness of the unoccupied house they have built. No matter how they fill the house with beautiful man-made treasures, that house will never be a home until the rare and beautiful treasures of life come and permeate its rooms.

What kind of home are you building?

Great God, help us be wise as we build our homes. Amen.

Talk It Over: *Your house is the ultimate representation of your life. What treasures fill your house? Is your house an empty box? Is it a home perfectly sized for your treasures?*

August 31 ~ "Wasteful" Love

While Jesus was in Bethany in the home of a man known as Simon the Leper, a woman came to him with an alabaster jar of very expensive perfume, which she poured on his head as he was reclining at the table. When the disciples saw this, they were indignant. "Why this waste?" they asked.

—Matthew 26:6-8

All this month we have talked about the importance of being wise with our resources and focusing on godly priorities. And here we see Jesus commending a woman who takes the most expensive perfume of her time and pours it on his head. The disciples are thinking about what this perfume could have been used for if it had been sold. Jesus says that there is a time when it is worth the investment to find and do the best for an honored guest.

I think the thing that was most valued by Jesus in that moment was not the perfume, but the woman's presence and reverence. She loved Jesus so much that she was willing to give up her most valued fragrance in order to show the love she had for him. This reminds us that the greatest value is in the love we share with one another.

God, there is no such thing as "wasteful" love, and we thank you that you have put people in our lives to teach us this. Amen.

Talk It Over: *Have there been times when you have expressed what others might call a "wasteful" love? Did the person understand the magnitude of the love you gave?*

September

DECISIONS, DECISIONS

Tim and Becky Eberhart

September 1 ~ First and Foremost

The human mind may devise many plans, but it is the purpose of the Lord that will be established.

—Proverbs 19:21

*L*iving with vision and intention is better than living without purpose. Few would disagree with that. The person who intentionally plans for an envisioned destination is more likely to arrive than the one who never intended anything. So, too, a marriage that is intentionally guided by a vision for life together has greater prospects of "arriving" than the marriage that lacks vision, direction, or purpose.

In the grand sweep of things, however, simply being effective goal setters and high achievers isn't enough. One of the meanings of the biblical definition of sin *(hamartia)* is "to miss the mark." A couple might envision, plan for, and achieve any number of intended goals (gaining early retirement, having influence within the community, being in style) and still be way off the mark. First and foremost, what matters is whether our plans correspond with God's purposes.

This month we will reflect upon the many plans, visions, and intentions that guide our relationship as we seek to move more closely to the heart of God's purposes.

Merciful God, save us from our many off-the-mark plans and establish in us enough vision, intention, and grace to join in your enduring purposes. Amen.

Talk It Over: *Take time individually to explore the following questions; then share. What visions/dreams/hopes, stated and unstated, guide our married life? How do we work to achieve them? Do they correspond with God's purposes?*

September 2 ~ God Is Good

Surely I know the plans I have for you, says the LORD, plans for your welfare and not for harm, to give you a future with hope.

—Jeremiah 29:11

Aligning our married lives with God's lasting purposes involves the same anxious uncertainty as the individual's leap into trusting God. Deep down, we yearn for our marriages to bring us happiness and pleasure and genuine intimacy. What we seek in marriage is profoundly connected to our innermost longings for life itself. Relinquishing control over something as significant as the fulfillment we seek in marriage to this One whom no one has ever seen (1 John 4:12) can feel like a blind leap.

The scriptures point beyond human vision to God the Creator, who breathes us into being (Genesis 2:7); God the Shepherd, who comforts us in danger (Psalm 23); God the Mother Hen, who desires to gather us in when we scatter (Matthew 23:37); and God the Compassionate Father, who embraces us when we return (Luke 15:20).

Not only can we trust that God plans for our good, but we also must know that only God's plans can provide the good we so deeply desire.

Steadfast God, help us trust you with our deepest needs. Amen.

Talk It Over: *Reflect upon your innermost longings for life and marriage. Share them with each other. Pray your partner might entrust all to God.*

September 3 ~ Seeking the Way

"Ask, and it will be given you; search, and you will find; knock, and the door will be opened for you. For everyone who asks receives, and everyone who searches finds, and for everyone who knocks, the door will be opened."

—Matthew 7:7-8

The discernment process can be—and usually is—difficult. Even if we've entrusted our relationship to God and even if we're willing to make God's purposes our plans, we're still often confused about the particular designs for our marriage in our time and place. What, specifically, would God have *us* do and be? How will we know?

Discerning the purposes of God in relation to one's marriage is a process and not a one-time-only disclosure. Like marriage itself, discernment happens over time, involving a genuine openness to God's leading, a long-term commitment (individually and together) to spiritual practices such as prayer, the study of scripture and Christian writings, sabbath/retreat, communal worship/fellowship, and a lifetime of learning how to listen—to yourself, to your spouse, to family, to friends and even enemies, to the world around, and to God.

Purposeful God, instill in us the confidence to ask, the discipline to seek, and the awareness to know when you've opened the door. Amen.

Talk It Over: *Individually, what spiritual practice(s) could you add to your daily/weekly/yearly schedule? Which could you practice together? Set aside time each week to communicate what you are learning/hearing.*

September 4 ~ Mysterious Ways

My thoughts are not your thoughts, nor are your ways my ways, says the LORD. For as the heavens are higher than the earth, so are my ways higher than your ways and my thoughts than your thoughts.
—Isaiah 55:8-9

Discerning God's purposes for our marriage requires us to believe, plan, and act somewhere between confidence and humility. We are assured of God's promise to find us in our seeking, and so we proceed with confidence in the answers we discern through prayer, scripture, listening, and so forth.

The scriptures themselves, however, caution against *overconfidence.* Exodus 3 portrays a God who will not be named, who is known only as the "I Am." The first two commandments warn against worshiping anything or anyone other than the one true God; and the third warns against misusing God's name for anything other than God's true purposes (Exodus 20:1-7). To move ahead with plans for our lives together, especially if we profess those plans to be true to God's purposes, requires a constant acknowledgment that we might be wrong.

Mysterious God, may your judgment resound when we replace your gift of simple faith with our own arrogance. Amen.

Talk It Over: *Have you ever acted upon what you thought was God's will only to realize later that you were wrong? Commit to humble hearts and prayers of repentance every time you believe, plan, or act in the name of God.*

September 5 ~ The Way

[God] has made known to us the mystery of his will, according to his good pleasure that he set forth in Christ, as a plan for the fullness of time, to gather up all things in him, things in heaven and things on earth.
—Ephesians 1:9-10

To be Christian is to believe that in the person of Jesus Christ, human confusion about God's purposes is met with the purposes of God made visible in human form. Christians discover the purposes of God by looking to the way of Jesus Christ. As tradition teaches, God became like humanity so that humanity might become like God.

Interesting enough, Jesus himself says very little about the married life, and when he does (i.e., Matthew 5:27-32), his actual counsel for married persons is really secondary to his grander message to all. Are we to imply, therefore—especially since Jesus himself never married—that marriage is unimportant in the broader scheme of God's purposes? Perhaps the importance of our marriage ranks precisely where Jesus places it—as secondary to God's grander purposes for all.

God in Christ, Emmanuel, you make known the way, you show us the truth, and you offer us life. May our marriage serve your grand purposes for all. Amen.

Talk It Over: *Share what the person of Jesus Christ means to you. In what ways has Jesus made the mystery of God available to you? Does your marriage rank ahead or behind the purposes of God made visible in Christ?*

188

September 6 ~ Love One Another

And this is my prayer, that your love may overflow more and more with knowledge and full insight to help you to determine what is best, so that in the day of Christ you may be pure and blameless, having produced the harvest of righteousness that comes through Jesus Christ for the glory and praise of God.

—Philippians 1:9-11

The way of Christ, who is the embodiment of God's will for humanity, is the way of love. Jesus invites us to "abide in my love, just as I have kept my Father's commandments and abide in his love. . . . This is my commandment, that you love one another as I have loved you (John 15:10, 12). In a marriage that seeks to serve Christ, the way of love will be the foundation upon which husband and wife unite, relate, communicate, and plan. God's purposes become our plans when the love we know in Christ becomes our lasting guide.

And what is love? In Christ, we know love to be a self-giving way of being/feeling/ thinking/acting, which works to promote wholeness and life in another. This kind of love is God's answer in Christ to our confusion of purpose and direction; it has the power to make us pure, and in it rests our hope for life eternal.

Praiseworthy God, may the love we know in Christ become the foundation of our marriage. Amen.

Talk It Over: *Does the love you know in Christ guide your lives together? In what ways does your spouse promote wholeness and life in you?*

September 7 ~ In God's Image

Then God said, "Let us make humankind in our image, according to our likeness." . . . So God created humankind in his image, in the image of God he created them; male and female he created them.

—Genesis 1:26-27

There is a famous Russian icon by Andrei Rublev that portrays the Holy Trinity seated around a table. Each person of the Trinity—God the Father,

God the Son, and God the Holy Spirit—is gazing into the eyes of another. Perhaps one of the meanings of the Trinity is that God does not exist as a solitary self but as related selves. God does not ultimately reside in any one of the persons but in the *space between*. God, in God's own self, is a relationship.

So, too, we do not exist as solitary selves, but in, through, and because of relationship. And as we grow deeper into the life of God, we find that God is ultimately not present in the solitude of our individual selves but in the space between. For "God is love, and those who abide in love abide in God, and God abides in them" (1 John 4:16*b*), and where does love abide if not in the *space between?* To be in loving relationship is to be in the image of God.

Loving God, ever renew in our marriage the likeness of your image. Amen.

Talk It Over: *How do you experience God in the space that is your relationship? Pray silently, gazing into the eyes of each other.*

September 8 ~ Mutual Giving

Like good stewards of the manifold grace of God, serve one another with whatever gift each of you has received.

—1 Peter 4:10

Love as we know it in Jesus Christ is the only way for two who are different to live in peace. Whereas difference by itself contains the potential of division, difference joined with love contains the promise of enrichment and growth. Love as the self-giving of one for another creates harmony rather than hostility amid different upbringings, talents, perspectives, tastes, and genders.

In this way, our differences as husband and wife are not problems but possibilities. That one is gifted here and another there need not be the basis for fighting but the probability of a broader vision for both. The mutual giving of personal gifts means the two are together smarter, more capable, and ultimately more complete. Marriage does not require sameness or the end of our unique selves. Marriage, grounded in love, is where our unique selves can be both given and received and thus made whole.

God of grace, in Christ you have given yourself to us that we might be made whole. May we pattern your love in giving our unique selves to each other. Amen.

Talk It Over: Take turns affirming the specific gifts your partner offers to your marriage.

September 9 ~ Two in One

I appeal to you . . . by the name of our Lord Jesus Christ, that all of you be in agreement and that there be no divisions among you, but that you be united in the same mind and the same purpose.

—1 Corinthians 1:10

In marriage, husband and wife unite "so they are no longer two, but one flesh" (Matthew 19:6). Two persons with separate hearts and minds intentionally join to form a new person with one heart and mind. Maybe a more accurate description is that in marriage, two become three, so that we are husband, wife, and the One who is our relationship. Regardless of how you add it up, being truly married means the two-in-one relationship has become more important than the single self.

Unity in marriage involves the constant giving of both persons for the good of the whole. If the husband puts himself, or the wife puts herself, ahead of the relationship, division arises and unity is destroyed. A marriage patterned after the way of Jesus Christ includes two persons who *both* submit personal plans, desires, and intentions to the overall good of the marriage. This is the way of unity, the way of peace, and the way of love.

Three-in-One God, unite us in giving ourselves to each other that we might be one. Amen.

Talk It Over: Identify areas of division in your marriage. Take turns offering how you might submit to the overall good of the relationship.

September 10 ~ When We Disagree

Some judge one day to be better than another, while others judge all days to be alike. Let all be fully convinced in their own minds. . . . Why do you pass judgment on your brother or sister? Or you, why do you despise your brother or sis-

191

*ter? For we will all stand before the judgment seat of God. . . . Let us then pur-
sue what makes for peace and for mutual upbuilding.*

—Romans 14:5, 10, 19

To seek unity in marriage does not mean we are in perpetual agreement. Few relationships, if any, exist without disagreements. One of us
wants pepperoni, the other black olives. She's Republican; he's a
Democrat. The husband would like to move back to the Midwest, but the
wife loves her job in the East. Being committed to unity does not entail the
elimination of all differences—of opinions, tastes, perspectives, or even
beliefs.

How we choose to express and act upon our disagreements is the cru-
cial issue. Those committed to unity in marriage must therefore also commit to communicating honestly but lovingly, directly but not in a way that
incites; and to acting with the hope of reconciliation and not further division. Maintaining unity means learning to disagree without passing judgment and to differ without despising. We must come to understand that
being right is far less important than being loving.

God of peace, help us speak and act in love, especially when we disagree. Amen.

Talk It Over: *Go to a local library or bookstore and pick up a book on marriage
that focuses on communication. Set aside time to read and discuss it together.*

September 11 ~ Seventy-seven Times

*Then Peter came and said to him, "Lord, if another member of the church sins
against me, how often should I forgive? As many as seven times?" Jesus said to
him, "Not seven times, but, I tell you, seventy-seven times."*

—Matthew 18:21-22

Being in relationship can bring immense joy. It can also bring tremendous pain. Inevitably, we hurt each other by what we do or say and by what
we don't do or say. At such times, the depth of our love for each other and
our ability to maintain unity is challenged.

The way of Christ is the way of forgiveness, which is itself the way to
restoring what has been damaged. In forgiving each other, we align with

the purposes of God, "who reconciled us to himself through Christ, and has given us the ministry of reconciliation; that is, in Christ God was reconciling the world to himself, not counting their trespasses against them, and entrusting the message of reconciliation to us" (2 Corinthians 5:18-19).

Forgiving God, give us the strength to forgive, the power to love, and the gift of reconciliation. Amen.

Talk It Over: *If forgiveness is how we respond when we are hurt, what is required of us when we are the transgressor? Is there a line for either of you between forgivable and unforgivable offenses? If so, what is that line?*

September 12 ~ The Simple Gift

You must understand this, my beloved: let everyone be quick to listen, slow to speak, slow to anger.
—James 1:19

Listening to another while she or he communicates is really quite basic, and yet it can be one of the most helpful gifts a person can give. The act itself involves very little, although most people are not good at it. Those who listen best say almost nothing, and yet what they communicate by their silence resounds in the depths of our beings.

Genuine listening means being fully present to another regardless of who she is, what he's done, or what she's saying. When we genuinely listen, we love in the way of Christ, for we shift attention from ourselves to another, from our voices to someone else's voice. This act of self-giving, so simple yet so profound, has the power to bring healing to the one who experiences great affirmation in being heard. A marriage nurtured by mutual listening is firmly grounded in the ways of God, who patiently listens to us without condition.

Attentive God, hear our prayer of love as we truly listen to each other. Amen.

Talk It Over: *For five minutes each, listen attentively to each other. The speaker is free to say whatever he or she would like or needs to express. The listener should maintain complete silence.*

September 13 ~ Bearing Fruit

Every good tree bears good fruit, but the bad tree bears bad fruit. A good tree cannot bear bad fruit, nor can a bad tree bear good fruit. . . . You will know them by their fruits.

—Matthew 7:17-18, 20

Identifying the fruit of our lives together can be a helpful guide in determining the overall health of our marriage. We might ask ourselves: What is born in us as individuals and as a couple as a result of our relationship? A healthy marriage, rooted in God's purposes as revealed in Jesus Christ, bears good fruit. Likewise, an unhealthy marriage, rooted outside of God's purposes, bears bad fruit.

The apostle Paul says the fruit of misguided planting is "fornication, impurity, licentiousness, idolatry, sorcery, enmities, strife, jealousy, anger, quarrels, dissensions, factions, envy, drunkenness, carousing, and things like these. . . . By contrast, the fruit of the Spirit is love, joy, peace, patience, kindness, generosity, faithfulness, gentleness, and self-control" (Galatians 5:19-23).

Notice that joy, peace, and all the other fruit cannot be had directly. Fruit proceeds from the tree. Seek first after God's purposes, therefore, and all these shall be added as well (Matthew 6:33, author's paraphrase).

Rooted God, open our eyes to see the true fruit of our marriage and nurture in us the desire to be grounded in you. Amen.

Talk It Over: *What is born in me and in us as a result of our uniting in relationship? Which fruit are signs of health? of disease?*

September 14 ~ Servants and Stewards

Think of us in this way, as servants of Christ and stewards of God's mysteries.
—1 Corinthians 4:1

To be servants of Christ means all that we are, including being married, belongs in service to the way of Christ. To be stewards of God's mysteries means that none of what we have, including our marriage, is meant to be an end in itself but a gift to be freely shared with all. Those who hope for final fulfillment in marriage itself, therefore, cannot help but be disappointed.

194

Stewardship of marriage involves using the goodness generated by our loving relationship for the good of others. "Look not to your own interests, but to the interests of others" (Philippians 2:4). Because God is Lord over all and the giver of all things, including our marriage, and because Christ has shown us the way, Christian marriage does not exist solely for the self-contained enjoyment of husband and wife but as a gift to the world. From God, to us, for others: the simple, eternal design.

Gift-giving God, use the uniqueness of our relationship and the goodness we have together to serve the needs of others. Amen.

Talk It Over: *How might you offer the goodness generated by your loving relationship to your neighbors, to your community, to the world?*

September 15 ~ Blessed to Be a Blessing

God blessed them, and God said to them, "Be fruitful and multiply, and fill the earth and subdue it; and have dominion over the fish of the sea and over the birds of the air and over every living thing that moves upon the earth."
—Genesis 1:28

God's blessing to men and women to have dominion over the created world has not been a particularly fruitful deal for the created world itself. Under our reign, the fish of the sea, the birds of the air, and all living things have suffered pollution, destruction, and the finality of extinction. Is this what God intended?

Humanity has understood "dominion" to mean domination. This is not the model of lordship we know in Christ, who "though he was in the form of God, did not regard equality with God as something to be exploited, but emptied himself, taking the form of a slave" (Philippians 2:6-7). Christlike dominion is not abusing power for self, but using power for the good of all. The time is ripe for us to repent of our exploiting God's created world and to reclaim our status as servants of life. This would be a blessing indeed—for *all* creation.

Creator God, plant in us the spirit of Christ that we might be a blessing to all the world. Amen.

195

Talk It Over: Consider how your lives influence the created world. Is your dominion a blessing or a curse? What can you do as a couple to be a blessing to God's creation?

September 16 ~ A Strange Love

Do not neglect to show hospitality to strangers, for by doing that some have entertained angels without knowing it.

—Hebrews 13:2

A closing blessing in the liturgy for Christian Marriage in *The United Methodist Book of Worship* says this: "Bear witness to the love of God in this world, so that those to whom love is a stranger will find in you generous friends." What an appropriately Christian way to send newlyweds into the world—commissioned together to a life of hospitality.

The Greek word for hospitality, *philoxenia*, literally means a love *(philo)* of the stranger *(xeno)*. Abraham and Sarah offered hospitality to three strangers, who were actually angels from God, by providing them a place of rest, nourishment, and a welcome presence (Genesis 18:1-8). Opportunities in marriage to provide love to strangers through these or other means are everywhere—at church or work, across town or across the street, in soup kitchens or in our own kitchens. Imagine if Christian couples everywhere spent time every week intentionally practicing hospitality. Love would increase, strangers decrease, and generous friendships abound.

Welcoming God, may those to whom love is a stranger find in us generous friends. Amen.

Talk It Over: Imagine if you were to spend time every week practicing hospitality to strangers. What would you do? When can you start?

September 17 ~ True Religion

Is not this the fast that I choose: to loose the bonds of injustice, to undo the thongs of the yoke, to let the oppressed go free, and to break every yoke? Is it not to share your bread with the hungry, and bring the homeless poor into your house; when you see the naked, to cover them, and not to hide yourself from your own kin?

—Isaiah 58:6-7

Oftentimes, the ideal Christian marriage is portrayed as the couple that regularly attends Sunday service, with the husband helping usher and the wife singing in the choir. This is religiousness, right? For the prophet Isaiah, all shows of religiosity detached from justice for the poor, food for the hungry, shelter for the homeless, and clothing for the vulnerable are—to say it gently—unimpressive in the eyes of God.

The problem for many of us first-world Christians is that by these standards our religious lives are far from impressive. Our "successful" churches reach out to young couples with rocking worship and praise, brand-new facilities, and we all "delight to draw near to God" (Isaiah 58:2). And inner-city poor still hunger, women and children around the world still suffer injustice, and displaced refugees still have no home. Like Isaiah, Jesus confronts our misguided religion: "Just as you did not do it to one of the least of these, you did not do it to me" (Matthew 25:45).

God of justice, open our ears to the cries of the poor and our eyes to plight of the needy. Amen.

Talk It Over: *How does your marriage benefit "the least of these"?*

September 18 ~ They Fell Down and Died

As for those who in the present age are rich, command them not to be haughty, or to set their hopes on the uncertainty of riches, but rather on God who richly provides us with everything for our enjoyment. They are to do good, to be rich in good works, generous, and ready to share, thus storing up for themselves the treasure of a good foundation for the future, so that they may take hold of the life that really is life.

—1 Timothy 6:17-19

Possibly one of the least commendable models of marriage portrayed in scripture is that of Ananias and Sapphira. The early Christian community, aware of the dangers of private ownership, committed to share everything in common. This couple, however, concerned more with their own livelihood than the good of the whole, chose to keep some back for themselves. Confronted by Peter, Ananias and Sapphira fell over and died (Acts 4:32–5:11). Of shame? Of regret over having been caught? By the judgment–justice of God?

Marriage, particularly in the affluent West, has become the unofficial beginning to the amassment and hording of private possessions. From the start, a couple genuinely seeking after the purposes of God is threatened by the dangers of idolatry, selfishness, pride, and false hope. Maintaining faithfulness to lives of self-giving, stewardship, hospitality, and care for the poor is ever more important and even more difficult.

Extravagant God, you freely give to us in perfect generosity. Guard us from possessiveness and so free us to share that we might take hold of the life that really is life. Amen.

Talk It Over: *Make a list of the possessions you most prize. Do they present any dangers to your marriage? to your Christian life?*

September 19 ~ Whom Will You Serve?

"Now therefore revere the LORD, and serve him in sincerity and in faithfulness; put away the gods that your ancestors served beyond the River and in Egypt, and serve the LORD. Now if you are unwilling to serve the LORD, choose this day whom you will serve, whether the gods your ancestors served in the region beyond the River or the gods of the Amorites in whose land you are living; but as for me and my household, we will serve the LORD."

—Joshua 24:14-15

Having led the Israelites out of captivity in Egypt to a bountiful homeland, the Lord promised the Israelites a hopeful future if they would stay faithful to God's ways. Though the decision seems simple enough, the Israelites were repeatedly enticed by the option to follow other gods and other ways.

Patterning our marriage after the way of Jesus Christ is obviously not the only possible option. Day after day, we come across proposals for relationships that glorify selfishness, dishonesty, materialism, hatred of the stranger, and disdain for the poor. Our allegiance to God is often compromised by the option to follow more enticing, or maybe just more common, ways. Nevertheless, God's promise for a hope-filled future remains, as does our daily opportunity to choose. "I have set before you life and death, blessings and curses. Choose life . . . so that you may live" (Deuteronomy 30:19-20).

Life-giving God, grace us with enough courage and wisdom to accept your promise of blessed life, this and every day. Amen.

Talk It Over: *Assess the strength of your marriage's faithfulness to the way of Jesus Christ. What commitments, beliefs, or behaviors keep you from deeper faithfulness? Decide together where you intend to go from here.*

September 20 ~ Two Are Better

Two are better than one, because they have a good reward for their toil. For if they fall, one will lift up the other; but woe to one who is alone and falls and does not have another to help.

—Ecclesiastes 4:9-10

Living God's purposes as made known in Jesus Christ is not easy. "For the gate is narrow and the road is hard that leads to life, and there are few who find it" (Matthew 7:14). Self-giving is counterintuitive, responsible stewardship can be overwhelming, hospitality takes time and energy, and caring for the poor requires leaving our "comfort zones" far behind. Is any of this actually possible?

God does not point us anywhere without providing a way; and in the experience of a loving relationship, we see the divine mind providing one of the more beautiful of ways. Marriage can be a means of grace in which those things we can't do as one alone become possible as two together. For "what is impossible for mortals," who rely on self-reliance, self-confidence, and self-motivation, "is possible for God" (Luke 18:27), who gives us relationship and the capacity to transform one another by encouragement, support, and love.

God of possibilities, we thank you for each other and for providing in our marriage a way toward greater faithfulness. Amen.

Talk It Over: *Share with each other how you have grown in faith since the day before your wedding day to today.*

September 21 ~ Keeping Accounts

Always be ready to make your defense to anyone who demands from you an accounting for the hope that is in you.

*—1 Peter 3:15*b

Christians have always been quite creative in developing specific ways to hold one another accountable. From the ordered life of monasticism to confession to spiritual mentors to small group Bible studies, committed persons have found the practice of accountability to be an essential part of maturing in the way of Jesus Christ. In giving a regular account of our lives to others and in opening ourselves to their loving response, we build into our lives the stability, support, and rhythm of responsibility we need to sustain growth along the way.

The relationship of husband and wife is a natural place to practice accountability. Each can provide for the other a listening ear, a caring presence, helpful feedback, and gentle reminders when needed. Practiced lovingly, accountability can nurture greater intimacy in our relationship, promote more sensitivity in learning how to help each other, and faithfully hold us to our commitments to grow in the way of Christ.

Gentle God, help us as we help each other grow closer to your loving ways. Amen.

Talk It Over: *Set aside regular time to clarify your commitments to the way of Christ, to share struggles and joys, and to offer each other help along the way. Begin today!*

September 22 ~ In a Spirit of Gentleness

If anyone is detected in a transgression, you who have received the Spirit should restore such a one in a spirit of gentleness.

—Galatians 6:1

Helping each other along the way toward greater faithfulness includes offering feedback, bringing up reminders, giving suggestions, and so forth. Most of us have experienced how helpful *and* how unhelpful this can be. Here, the potential blessing of mutual upbuilding in a relationship runs parallel to the potential curse of tearing each other down. Those we love the most are the very ones we can and often do hurt the most. The closer we become, the more damaging our words or actions can be.

We increase the likelihood that our feedback, advice, and even our corrections will be helpful and not hurtful when we act in a spirit of gentleness. Practicing Christlike accountability does not involve unbridled criticism of our partner, which is often grounded in a spirit of anger or selfishness and likely to create division. By contrast, the spirit of gentleness, motivated by love, is our surest path to restoration.

Tenderhearted God, may our attempts to help each other be firmly grounded in your gentle spirit. Amen.

Talk It Over: *Take turns sharing what is helpful and what is hurtful from your partner in the process of holding each other accountable.*

September 23 ~ Humble Wisdom

A scoffer who is rebuked will only hate you; the wise, when rebuked, will love you. Give instruction to the wise, and they will become wiser still; teach the righteous and they will gain in learning.

—Proverbs 9:8-9

True wisdom is revealed in a person's capacity to humbly accept guidance and learning from another. We grow in faith through the practice of accountability only when both husband and wife willingly submit themselves to each other for mutual correction. Without granting others the authority to offer instruction, and without the wisdom to genuinely listen to what they say, we cannot and will not grow in faithfulness to the way of Jesus Christ.

"Whoever heeds instruction is on the path to life, but one who rejects a rebuke goes astray" (Proverbs 10:17). Therefore, "all of you must clothe yourselves with humility in your dealings with one another, for 'God opposes the proud, but gives grace to the humble'" (1 Peter 5:5*b*).

201

Gracious God, grant us the good sense to invite others to look after us and the humility to accept what they see. Amen.

Talk It Over: *In the spirit of gentleness, identify for your partner areas of possible growth. Then, in the spirit of humble wisdom, listen quietly to what each other has to say.*

September 24 ~ One Day at a Time

Come now, you who say, "Today or tomorrow we will go to such and such a town and spend a year there, doing business and making money." Yet you do not even know what tomorrow will bring. What is your life? For you are a mist that appears for a little while and then vanishes. Instead you ought to say, "If the Lord wishes, we will live and do this or that."

—James 4:13-15

Conventional wisdom advises us to look to the future, to identify goals, and to construct plans to get us from where we are to where we'd like to be. We are taught to dream about our lives five, ten, and twenty-five years from now and then to do whatever it takes today to secure those dreams.

The problem with conventional wisdom is its origin in self-indulgent fear. We fear the future, in particular *our* future, and so we waste time and energy trying to control tomorrow at the expense of countless opportunities to be faithful to the way of Christ today. Welcoming the stranger, listening with an attentive presence, discerning God's purposes through spiritual discipline, meeting the needs of the poor—such things can only be done in the present. Therefore, "do not worry about tomorrow, for tomorrow will bring worries of its own. Today's trouble is enough for today" (Matthew 6:34). True wisdom is living God's purposes in the way of Jesus Christ one day, one hour, one moment at a time.

Ever present God, awaken us to the possibilities of today. Amen.

Talk It Over: *Confess ways in which worry over tomorrow has kept you from faithfulness today.*

202

September 25 ~ Basic Training

Now, discipline always seems painful rather than pleasant at the time, but later it yields the peaceful fruit of righteousness to those who have been trained by it.
—Hebrews 12:11

What we repeatedly do orders the foundation of who we become. Like the athlete who practices for hours day after day, repeating the same drills over and over until they become second nature, so too those who practice the way of Christ day after day grow into persons in whom the "peaceful fruit of righteousness" is deeply embedded in their bones.

Now, in the same way that a four-mile run after weeks—maybe even years—of doing nothing feels almost unbearable, so too does self-giving, hospitality, watching over one another in love, and so forth seem hard to us at first. And in the same way that the athlete some days "feels" like practicing and some days does not, so too do we some days "feel" like following God's purposes and some days not. The point is to keep practicing, to keep trying to live faithfully, so that eventually the way of Christ becomes not just our second but our essential nature.

God of yesterday, today, and tomorrow, train us in your nature until loving-kindness becomes our way in the world. Amen.

Talk It Over: *Commit to practice an act of self-giving once a day for the next week.*

September 26 ~ By Grace Alone

Speak evil of no one . . . avoid quarreling . . . be gentle, and . . . show every courtesy to everyone. For we ourselves were once foolish, disobedient, led astray, slaves to various passions and pleasures, passing our days in malice and envy, despicable, hating one another. But when the goodness and loving kindness of God our Savior appeared, he saved us, not because of any works of righteousness that we had done, but according to his mercy.
—Titus 3:2-5

The inevitable danger lurking near all who seek to grow in faithfulness is spiritual pride. Maybe we've found success reading scripture together,

203

or maybe we've disciplined ourselves to serve at a soup kitchen once a week, and now people admire us and deep down we've begun to think of ourselves as better than all the rest. Few of us can resist this temptation.

Basic to the gospel message is the affirmation that "while we still were sinners Christ died for us" (Romans 5:8). We do not earn God's favor by working hard at discipline or accountability or even self-giving. We know the way because God in Christ first loved us, and we become more loving and gentle and gracious ourselves not because of our own merit, but in response to the grace of God still at work in us. In the order of salvation, grace is the first, the middle, and the last word. So there really is no place for pride, only gratitude.

Merciful God, guard us from pride by filling our hearts and minds with gratitude. Amen.

Talk It Over: *Confess your tendencies toward spiritual pride. Discuss how you may hold each other accountable to lives of gratitude.*

September 27 ~ The Way of the Cross

Then the mother of the sons of Zebedee came to him with her sons, and kneeling before him, she asked a favor of him. And he said to her, "What do you want?" She said to him, "Declare that these two sons of mine will sit, one at your right hand and one at your left, in your kingdom." But Jesus answered, "You do not know what you are asking. Are you able to drink the cup that I am about to drink?" They said to him, "We are able."

—Matthew 20:20-22

To affirm the *whole* gospel story is to acknowledge that the way of Christ leads to the way of the cross. We prefer to omit the cross. Affirming God's unending love is easy. Praising Christ's victory over sin and death is exhilarating. Even following with the disciples in claiming Jesus' lordship gives us a sense of identity and belonging. We, too, want to sit beside Christ when all is said and done. But do we really know what we are asking? And are we truly able to affirm what self-giving love entails and where following Jesus to the end leads?

Jesus says, "If any want to become my followers, let them deny themselves and take up their cross and follow me. For those who want to save their life will lose it, and those who lose their life for my sake, and for the sake of the gospel, will save it" (Mark 8:34-35).

Suffering God, grant us the grace to love as you love no matter the cost and to the very end. Amen.

Talk It Over: *What have you sacrificed as a result of your commitment to the way of Christ? What are you willing to sacrifice?*

September 28 ~ Blessed Persecution

"Blessed are those who are persecuted for righteousness' sake, for theirs is the kingdom of heaven. Blessed are you when people revile you and persecute you and utter all kinds of evil against you falsely on my account. Rejoice and be glad, for your reward is great in heaven, for in the same way they persecuted the prophets who were before you."

—Matthew 5:10-12

The way of Christ is not the chosen way for all. Clearly, there are those who are not committed to self-giving love at all costs but rather to self-serving gain no matter the price. To such persons, faithfulness to the way of Christ is absurd. For "God chose what is foolish in the world to shame the wise" and "what is weak in the world to shame the strong" (1 Corinthians 1:27).

A couple whose way is guided by Christ will likely face resistance, ridicule, even persecution from persons who perceive this way to be a threat. Like the prophets, our standing against persons and structures that breed hatred of others, that promote the worship of things, that "trample the head of the poor into the dust of the earth" (Amos 2:7) may lead toward the way of the cross.

But "happy are those...whose hope is in the LORD their God, who made heaven and earth . . . who keeps faith forever" (Psalm 146:5-6).

Faithful God, stand with us as we seek to stand for you. Amen.

Talk It Over: *How might you speak out and stand up for the way of Christ at work, in your community, in the world?*

205

September 29 ~ Radical Love

"You have heard that it was said, 'You shall love your neighbor and hate your enemy.' But I say to you, Love your enemies and pray for those who persecute you, so that you may be children of your Father in heaven; for he makes his sun rise on the evil and on the good, and sends rain on the righteous and on the unrighteous."

—Matthew 5:43-45

Following the radical way of Jesus Christ can bring enemies. Some may resist or oppose who we are, what we say, and where we stand. At such times, we are tempted to return dislike for dislike and give in to what we want to do: to hate them. Following the radical way of Jesus Christ, however, requires us to do the most radical thing of all: to love them.

For us to commit so deeply to self-giving love that we meet resistance, and then turn around and hate our enemies is to betray our foundational commitment, deny Christ, and become the enemy ourselves. The crusades, Inquisition, witch trials, and every act of violence raged by Christians *in the name of Christ* are all lamentable examples of such betrayal. The way of Christ, seen on the cross, is self-giving love, even of enemies, to the very end.

Radical God, do not let us be overcome by evil, but strengthen us to overcome evil with good (Romans 12:21). Amen.

Talk It Over: *As a couple, who are your enemies? Are they enemies because of your faithfulness or your sinfulness? How specifically might you love them?*

September 30 ~ Take Courage

"In the world you face persecution. But take courage; I have conquered the world!"

—John 16:33

The good news for all who profess Jesus as Christ is the assurance that in Jesus' resurrection to life from death on the cross, God pronounces that self-giving love is the enduring way that will never fail and can never be

206

defeated. This is the hope and the promise for all who commit to love, who suffer for love, and who last in the way of love, because "love never ends" (1 Corinthians 13:8). Neither suffering nor injustice nor death itself is the end, for we are convinced "that neither death, nor life, nor angels, nor rulers, nor things present, nor things to come, nor powers, nor height, nor depth, nor anything else in all creation, will be able to separate us from the love of God in Christ Jesus our Lord" (Romans 8:38-39). So take courage. God's purposes, known to us in the way of Jesus Christ as self-giving love, are the way of eternity.

Almighty God, we praise and thank you for your promise of eternal life, sealed in the resurrection of Jesus and available to all who follow in his way. Amen.

Talk It Over: *Hold one another accountable to speaking words and living lives of hope.*

October

DESIRABLE ADJUSTMENTS
James Chongho and Karen Eunsook Kim

October 1 ~ Come Closer to Christ

But God demonstrates his own love for us in this: While we were still sinners, Christ died for us.

—Romans 5:8 (NIV)

When Queen Elizabeth II married Sir Philip, it was said that the Archbishop of Canterbury advised, "Each of you, come closer to Christ. Then you will truly be close to each other."

When we come closer to Christ, we experience the grace of God. It is God's grace that brings and binds us together as one, as husband and wife. If we ignore our weaknesses and rely solely on our own strengths, a marriage will not last long. Self-righteousness is one of the main sources of marital conflict. Having the ability to humbly admit and acknowledge our shortcomings to our spouses is one of the most important ingredients for success in marriage. "While we were still sinners, Christ died for us." As we come closer to Christ, admitting our shortcomings becomes not only easier but desirable.

This month we will explore some of the other desirable "adjustments" Christ helps us make in marriage—in our attitudes and in our actions—as we come closer to him. The result is a stronger relationship, a relationship built on the love of Christ.

Dear Lord, help us look at each other with the heart of Christ. Amen.

October 2 ~ Being the Right Person

The LORD God said, "It is not good for the man to be alone. I will make a helper suitable for him."

—Genesis 2:18 (NIV)

Husband and wife were created to be each other's helper. The helper God created for man was not a hired worker. The helper that God created for man is one who enables and empowers man to be whole as a partner. In Proverbs, we read that "he who finds a wife finds what is good and receives favor from the LORD" (18:22 NIV). Why did God make one wife instead of ten friends when man was alone? This "one" is everything that man needs to be a whole being.

No marriage is perfect. No one is perfect. Success in marriage is not finding the right person, but rather being the right person for each other. Marrying someone is one of the most holy and courageous choices we make in our lives. When we said yes to each other, we did not say yes because we were perfect for each other. We said yes because of our will-ingness to risk who we are and what we will become, trusting that God will help us.

Dear Lord, we thank you for providing a helper to make us whole. Amen.

Talk It Over: Make a list of ten things you would like your spouse to help you with (chores, tasks, projects, and so forth), and share your list.

October 3 ~ I Love You for You

God saw all that he had made, and it was very good.

—Genesis 1:31 (NIV)

In the beginning, God said that "it was very good." Indeed, it should be very good. It is God's will and commandment for us. Optimum goodness happens when we become what God intends for us to be. In marriage, God's intention for us is to help each other grow into perfect love.

In Kahlil Gibran's book *Jesus the Man*, Jesus said, "Others love you for themselves, but I love you for you." Love happens when we learn this truth. We always struggle in marriage when we force our spouse to become what we want him or her to be. Success in marriage happens when we help each other become the best of who we are and who we can become.

Dear Lord, sometimes we become very selfish without realizing it. Help us love each other as you have loved us. Amen.

Talk It Over: *Find a quiet place and talk about your dreams. Help each other come up with a plan to begin living out your dream.*

October 4 ~ Return to Sender

God saw all that he had made, and it was very good. And there was evening, and there was morning.
—Genesis 1:31 (NIV)

There are good times and bad times. At times we love, and at times we argue and fight. At times our children can be loving, and at other times not so loving. That is why it is so important for us to always return to our Sender who said, "It was very good." It was very good when we got married. It was very good when we had the child. It was very good in the beginning. Reminding ourselves that it was God who made us come together in the first place always helps us be more mindful of God's original blessing.

One time a while ago, we were on a family trip and had a long distance to travel. I remember driving and hearing the noise of my wife snoring. I looked at her and found a woman entering middle age, losing her youthful beauty. For a moment, an unhappy thought passed through my mind, but I soon realized that her aging was not only natural but due to her sacrificial dedication to our family. I had to stop the car on the highway shoulder to give her a kiss.

211

God made us lovable by loving us. We, too, can make one another lovable by loving one another.

Dear Lord, help us always come back to the realization that it is you who started and blessed our family. Amen.

Talk It Over: *Look at your wedding video and/or photos together. Talk about your "beginning."*

October 5 ~ Do Not Sin in Your Anger

"In your anger do not sin": Do not let the sun go down while you are still angry, and do not give the devil a foothold.
—*Ephesians 4:26-27 (NIV)*

Norman Wright said that marriage is the only race in which two racers can both win. But in reality, we sometimes find ourselves racing against each other. I remember one Sunday morning when my wife made a critical comment about my ministry. I was upset. Instead of focusing on Sunday morning service preparation, I thought about getting back at her. On holy Sunday morning, I was concentrating on how to get back at my wife. The thought of getting back at my wife was still on my mind even during my sermon time. When I was preaching, I told the congregation what was on my mind, saying, "I know Jesus told us to love our enemies, but this morning my enemy happened to be my wife. I am still trying to figure out how to get even with my wife!" The whole congregation went into an uproar of laughter.

It is perfectly all right to argue and even get angry at each other, but in the end we must create a win-win situation by working out our problems in a wise and productive manner. Many times we are too serious about minor things. Sometimes finding humor in our seriousness can bring healing into situations.

Dear Lord, help us always be mindful that we both can be winners even in the midst of arguments. Amen.

Talk It Over: *Talk about "rules" that can help your future disagreements be fairer and more constructive.*

212

October 6 ~ Rules of Communication

Do not let any unwholesome talk come out of your mouths, but only what is helpful for building others up according to their needs, that it may benefit those who listen.

—Ephesians 4:29 (NIV)

Words can hurt us. Communication is one of the most difficult problems married people face. It requires practice and intentional discipline. There are several biblical principles or rules of communication.

First, we have to listen carefully to our spouse before we talk. It is written in Proverbs that "he who answers before listening—that is his folly and his shame"(18:13 NIV). Most of the time, conflict arises because we do not respect this principle.

Second, we have to ask, "Is it helpful?" We have to discern whether what we have to say will help or hurt our spouse. It is also written in Proverbs, "Gold there is, and rubies in abundance, but lips that speak knowledge are a rare jewel"(20:15 NIV).

Third, we have to find an appropriate time to make good communication. "A man finds joy in giving an apt reply—and how good is a timely word!"(Proverbs 15:23 NIV). How good is a timely word!

An old saying states it well: "A wise word can pay off a million-dollar debt."

Dear Lord, help us know when to speak and when to listen. Bless our lips to be an instrument of joy and goodness. Amen.

Talk It Over: *Help each other be mindful of three questions to consider before speaking: (1) Have I listened carefully? (2) Is what I have to say helpful? and (3) Is this the right time?*

October 7 ~ Eyes on Me and Lips Sealed!

Instead, speaking the truth in love, we will in all things grow up into him who is the Head, that is, Christ.

—Ephesians 4:15 (NIV)

213

It is very important that we have a goal and purpose in our lives. Sometimes we just float around purposelessly. Instead of a "called" life, we sometimes are living in a "driven" life or "pushed into" life. I remember when my oldest daughter was four or five years old. When I was reading a newspaper instead of paying attention to what she had to say, she shouted, "Daddy! Eyes on me and lips sealed!" Sometimes God speaks to us through our children, and sometimes through our spouses; and we must always be prepared to listen.

Our challenge is to grow up into Christ—to keep our eyes on Christ in order to grow up into Christ. We need each other to help each other grow. Marriage is a God-given calling. Having a family is a God-given calling. It is not something we are being pushed into. We may sometimes feel that way, but it is not so. Success in marriage depends on our willingness to make it God's calling for our families to grow up into Christ. And one of the ways we do this is by listening to each other.

Dear Lord, help us fix our eyes on Christ so that we may grow up into Christ, and help us always be prepared for a word from you from each other. Amen.

Talk It Over: *Set aside time for one of you to talk freely and the other to pay attention and listen.*

October 8 ~ Partners in Ministry

Paul stayed on in Corinth for some time. Then he left the brothers and sailed for Syria, accompanied by Priscilla and Aquila.
—Acts 18:18 (NIV)

The names Priscilla and Aquila appear five times in the Bible—always together. Priscilla and Aquila not only worked together, but also engaged in ministry together. They were not only a good wife and husband but also two of the best Christian workers in the early church. I know of many couples who work together and have a terrible time both in business and at home. But Priscilla and Aquila were successful in doing both together. What was their secret? They made Christ the priority in their life together.

JOY, the abbreviation of a mission organization, stands for "Jesus first. Others second. You third"—which reveals the secret of happiness that can also be applied to our family life.

Dear Lord, we want to be like Priscilla and Aquila. Help us be "partners in ministry" by putting Christ first. Amen.

Talk It Over: *Choose a mission or service project that you can do together (or as a family, if you have children).*

October 9 ~ Confidence and Courage

And hope does not disappoint us, because God has poured out his love into our hearts by the Holy Spirit, whom he has given us.

—Romans 5:5 (NIV)

Mother Teresa once said that we need to gain the confidence that God loves us. She also said we need to regain courage to love others. Our families are in much need of this courage and confidence. Our human energy of love and will for love can easily be drained out. This is precisely why the Bible said that God loved us first, and that it is God who has poured his love into our hearts.

Humbly recognizing that it is God who loved us first gives us both the confidence and the courage to love. Saint Augustine said that by loving us, God made us lovable. This principle of love applies to all of us. When we gain this confidence from being loved, we will all become lovable and gain the courage to love.

Dear Lord, we thank you for making us lovable by loving us first. Amen.

Talk It Over: *Each of you make a list of twenty things that make you proud of your spouse; then share your lists.*

October 10 ~ As Good as It Gets

The man said, "This is now bone of my bones and flesh of my flesh; she shall be called 'woman,' for she was taken out of man."

—Genesis 2:23 (NIV)

What Adam shouted when he saw Eve can be translated as, "This is the best of who I am and what I can become!" This is far away from the male chauvinistic translation saying that woman is inferior because she was taken out of man. Adam was excited to see Eve because she represented the best of what he could become together with her.

In the Oscar-winning movie *As Good as It Gets,* Helen Hunt asks Jack Nicholson to say something nice about her. Nicholson replies, "You make me want to be a better man." This is one of the highest compliments one can be paid. It is a wonderful thing to be the inspiration for someone's desire to become a better person. And this is how Adam viewed Eve. This is what people in love should do for each other: help each other strive to become better.

Dear Lord, thank you for giving me someone I can encourage to become the best of what he or she can be. Amen.

Talk It Over: *Surprise your spouse sometime this week with an encouraging note tucked into a briefcase, taped on the dashboard, or attached to a mirror or refrigerator. Do this periodically to inspire your spouse to keep growing.*

October 11 ~ The ABCs of Love

Love is patient, love is kind. It does not envy, it does not boast, it is not proud. It is not rude, it is not self-seeking, it is not easily angered, it keeps no record of wrongs.
— *1 Corinthians 13:4-5 (NIV)*

The A of love is *accept*—accepting a spouse as he or she is. It has been said that love is gently holding the other's hand in his or her journey of finding self. Yes, men are from Mars and women are from Venus. Therefore, the first rule of happiness is accepting each other.

The B of love is *believe.* And the C of love is *care.* A long time ago, our dryer broke down. We had to hand-squeeze and hang dry all our laundry. It was a very tiresome and time-consuming task. Initially, we complained and blamed each other for our unfortunate situation. But soon enough we realized that we were having fun. We also realized that we needed each other to hand-squeeze our towels and other large clothing. It was one of those rare "picture-perfect moments" in our lives. Believing in and caring for each other helps us through our everyday trials.

216

The D of love is *desire*—in other words, expecting each other to become the best we can be. As John Lennon sang and Robert Browning wrote, "Grow old along with me! The best is yet to be." We desire the best of each other.

The E of love is *erase*—forgiving and forgetting each other's wrongdoings and shortcomings.

How would you complete the ABCs of love?

Dear Lord, we know that love is all that matters. Enable us to remind each other that the best is yet to come. Amen.

Talk It Over: *Keep these three S's in your life together: (1) a* secret *romantic place for each other, (2)* stimulus *to make your life exciting, and (3) some* fun!

October 12 ~ Love Is as Love Does

If anyone says, "I love God," yet hates his brother, he is a liar. For anyone who does not love his brother, whom he has seen, cannot love God, whom he has not seen.

—1 John 4:20 (NIV)

I know of a retired army man who did not know how to express his love for his wife. But on his deathbed he asked his son, "Please tell your mother that I love her." His wife was happy to hear this, but all her life she suffered from a deficiency of love. A song is not a song until someone sings it. Love is not love until it is shared. Love is as love does.

One day when they were little, out of nowhere, my younger daughter, Eunice, asked her older sister Anna, "Sister, do you love me?" Surprised by this sudden and awkward question, Anna shrugged her shoulders and responded with a smile, "Of course, I do. I love you, Eunice. I'm your sister." Hearing this, Eunice said, "Thank you, sister." She needed to hear her sister's love for her.

Even as adults, we need to know that we are loved. It's a need we never outgrow.

O Loving God, we all need to love and be loved. You made us capable of loving. Help us realize that we need each other. Amen.

217

October 13 ~ I Am What God Thinks of Me

But now, this is what the LORD *says—he who created you, O Jacob, he who formed you, O Israel: "Fear not, for I have redeemed you; I have called you by name; you are mine."*

—Isaiah 43:1 (NIV)

"I am not what others think of me. I am neither what I think of myself. I am what God thinks of me." This was part of a faith statement read during one of the World Council of Churches worship services prepared by a women's group.

When my children were growing up, I paid more attention to my younger daughter, Eunice, because she received less attention from people. I sometimes caught myself making exaggerated gestures of love toward Eunice. One day when she was three years old, I hugged her and asked, "Why are you so beautiful?" in order to boost her self-esteem. Without hesitation she responded, "Daddy, don't you know that I am beautiful because God made me?" I was dumbfounded. That was her saying, "Daddy! I am beautiful not only because you love me; I am beautiful because God loves me."

Healthy couples and families encourage one another to see themselves as God sees them.

O loving God, we give thanks for your love. Through your love we find ourselves and discover how precious we are. Amen.

Talk It Over: Point out three God-given qualities or characteristics of your spouse that you appreciate and value.

October 14 ~ Sharing Burdens

Moses' father-in-law replied, "What you are doing is not good. You and these people who come to you will only wear yourselves out. The work is too heavy for you; you cannot handle it alone."

—Exodus 18:17-18 (NIV)

I remember often shouting to my wife, "Do you have any clue what I am going through at work?" She would reply, "Do you have any idea what I am going through at home?" We were both overburdened with our hard work. Why is it so difficult to share our burdens and hardships with the one we love the most?

Psalm 46 reminds us, "Be still and know that I am God"(v. 10). Realizing that we are not God but rather mere human beings is a lifesaving gospel. This revelation enables us to give our burdens to God rather than taking them on all by ourselves.

O God of Love, strengthen us to share our burdens together in love. Amen.

Talk It Over: *Share a burden or hardship with your spouse and talk about ways your spouse may offer encouragement and/or help.*

October 15 ~ You Are Never Alone

"Come to me, all you that are weary and are carrying heavy burdens, and I will give you rest. Take my yoke upon you, and learn from me; for I am gentle and humble in heart, and you will find rest for your souls. For my yoke is easy, and my burden is light."

—Matthew 11:28-30

I remember seeing a Christmas card from Boys Town, an orphanage for boys, with a picture of a young boy carrying an even younger boy on his back. Printed at the bottom of the picture were the words, "He ain't heavy, Father! 'Cause he's my brother." (The term *father* was in reference to the priest in charge of Boys Town.) I am sure that each boy carried a heavy heart growing up without parents. But the older boy was smiling.

Former Archbishop of Brazil, Dom Helder Camara, champion of love and justice for poor people, prayed, "Lord, when the cross falls on us full force it crushes us. . . . When you come along with the cross you embrace us." We all carry our own crosses: some small, some too big. But we are never alone in carrying our crosses. Christ is there for us.

O God of Love, we thank you for being with us when we carry our own crosses. Amen.

219

Talk It Over: Talk about a time when Christ helped each of you carry a burden—perhaps one you're still carrying now.

October 16 ~ Being a Servant

"Whoever wishes to be great among you must be your servant, and whoever wishes to be first among you must be your slave; just as the Son of Man came not to be served but to serve, and to give his life a ransom for many."
—Matthew 20:26-28

One day my seminary professor entered class with a big smile on his face. After announcing that he had just been to the admission review committee, he told us how, as usual, nearly all of the recommendations written for the applicants said that the students were strong and able leaders. On that particular day, however, a recommendation for one of the applicants said that this particular student was not much of a leader, but was a very good follower. The professor was so overjoyed by this remark that he recommended the committee accept the applicant without further review. "We need at least one good follower in this school where everyone claims to be leaders," he said.

A good leader is also a good follower. Christ was a great leader, but he also was an obedient and faithful servant of God. In addition to being servants of God, we need to be servants for one another—especially for our spouses.

O merciful God, help us empty ourselves so that we may become servants for each other. Amen.

Talk It Over: Give each other a foot massage!

October 17 ~ Love Begins at Home

Be kind and compassionate to one another, forgiving each other, just as in Christ God forgave you.
—Ephesians 4:32 (NIV)

Our marriages need regular "health checkups." A periodic checkup helps us find problems, illness, and wounds that, if ignored, can destroy our relationship. Living in the same house under the same roof doesn't necessarily make a house a home. Because we tend to take each other for granted, we often fail to see each other's wounds and hurts.

My wife and I are both in the helping profession. For many years, I assumed that my wife could handle her problems well by herself. Likewise, I believed that she didn't have a clue about the kind of emotional wounds I carry as a pastor. As I later discovered, neither is true. Regardless of our assumptions, we all are in need of tender, loving care.

A preacher's kid once came to me for counseling, saying, "I just want my father to be the same at home as he is at church!" Unfortunately, we're often more compassionate toward "outsiders" than we are toward our own spouses and children. And yet, unless we learn to be kind and compassionate to each other at home, forgiving each other, we will never fully discover our ability to love others.

Dear Lord, help us learn kindness from you. Let loving-kindness flow so freely at home that it overflows to others who are in need of your love. Amen.

Talk It Over: *What are some ways you can express "tender, loving care" to your spouse? to your family? Once a week, turn off the television and have a "family time"—a time of talking and listening to one another; a time when everyone is respected and heard.*

October 18 ~ Love Is Hard Labor

Be very careful, then, how you live—not as unwise but wise, making the most of every opportunity, because the days are evil. Therefore do not be foolish, but understand what the Lord's will is.

—Ephesians 5:15-17 (NIV)

The poet Rainer M. Rilke wrote, "Love is hard labor. God knows this is true." Marriage requires hard work and discipline. Sadly, the majority of couples today are unwilling or unable to "work at it." Perhaps this is why the divorce rate among couples married for three to five years is more than 50 percent; and, unfortunately, the divorce rate of Christians is no lower than that of other couples.

221

Love is not what we say but what we do. Supposedly, the "love chemical" that makes a man's and a woman's heart pump for physical love for each other lasts only thirty months. After that, we need hard labor and discipline to keep our love working. Not only that, but we also need the grace of God to make marriage work as it should.

I remember a time long ago when our children were ill. My wife lost weight and was emotionally drained. Instead of allowing the situation to put a strain on our relationship, I decided to do all I could to ease her stress and make her smile. So, each evening before I left my office for home, I came up with a joke that would make her laugh. It's hard to come up with a good joke every day, but my hard labor paid off with a good return.

Grace is there when we do our best out of love. And laughter is an effective medium to experience healing and grace.

Dear Lord, let us be mature about love, realizing that it is hard work that requires discipline. Amen.

Talk It Over: *Talk about ways you can "work" on your marriage—everyday ways as well as periodic things such as a weekend getaway or marriage retreat. If you do not already exercise together, why not try this fun and healthy way to improve both your mental and physical strength to serve each other better?*

October 19 ~ You Are Beautiful

My lover spoke and said to me, "Arise, my darling, my beautiful one, and come with me."

—*Song of Songs 2:10 (NIV)*

Love is telling your wife or husband, "You are beautiful." Saint Augustine said, "By loving us He made us lovable." God made us lovable by loving us first. This is why we are beautiful. And by telling our spouses that they are beautiful, they will become beautiful. Try it!

It is said that even porcupines think their children are beautiful. Beauty is in the eye of the beholder. I still remember what my three-year-old twin sons told my widowed mother a long time ago. They asked their grandmother why she didn't have a boyfriend. She told them, "Who would like an old grandma like me?" My kids were puzzled for a moment, and with a protesting voice both of them shouted, "Grandma, you are beautiful! Grandma, you are beautiful!" And they were as sincere as an adoring spouse expressing love for his or her beloved.

We are beautiful because we are loved by God. And that's what makes us beautiful to each other. Have you said, "You're beautiful" lately? Remember, everyone needs to hear the words "You are beautiful."

Dear Lord, thank you for making us beautiful. Thank you for making us lovable by loving us first. Amen.

Talk It Over: *Say, "You're beautiful" in a unique way. Play some romantic music and dance together! Take turns letting each other lead.*

October 20 ~ The Season of Singing Has Come

See! The winter is past; the rains are over and gone. Flowers appear on the earth; the season of singing has come, the cooing of doves is heard in our land.
—*Song of Songs 2:11-12 (NIV)*

Love is helping our spouses experience the fullness of God's blessing in the world. Love is reminding each other that the winter is past, the rains are over and gone. Most of us do better in an encouraging environment. Love encourages the other person to make the best of their God-given talent.

I remember during a Chicago winter some years ago, one of my elderly neighbors who lived alone was trying to drive out of her driveway despite the barrier of snow left by the city snowplow. After great effort, she was still unsuccessful. As a veteran of nearly two decades of harsh Chicago winter, I knew that I if I tried, I could get her out easily. But instead of doing it for her, I told her to follow my instructions: depress the gas pedal slowly until you come close to the snow pile and then accelerate. She tried, but failed. I encouraged her to try again. This time, when she was getting close to the snow pile, I yelled, "You can do it! You can do it! Yes! Yes! Yes! You did it! You did it!" She made it. She came out of her car with a big smile and told me, "I guess I just needed someone to tell me that I could do it."

Sometimes we just need someone to tell us that we can do it.

O God of love, help us be instruments of encouragement for each other and others. Amen.

Talk It Over: *Tell your spouse the things you love about him or her. Then, sometime this week, write an encouraging note to your spouse. Send it to his or her workplace or mail it to your home address.*

October 21 ~ Expecting the Best from Each Other

When I called, you answered me; you made me bold and stouthearted.
—Psalm 138:3 (NIV)

In 1 Kings of the Old Testament, we see Elijah sitting down and praying under a broom tree in the desert where he might die. Even Elijah, one the greatest prophets, experienced depression. But an angel of God came to give him a word of encouragement and food and drink. This enabled Elijah to get up and continue his journey.

When I entered seminary, I was filled with an inferiority complex. Everyone seemed to be smarter than me. I feared that I might not graduate. One day after my Old Testament class, my professor asked me to come see him. I imagined the worst: not making a passing grade in his class. With a discouraged look, I entered his office. "Mr. Kim, how are you doing?" he asked. I said, "Well, OK, sir, but I do not expect too much from myself this semester." Suddenly, this big, aging man grabbed me and shook my shoulders as he affirmed me, "But I do! I do expect a lot from you." It was a life-transforming moment. I was no longer the same.

Encourage each other by expecting the best from each other—not in a demanding or unrealistic way, but in a loving and affirming way. Remember, a simple word of encouragement can change a person's life.

Dear Lord, all of us need to hear that we are OK. Open our hearts and minds to hear and say encouraging words to each other. Amen.

Talk It Over: *What do you expect of each other? What possibilities do you envision for each other? Take time right now to tell each other all that you know the*

224

other is capable of being, doing, and becoming. Plan to surprise each other—and/or a family member—sometime in the near future by attending one of his or her games, concerts, or other special events; or plan a special celebration in honor of some particular achievement.

October 22 ~ The Journey of Coming Home

Rather, clothe yourselves with the Lord Jesus Christ, and do not think about how to gratify the desires of the sinful nature.

—Romans 13:14 (NIV)

In Odysseus's journey of coming home, he encounters many enemies. But not all his enemies are giants and mighty monsters. His journey of coming home is also a spiritual wandering, as well as a battle with temptations. Some of these include the song of the sirens, the lotus fruit, and Calypso's promise. The song of the sirens arouses erotic energy but ultimately ends in death. Lotus fruit is so delicious and sweet, but it leads people to forget their journey home. Calypso's promise is a promise of never aging: "Stay with me; you'll never grow old." But it will lead to the loss of Odysseus's touch with reality. All those sweet temptations are more deadly than the giants and monsters.

Some say these temptations are what many men and women are faced with. It was same with Adam and Eve. The forbidden fruits looked desirable and pleasing. A journey of coming home is coming to appreciate who we are and what we have. This is the greatest challenge.

Dear Lord, we want to come home to each other (and our children). Enable us to journey with courage and faith. Amen.

Talk It Over: *Plan a special "coming home" evening for just the two of you. Tell each other all that you appreciate about each other and your life together. Celebrate your love. If you have children, plan another "coming home" evening for the whole family when you can celebrate your life together and affirm every family member. Do something fun together, such as camping out in the backyard or living room! You might even make this a monthly event.*

225

October 23 ~ In All Things Charity

And now these three remain: faith, hope and love. But the greatest of these is love.

—1 Corinthians 13:13 (NIV)

"In Essentials Unity, In Nonessentials Liberty, In All Things Charity"—this was the main theme of the 1996 United Methodist Church General Conference held in Denver, Colorado. It's a wonderful principle. Many times we sweat the unimportant things. Sometimes marital problems arise from issues that really mean nothing in the long run.

Healthy relationships seek unity, not uniformity. Sometimes people who force others to conform have a need to control others. This isn't love. When spouses do not allow liberty in nonessential matters, the relationship suffers from lack of breathing space. Sometimes nothing really matters except loving each other. Allow each other space, and accept each other's differences.

Dear Lord, give us wisdom to know our differences and maturity to celebrate them. Amen.

Talk It Over: *Talk about your differences and find a way to celebrate them today.*

October 24 ~ What You Need Is What You Got

"My grace is sufficient for you, for my power is made perfect in weakness."
—2 Corinthians 12:9 (NIV)

"What you need is what you got." This is the title of a Pueblo blessing that is given to young people by the elders in the community. This blessing reminds young people to hold on to what is good and what they believe. The end of the blessing warms the heart: "Hold on to life—even when it is easier letting go. Hold on to my hand—even when I have gone away from you." As an old spiritual song says, "Hold on and keep on holding on."

When Paul prayed fervently about his illness, God gave him an answer saying, "My grace is sufficient for you, for my power is made perfect in weakness." If we open our hearts and minds to God's blessing, we will be overwhelmed by its abundance. Look again and again. You will find sufficient blessing from each other.

Dear God of Grace, we thank for your abundant grace poured upon us. Amen.

Talk It Over: *Talk about the ways God has blessed you—as individuals and as a couple/family. Take time to give thanks together for your blessings.*

October 25 ~ Life Is a Live Show

To this you were called, because Christ suffered for you, leaving you an example, that you should follow in his steps.
—1 Peter 2:21 (NIV)

In her book *The Couple's Journey,* Susan Campbell reports some of the common characteristics of a successful marriage. One characteristic is that couples try to make the best of a bad situation and learn from the experience. She concludes that success in marriage is loving what you have, rather than getting what you want.

Life is a journey. Marriage is taking that journey together, not knowing what's ahead. This can make life challenging and chaotic at times. Sometimes we ask ourselves, "Would you have done this if you knew what it would be like?" Yet life is not a dress rehearsal; it is a live show. We just have to learn as we go along.

One man who has been seasoned with life told me, "By the time you think you know what life is all about, you are ready to die." Don't expect your husband or your wife to know everything. We are all students of life, especially when it comes to loving someone.

Dear Lord, we thank you for letting us take this journey together. Help us be patient with each other and be mature enough to gently hold each other's hand in our journey of finding ourselves. Amen.

Talk It Over: *Take a "journey" into your past together and talk about some of the things you have learned along the way. How has God's grace sustained you through the uncertainties and challenges?*

October 26 ~ Drink Water from Your Own Cistern

Drink water from your own cistern, flowing water from your own well.
—Proverbs 5:15

There is a story about a man who wanted to safeguard his well from his neighbors; so, he covered and locked his well. After his neighbors went away in search of water, he reopened the well only to find that the well had dried out.

Our love is like a well of springwater. We must drink from it every day if we don't want it to dry out. That is why Proverbs says, "Drink water from your own cistern, flowing water from your own well." Actually, the word *well* refers here to one's wife—or husband, as the case may be. "Drink" as often as you can, and your well will never dry out. It will bring more and more refreshing water for you.

Dear Lord, we know that we are sufficient for each other. We thank you for giving us a well of love. Amen.

Talk It Over: *Talk about what it means to "drink from the well of love" every day so that it does not dry out. In what ways can you do this? Brainstorm a list of ideas and try to use one or more each day.*

October 27 ~ We Learned It All in Kindergarten

If anyone has material possessions and sees his brother in need but has no pity on him, how can the love of God be in him? Dear children, let us not love with words or tongue but with actions and in truth.
—1 John 3:17-18 (NIV)

Robert Fulghum's book *All I Really Need to Know I Learned in Kindergarten* has touched many of us because it helps us see extraordinary truths in elementary teachings. He reminds us that wisdom is not at the top of the graduate school mountain but at the Sunday school playground.

What were some of the things we learned in kindergarten? Share everything. Play fair. Don't hit people. Put things back where you found them. Clean up your mess. Say you're sorry when you hurt somebody. The list goes on, naming those universal things we tell our young children.

Aren't these the things we need to be a functional family? Aren't these the things we need to achieve a better world? Aren't these the things we need to be better husbands and wives? Let's be decent, mature married people by practicing what we learned in kindergarten.

Dear Lord, our problem is not that we do not know how to make our marriage work, but that we do not always practice what we already know. Help us live out the values and principles we learned long ago. Amen.

Talk It Over: *What were some of the basic principles you learned as a young child that are necessary for a successful marriage? Do you practice these principles in your marriage on a regular basis? If not, why not?*

October 28 ~ Love Is a Journey

Consider it pure joy, my brothers, whenever you face trials of many kinds, because you know that the testing of your faith develops perseverance.
—James 1:2-3 (NIV)

A sage once said, "A journey of a thousand miles starts under one foot." No matter how long the journey, one can only get there by taking one step at a time. Every good thing takes time. And along the way, we all experience trials and difficulties. This is why it's so exciting to stop and recognize the growth we're experiencing along the way. Our spouses are precious because they are journeying with us.

When I was in high school, I asked my youth group teacher, whose wife had been ill for a long time, whether he loved his wife. He smiled and said, "I do more than love my wife. I am her best friend." I did not really understand what he meant then. Now I do. He was her friend who was journeying through life with her, both in good times and bad.

When we journey together, we learn to be patient with each other and to rely on each other—both in good times and bad.

Dear Lord, help us be patient with each other as we face both the good and the bad on our journey together. Amen.

Talk It Over: *Talk about some of the good and the bad times you've experienced on your journey together thus far. Looking back, what growth did you experience as a* *result of these times? What effects did these experiences have on your relationship? Plan an exciting and fun "adventure" to celebrate your journey together, such as going mountain hiking, starting a new project or joint hobby, or something else.*

October 29 ~ Being an "Angel" for Each Other—and Others

As the body without the spirit is dead, so faith without deeds is dead.
—James 2:26 (NIV)

Perhaps you remember the best-selling book *Random Acts of Kindness.* According to the book, "angels" are also people who commit small random acts of kindness to strangers. Because married life sometimes becomes mundane and routine, it can brighten our days if we learn to become "angels" for each other. You'll find that doing random acts of kindness for your spouse can bring much excitement to your relationship—such as surprising your spouse at work or home with flowers or his or her favorite dessert.

The Grace of God works when we share random acts of kindness and love—with each other and with others.

Dear Lord, we thank you for giving us sharing hearts. Amen.

Talk It Over: *Make a commitment to practice random acts of kindness for each other regularly. If you have children, the whole family can commit to practicing random acts of kindness for strangers. When my wife worked as a school social worker, our whole family prepared and delivered Christmas gifts to underprivileged children each year. It was a very rewarding experience for all of us. It helped our children not only to learn the joy of sharing but also to appreciate what they had.*

October 30 ~ Love Is Allowing Yourself to Be Challenged

"Now that I, your Lord and Teacher, have washed your feet, you also should wash one another's feet. I have set you an example that you should do as I have done for you."

—John 13:14-15 (NIV)

I had the opportunity to converse with an African American gentleman who said that he had divorced about ten years ago and had not yet met the "right" woman. He said that women in the United States have changed quite a bit. I knew exactly why he was saying this to me. He was hoping that I, being an Asian woman, might have a different view from that of a typical American woman. I thought of another gentleman I used to know who always longed for a foreign wife, thinking she would please him better than an American woman. So I told this gentleman that all women, regardless of the country in which they live, strive for equal status with men. Even though the issues at hand may be different, all wives challenge their husbands for an equal and fair relationship. We have come a long way as women, and we have a long way to go; and there is no going back. I told this gentleman that although my husband may not be perfect, I live with him because he is willing to accept the challenge of equality in our relationship, even though it is not always convenient for him to do so.

Love is the willingness to challenge and be challenged to help one another to become the best we can be for each other.

Dear Lord, give us the courage to challenge each other to change, and give us an understanding heart to embrace the things that cannot be changed. Amen.

Talk It Over: *What have been and/or are some of the challenges in your relationship? How have you each been challenged to change?*

October 31 ~ God Loves You, and I Am Trying

"A new command I give you: Love one another. As I have loved you, so you must love one another. All men will know that you are my disciples if you love one another."

—John 13:34-35 (NIV)

While on the road, I saw a bumper sticker that said, "God loves you, and I am trying." I nodded my head in agreement. In the comic strip "Peanuts," innocent young Linus shares his dream of one day becoming a doctor. Upon hearing this, Lucy tells him that he can never be a doctor because he doesn't love people. Linus shouts at Lucy, saying, "I love

231

human beings; it's people I can't stand!" Loving human beings in general is not that difficult, but loving real people is not easy.

Likewise, loving our spouses is not always easy. There is a saying, "If you can't love them, leave them alone." God's love, however, is "in spite of" love, not "because of" love. This kind of love is hard for us humans, who naturally love others "because of. . . . " Yet God can teach us "in spite of" love. If we will practice it in faith, God will help us. God will bless our trying hearts.

No marriage is perfect. But remember this: Most relationships can improve greatly if we invest in making some simple, thoughtful, "desirable" adjustments.

Dear Lord, we thank you for your love. Help us make all the "desirable adjustments" we need to make in order to love each other as you have loved us. Amen.

Talk It Over: *Talk about the "desirable adjustments" you've identified this month that would be beneficial to your marriage. What will you each make a sincere effort to do in order to improve your relationship? Make a commitment to earnestly strive to make these adjustments in the days and weeks to come. We encourage you to put your commitment in writing and discuss your progress periodically.*

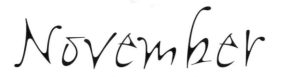

MARRIAGE UNDER FIRE

Bill and Katie Treadway

November 1 ~ Always Changing

May your unfailing love rest upon us, O LORD, even as we put our hope in you.

—Psalm 33:22 (NIV)

Katie and I were relatively young when we were married. She was twenty-two and just out of college, and I was twenty-three and one year removed from my own college graduation. We had known each other for a little more than three years—and thought we really "knew" each other well. What we did not—and could not—appreciate at the time was how much each of us would change as time passed.

Now, more than seven years later, experience has shown us that change is perhaps the only constant of our marriage. Changes in career paths, health, financial circumstances, housing—all of them influence our marriage. Even positive changes such as getting a better job or buying our first house put stress on our relationship and require us to come together as a couple to respond to the changes.

This month we'll consider some of the many changes and stresses that are common to all marriages—things that can either build us up or tear us down. You might say that our marriages are "under fire" each and every day, and how we respond determines whether we will be defeated or made stronger. Remaining mindful of the presence of God through the myriad changes we experience can transform change from a dreaded reality of life into a treasured opportunity for growth in relationship to our marriage partner and to God.

God, may we always turn to you as we face change together, strengthening our bond of love. Amen.

Talk It Over: *What changes have you and your partner undergone together in your marriage? How did each of these affect your relationship? Name some couples you know (or know of) who have handled changes well throughout their relationship. What characteristics have helped them respond positively to changes in their relationship? Knowing that the way that each one of us handles change is unique, discuss with your partner ways that you are willing to respond positively to changes in your partner.*

November 2 ~ Arguments

Be angry but do not sin; do not let the sun go down on your anger.
—Ephesians 4:26

As human beings with feelings and opinions, we're bound to disagree and argue at times. The real issue is *how* we deal with our disagreements. Though it may feel good initially to let go angry words and emotions, heated confrontations always leave a bitter aftertaste that can fester if it isn't dealt with openly.

Many of us have a competitive instinct—encouraged by our culture—that causes us to approach arguing with our spouse as one more contest to be won. But that approach leaves us "playing against" the person who is supposed to be our closest ally. Over the course of time, this kind of negative competition can only alienate us and undermine our relationship.

The scripture doesn't make distinctions between who is right and who is wrong—it doesn't say, "don't let the sun set, unless you're right." Rather, the scripture counsels us to resolve angry emotions. The tragedy is not in having occasional arguments, but in allowing them to grow and fester rather than resolving them in love.

God, remind us to resolve our arguments in love for the sake of our enduring love together. Amen.

234

Talk It Over: How do you and your spouse typically deal with arguments? In what ways do you fight fairly? In what ways do you fight unfairly? What effective ways of resolving arguments have you found—irrespective of who is "right" or "wrong"? How do you prevent the sun's setting on your anger?

November 3 ~ Bad Decisions

Fools say in their hearts, "There is no God." They are corrupt, they do abominable deeds; there is no one who does good. The LORD looks down from heaven on humankind to see if there are any who are wise, who seek after God.
—Psalm 14:1-2

Sometimes we feel like our married life has been a series of bad or at least "less than perfect" decisions. We married young—right out of college. We took out student loans to live on during graduate school. We had children while we were still students. We bought too much of a house for our financial situation. We haven't "bottomed out" completely, but it is obvious that our lack of forethought has contributed to many of our marital frustrations.

When we are young and in love, we often do not make wise choices. Yet God invites us to entertain wisdom. To follow God is to set aside our foolish ways with repentance and live the life God has called us to live. In God's grace, God forgives our foolishness. For our marriage to thrive, we must seek God's wisdom and forgiveness. We can give thanks that we are forgiven.

God, grant us your wisdom and guidance in the decisions we make. May we forgive ourselves for our wrong decisions. Renew our life with your wisdom. Amen.

Talk It Over: What are some foolish decisions you and your partner have made together? Looking back, why do you think you made these decisions? Are you able to forgive yourselves now? Why or why not? How can you seek God's wisdom in your future decisions? List concrete examples.

November 4 ~ Children

For surely I know the plans I have for you, says the LORD, plans for your welfare and not for harm, to give you a future with hope.
—Jeremiah 29:11

I realized what incredible gifts of God children are as I held our daughter in my arms for the first time. But as all parents soon learn, children also carry with them a great burden of responsibility—a burden that all too often begins to wear on the fabric of the marriage relationship.

Little did I know at the time, but that sweet little angel who somehow wrapped herself around our hearts within seconds of our first gaze would grow up to be very independent and stubborn as a three-year-old. There are evenings when I am convinced she belongs to someone else! As she whines and yells and sasses, our marital roles turn strictly to parental roles; and when she is finally sweetly sleeping, we are worn out. Each other's needs are easily set aside as we race to our pillows to recharge for the next day's challenges.

Since another daughter joined our family one year ago, we've come to understand even more that children require an enormous amount of energy and attention! And, if we're not careful, our spousal relationship suffers because we're so busy being "Mommy" and "Daddy." The only sure safeguard is devoting regular time and attention to each other. Sometimes this time has to come late at night or in a few hours while the children are with the baby-sitter. Though searching for time to be together can be both exhausting and frustrating, we have found that this is an essential commitment to maintaining a healthy and growing marriage.

Remember, God can work to join us to each other, even when we are convinced that children are plotting to divide us.

God, thank you for blessing the two of us with your beautiful and wondrous creation(s). Thank you for guiding our life together even when we are overwhelmed by life's demands. Amen.

Talk It Over: *What "plots against" your and your spouse's time together? How do you renew yourself in life's chaos? How do you renew yourselves as a couple? How difficult is it for you to place your trust in the words of Jeremiah when life is chaotic? Why? How do you feel "joined together" through the vocation of parenting?*

November 5 ~ Communication

"And do not swear by your head, for you cannot make one hair white or black. Let your word be 'Yes, Yes' or 'No, No'; anything more than this comes from the evil one."

—Matthew 5:36-37

236

Few clichés are more prominent in our society than the lip service paid to the importance of "communication." Newspaper advice columnists, afternoon television talk-show hosts, and self-help book authors devote as much attention to communication as to any other topic. With all the attention given to the issue, why, then, does communication remain such a stumbling block in our married lives?

Perhaps it is because communication is so central to the success of any relationship that nothing can substitute for the genuinely difficult work of clean, honest communication between two people. *Knowing* the rules doesn't necessarily translate into *following* them in the nitty-gritty of daily life.

When Jesus said, "Let your yes be yes and your no be no," he was talking about communication free of the masks we so often wear—communication that is honest and true. Especially with our spouses, we should constantly strive for this level of honesty and integrity in all our communication. Our hard work is rewarded with increasing levels of integrity and intimacy not only in our relationships with our spouses, but in all our relationships.

God, free us from the masks that hide our true selves so that we may communicate honestly with our spouses, revealing your perfect image that dwells in each one of us. Amen.

Talk It Over: *How would you characterize your communication with your spouse? On a scale of 1 to 10 (1 = very little), how conscious are you of the verbal and nonverbal communication between you and your spouse? Brainstorm together some practical strategies for increasing the integrity and intimacy of your communication.*

November 6 ~ Debt

Keep your lives free from the love of money, and be content with what you have; for he has said, "I will never leave you or forsake you."
—*Hebrews 13:5*

Let's see . . . we owe the bank money for student loans, for the house, for a credit card, and for a car. We owe our parents money for helping us out when things were tough. We are definitely in debt. It is a constant point of stress—not the place where we want to be. What's even more frustrating about this situation is that neither of us puts a lot of trust in this "entity" we call money.

As a couple, we have a shared goal of communicating the important things in life—the kingdom of God, for example. Yet we are constantly reduced to an "in-the-red" life-style that demands making money be our primary focus in life.

To successfully be free to live the life of Christ, we must faithfully pay off our debts. We believe God will provide for our needs. But we also recognize that until the two of us jointly make wise decisions to alleviate debt, we will be slaves to that which keeps us from loving God completely.

God, help us live a life of service to you and to others, not to our debts. Amen.

Talk It Over: *Are your debts holding your marriage "hostage" in any way? Talk about some times when debt has come between you and your partner, and how you handled that situation. Are there alternative ways you could have handled the situation? Make a list of all your debts. Which ones are the results of meeting needs? Which ones are the results of poor decisions? Are there ways you can work together as a couple to gain freedom from debt?*

November 7 ~ Family/In-laws

Pursue peace with everyone, and the holiness without which no one will see the Lord.

—Hebrews 12:14

What happens when you blend two families together who otherwise have nothing in common and would almost certainly never have met without a marriage? The ideal would be a completely harmonious union in which two separate families blend together seamlessly. That, however, has not been our experience. We haven't achieved the ideal union of families, but neither has the process been a total disaster.

Fortunately, our families have understood our need to find some middle ground—sharing and blending holiday traditions, vacation time, and time spent with the grandchildren. Our seven years of marriage are only a beginning in bridging our two family worlds. But through the process each of us has learned how to compromise, how to accept as "family" persons who are not like us, and how to be a part of new family units. It is not always simple and pleasant, but the results have been worth the effort.

God, help us reach out and embrace each other's family, loving them as our own. Amen.

Talk It Over: *How have the two of you bridged the family worlds from which you come? What has been difficult? What has been easy? How has/might accepting your partner's family as your own strengthened your relationship as a couple? Are there relationships among your different family units that need healing and special attention? What steps might begin that process?*

November 8 ~ Finances

Two are better than one. . . . For if they fall, one will lift up the other.
—Ecclesiastes 4:9a, 10a

No other topic has generated more frustration, more gut-wrenching conversations, or more confusion in our marriage than finances. Katie and I did not get very far into our marriage before we came face-to-face with financial pressure.

Finances continue to be a challenge for us. We both attended graduate school after we were married; and now we face the reality of repaying our loans as well as trying to pay for a house, a car, and our children's needs. What's more, it seems that when one of us is intent on saving, the other yearns to spend money, and vice versa. We hem each other in, creating a balance that sometimes works and sometimes leaves us in tension with each other.

Though we've come to no magic formulas, we have learned that working separately only keeps us stuck. When we work together, we're reminded that two really are better than one, "for if they fall, one will lift up the other." In the ebb and flow of dealing with financial responsibilities, we've found this to be true. The two of us together are stronger, and wiser, than either of us is on our own.

God, remind us that no matter what challenges we face, we face them together in you. Amen.

Talk It Over: *How do your individual ideas about money fit with your part-ner's? Where are the balances and imbalances in your dealings with money? Name some times when financial issues have come between you. How did you resolve the issues? List some proactive steps you can take to keep these issues from coming between you again.*

November 9 ~ Finding Balance

Therefore a man leaves his father and his mother and clings to his wife, and they become one flesh.

—*Genesis 2:24*

Most all of us want to live up to the ideal of joining together so that we are no longer two separate persons but an entirely new entity in marriage. Of course, this doesn't happen magically the day we open a joint bank account or move into the same home. Making two persons into "one" in marriage takes work—constant, hard work.

Sometimes we forget that though our intimacy and unity truly make us one, we are still two unique individuals with unique needs, gifts, and wants. In the struggle to become one, we do well not to forget the two real persons involved.

In marriage, as in all of life, we constantly seek balance—balance between working on the "oneness" of the relationship and nourishing the uniqueness that drew us together in the first place. There is no science for this, no quick-start guide. Instead, we must rely on experience, communi-cation, and a sense of abundant grace to find and maintain the balance needed for the long term.

God, thank you for bringing us together as two individuals who wish to balance our unique interests with the unity of seeking your kingdom. Grant us your abundant grace in our love for each other and for ourselves. Amen.

Talk It Over: *Discuss with your partner what is the proper balance in your mar-riage between unity and uniqueness. How can you achieve and maintain this balance? Make a list of what tends to push your relationship out of balance. How do/can you deal with each of these?*

240

November 10 ~ Forgiveness: Seeking Reconciliation

Create in me a clean heart, O God, and put a new and right spirit within me. Do not cast me away from your presence, and do not take your holy spirit from me. Restore to me the joy of your salvation, and sustain in me a willing spirit.
—Psalm 51:10-12

In our marriage, hurtful words and thoughts are often more common than we would care to admit. Sometimes we say words without any intent to hurt, while other times we say words with every intent to cause pain. Whether intentional or not, we must seek the reconciliation of our relationship through the forgiveness exemplified by none other than the Christ in whom we place our faith. To forgive demands both a conscious effort to change our behavior and a genuine reception of the other's forgiveness.

Dear God, at our deepest hurt and hurtfulness, teach us to forgive as we have been forgiven. Amen.

Talk It Over: *Discuss openly the times when you have consciously hurt your spouse. Why did you do it? When did you realize the need to ask forgiveness? Were you willing to change your behavior? Why or why not? How was your request for forgiveness received? Talk about what a reconciled relationship would look like. Can trust be regained? Compare this relationship to the reconciliation of God with all of us who are sinners.*

November 11 ~ Forgiveness: Confronting Mistakes

Then Peter came and said to him, "Lord, if another member of the church sins against me, how often should I forgive? As many as seven times?" Jesus said to him, "Not seven times, but, I tell you, seventy-seven times."
—Matthew 18:21-22

We all make mistakes. That is not news to any of us. But what about when one of those inevitable mistakes is hurtful to your partner?

Perhaps it was a last-minute change of plans that preempted a long-standing evening with your spouse. Or perhaps it was a comment passed

241

on to your partner's friend that was meant to be held in confidence. Whatever the particulars, at this point the mistake takes on added significance since it influences your marriage relationship.

It's easy to say that when mistakes happen we simply need to forgive, forget, and move on. It's another thing altogether to actually forgive our spouse when we are hurt significantly by a mistake she or he has made. Yet, unless we forgive—truly forgive and not allow the wound to fester—we risk weakening and eventually destroying all trust.

Confronting a hurtful mistake may be difficult, and even painful, but not nearly as difficult or painful as trying to rebuild lost trust. Perhaps Jesus' admonition to forgive without keeping score finds its most powerful expression in the marriage relationship.

God, give us the courage to forgive each other, and restore our trust. Amen.

Talk It Over: *When has "keeping score" of past mistakes caused trouble in your marriage? How did you and your spouse deal with these issues? What have you learned about your own ability to forgive through your marriage? What makes it difficult for us to follow Jesus' admonition to forgive again and again?*

November 12 ~ "Growing Up"

When I was a child, I spoke like a child, I thought like a child, I reasoned like a child; when I became an adult, I put an end to childish ways. For now we see in a mirror, dimly, but then we will see face to face. Now I know only in part; then I will know fully, even as I have been fully known.
—1 Corinthians 13:11-12

I have a confession to make. I am not a good housekeeper. No, let's rephrase that. I am a lousy housekeeper. I get sidetracked by "fun" stuff to the point that the work (and dishes, and dust, and dirt) piles up. Bill and I see things very differently. He's not a neat freak, but he does know what clean should look like. And although we share responsibilities (he does laundry, I handle dishes, and so forth), we sometimes argue about whether or not our responsibilities are equally shared. I am learning that I need to "grow up" a bit and accept my household duties as a part of the promise I made before God to Bill on our wedding day. The vows didn't

242

exactly say, "in filth and in shine," but they did say that we would respect each other. Cleanliness is one of those "respect" issues that my personality often overlooks. But if our relationship is to model a vision of the kingdom of God, I want to respect my partner's needs just as he wants to respect mine.

God, bring us into full maturity as a couple. Amen.

Talk It Over: *What are the "respect issues" in your relationship? How can you work together to address them? We may not see fully the vision of the kingdom of God, but as Christians it is our hope that marriage can help us catch glimpses of it. What are ways your marriage hinders this glimpse? What are ways your relationship brings the kingdom of God into focus?*

November 13 ~ I Will Not Change You

Now there are varieties of gifts, but the same Spirit; and there are varieties of services, but the same Lord.
—*1 Corinthians 12:4-5*

The greatest thing I learned in premarital counseling was that I should never try to change my spouse. At the time, I couldn't see how this would be an issue, but as the first year of marriage suddenly becomes the seventh, the list of things I would like to change multiplies frequently. The more we know our spouses, the more we become aware of the great divide in the way we do things. The hardest lesson I have had to learn is that Bill is a unique and blessed child of God who I must allow to be fully the one God has made him to be (rather than the one Katie wants to make him to be). When change does not come, I want my eyes to recognize the giftedness he already possesses.

God, allow me to see my spouse with the lenses of your grace. Amen.

Talk It Over: *How would lenses of grace enable you to see your spouse differently? How can you see your spouse as an important part of the Body of Christ, gifted by the same Spirit who has called you into service?*

243

November 14 ~ Illness

"I will never leave you or forsake you."

—Joshua 1:5c (NIV)

"In sickness and in health . . . " When I repeated those words after the minister who officiated our wedding, I don't think that I really understood what they might mean. Up to that point, both Katie and I had been blessed with excellent health—not even a single broken bone between us.

As time passed, small health concerns began to crop up—a cholesterol reading that remained too high even after a dramatic shift of diet; blood pressure a few notches into the red; and chemical imbalances resulting from the complex process of carrying and birthing children. The list of infirmities has grown dramatically since I promised my spouse that I would love her "in sickness and in health." I'm certain that as time continues to pass, those words will take on even more depth for me. Even more meaningful, though, is the knowledge that we made a sacred promise one to the other and to God, that sickness of any sort would not change our care and faithfulness toward each other.

God, bind us together in sickness just as in health. Amen.

Talk It Over: *Have you experienced any illnesses or medical difficulties—with parents, children, or each other—that have influenced your life as a couple? How did these experiences affect your relationship? Are there ways you could have handled these together more effectively? What can you do to be prepared as a couple for future health issues you may face?*

November 15 ~ Infertility

A friend loves at all times.

—Proverbs 17:17

It's not fair. With all of the babies in the world, there is no reason a happily married couple wishing for children wouldn't wonder, *Why not us?* When Bill and I started "trying" to conceive our first child, I began to worry that we would never be able to have children. As someone who had

244

wanted to be a mother from the time I could say "baby," I didn't understand how month after month I "failed" to conceive. That year of "trying" was very trying on our relationship as well. My preconceptions of marriage had been gathered from watching my own parents, who had children. I was (and am) still learning that marriage is more than parenting; it also is about loving strength for each other in *all* circumstances—with or without children.

God, grant us grace to embrace the love you have given the two of us, even when things do not go as we would plan. Amen.

Talk It Over: *What preconceptions did you bring to your marriage? How has your experience in marriage changed some of these? How might you engage in parenting as a couple even without having children of your own? In what ways is your marriage—and every marriage—about "loving strength"?*

November 16 ~ In-laws

A friend loves at all times, and kinsfolk are born to share adversity.
—Proverbs 17:17

I have a friend whose marriage is constantly challenged by her mother-in-law. It's the standard story: her husband is his mother's youngest son who, in her eyes, can do no wrong. He married a good woman, but no one is quite good enough for her son. Visits to her house usually involve a pre-arranged schedule to which neither my friend nor her husband feels free to challenge—given that the mother-in-law becomes openly hostile when she feels she is not being shown the proper respect. Yet marriage is not intended to pit son against mother, nor does it insist that husband and wife be divided in love.

Marriage calls us to love and support our spouses. As a household of faith, we are to model the kingdom of God by seeking peace and modeling the love of Christ to our extended families. This challenge is our calling as Christians who are united with the incredible gift of God's love to us.

God, help us be sensitive yet firm when confronting a family relationship that threatens to divide us. Amen.

245

Talk It Over: Does your partner have any family relationships that challenge your marriage relationship? How have the two of you attempted to resolve these? Have you ever felt "divided" in your allegiance to your spouse and your larger family? How did/can you strive for peace in this situation?

November 17 ~ Living with Uncertainty

The LORD went in front of them in a pillar of cloud by day, to lead them along the way, and in a pillar of fire by night, to give them light, so that they might travel by day and by night.

—Exodus 13:21

Most of us would like to see more clearly into the future. What will our careers hold in five or ten years? Where will we be living? Many of us, however, find ourselves looking into a future made uncertain for one reason or another, with little other than faith, hope, and love to sustain us.

Married couples of all ages and financial brackets find the future much too uncertain for comfort. Career, finances, and health can change without forewarning, prompting the need for radical life changes—relocation, rebudgeting, ongoing health care. Try as we might to prepare for and insulate ourselves from seemingly random happenstance, at some point all of us are vulnerable.

I imagine that is very much how the refugee slaves from Egypt must have felt. With little more than a vague sense of God's presence and leadership much of the time, they were asked to forge their way into an uncertain and perilous-looking future. Of course, the story is one of both tragedy and triumph—tragedy for those unable to grasp God's vision and continue toward it, and eventual triumph for those who stayed the course in faith.

Like that band of liberated slaves who carried the germ of a nation-to-be, we have the choice to remain faithful both to our wedding vows and to our understanding of God's vision for our relationship in the face of uncertainty, or to return to "Egypt" and the certainty of that life. Though we cannot yet see the end, we are promised grace enough to sustain us if we remain faithful on the road.

God, as you have led those before us through uncertain times, go before us now as we look to you in faith. Amen.

Talk It Over: List some of the uncertainties you have faced as a couple and how you dealt with each. In what areas of your marriage are you feeling called toward the unknown? How have you responded toward this calling?

November 18 ~ Loss of Hope

But those who wait for the LORD shall renew their strength, they shall mount up with wings like eagles, they shall run and not be weary, they shall walk and not faint.

—Isaiah 40:31

And now faith, hope, and love abide, these three; and the greatest of these is love.

—1 Corinthians 13:13

There is a point in every relationship when you wonder if continuing in the relationship is worth it. Is your partner's and your own happiness worth the time, the heartache, the confusion, and the energy to which you have given yourself? The alternative of single life looks so attractive when accountability is not required and your time is your own.

The loss of hope in a relationship is the point when we say to ourselves, and sometimes to our partner, "I can't do it anymore. It may have been worth it at one time, but I can't uphold my part of the covenant. I can't work and fight for us anymore. The end is here." I like to believe that God is a God of hope, a God who sees our need to relate and to give and receive love, even when we are blinded to this reality and overcome with exhaustion. God has called us into relationship with each other and will give us strength when our hope is waning.

God, your love has called us together. Be our hope when we lose hope for our relationship. Amen.

Talk It Over: Have you ever lost hope in your relationship? When? Why? What rekindled (or would rekindle) your hope for your marriage? Why do you believe God has called you into relationship with each other? How can you honor God's call?

247

November 19 ~ Loss of Job

But God proves [God's] love for us in that while we still were sinners Christ died for us.

—Romans 5:8

Our marriage has endured one stress after another. Some of these stresses have been good, such as the births of our girls, but some have been hard. Just after our first daughter was born, Bill lost his job. He had just earned his master's degree and was working temporarily as an editor while teaching as an adjunct at a local college in the evenings. His temporary job ended without much notification and we found ourselves in a financial bind. I felt guilty because I had just quit my job to assume the roles of parent and student. Bill felt responsible because he wanted to support us financially. Not knowing what else to do, he respected my desire to stay home with our daughter, and he took his master's degree to the checkout line of a local grocery store where he made minimum wage.

Looking back, I realize I more fully discovered the intense generosity and care of my husband in that difficult situation. Putting my feelings before his own was probably one of the hardest things he had ever done. I saw and learned much about the extent of his love for me and for our daughter in his self-sacrifice. I think that for him and for me, it is the example of Christ's self-sacrificial love that enables us to put aside our own self-interests in order to provide for the needs of others.

God, give us eyes to see the love and care that we have for each other. Amen.

Talk It Over: *What is the hardest thing you've ever had to do for your partner? How did your love for your spouse help you get through the experience? How is the love in your relationship similar to Christ's love for us? In what ways can you learn to love your spouse as Christ loves us?*

November 20 ~ Miscarriage

"Be still, and know that I am God!"

—Psalm 46:10a

When I was pregnant, I joined one of those Internet chat groups. It's a great way to compare notes and make friends when you don't have any pregnant friends nearby. But as we shared morning sickness stories and ultrasound hopes, it never failed that one of us miscarried. The sadness of that one became the sadness of the whole community.

Loss of any kind is difficult on relationships, but when a baby is lost—even before it is ever known—the stress is great. Some of us prefer to grieve alone whereas others look to anyone and everyone for consolation. The shared truth, however, is that death stings and grief never leaves us. Wanting to know why it happened is common, but the answer is always ambiguous. We don't know why these things happen, but when they do, I pray our relationships can know that God is with us—all of us.

God, though we may grieve, may we be aware of Emmanuel, God with us. Amen.

Talk It Over: *If you have ever lost a child, did you grieve differently than your spouse? How did your love withstand the pain of losing a child? How did/do you know Emmanuel, God with you? Discuss ways to be aware of God's presence when the stress of life and death are great.*

November 21 ~ Not Enough Time Together

"Don't urge me to leave you or to turn back from you. Where you go I will go, and where you stay I will stay. . . . May the LORD deal with me, be it ever so severely, if anything but death separates you and me."
—Ruth 1:16-17 (NIV)

Our culture speaks of "quality time" as being more important than the quantity of time spent together, but I really don't buy it. I have found that our relationship begins to wither when we try to cram too much into too little time, leaving our life together feeling cramped and pinched rather than spacious and open.

Katie and I have different work schedules, which means that often our "free time" cannot be spent together. When this happens for days and even weeks on end, the stress on our relationship becomes apparent. We've discovered no magic formulas to alleviate this situation. What we have discovered is that we must be intentional about carving out time

249

together and setting strong boundaries around that time to protect it from encroachment. It's not an easy thing, but it is necessary to keep our relationship vibrant and growing.

God, bring peace to our relationship when life seems to be moving too quickly. Amen.

Talk It Over: *What variables affect the time you are able to spend with your spouse? What kind of intentional time do you make to be with your spouse?*

November 22 ~ You Don't Bring Me Flowers Anymore

Then the L ORD God said, "It is not good that the man should be alone; I will make him a helper as his partner."
—Genesis 2:18

Remember the days? He brought me flowers! She sent me a love note! He kissed me in such a sweet way! She and I went on long walks and just talked the night away! We went on dates!

Marriage often becomes so routine that we begin to ignore the special things that brought us together in the first place. We don't have time to linger in our kisses, go for long walks, or stay up late to talk about what is important. "Life" preoccupies us instead of our spouse. We are divided by monotony, routine, the ordinary. But the truth of the matter is that whatever the excuse for missed time with our spouse, a loss of romance is a place of pain.

As humans, we want to know we are special, and we *need* to know we are important to another human being. God created us for each other to love and to care. Romance may just need to step up a notch on the priority list!

God, renew our romance so that our relationship can reveal the truth that you value us, your beloved creation. Amen.

Talk It Over: *What do you miss from your dating days? In what ways do you keep romance alive? You are married to an incredible creation of God. How do you feel about that? Tell your spouse!*

November 23 ~ Respecting Differences

For just as the body is one and has many members, and all the members of the
body, though many, are one body, so it is with Christ.

—1 Corinthians 12:12

I always had the notion that two people who love each other should be
the same—like the same things, believe the same way, and have the same
friends. Of course, by marriage's educational nature, I quickly discovered
otherwise! I've had a very difficult time coming to terms with our differences. Bill likes hiking and bluegrass. I like yoga and crafts. Bill is a modern contemplative with a heart for justice and a head for reason. I am a
mainline Protestant in love with tradition and the vision of God's kingdom. I enjoy the company of friends. Bill enjoys the company of family. We
are different "just enough" that our puzzle pieces don't quite interlock
unless they are wedged together forcibly.

Yet I'm learning that it's not of utmost importance that we fit perfectly
together. I'm realizing that love does not always have to agree—but it does
always respect the other. Respecting our differences rather than fighting
to wedge them into the wrong puzzle space nurtures our relationship,
allowing us to be "more" than "the same."

God, may we nurture each other's differences so that we may grow in our love and
respect for each other. Amen.

Talk It Over: *As your marriage has progressed, what differences have emerged*
between the two of you? Do you find yourself trying to reconcile differences or
respect them? Why? Do you believe that couples must be "alike" in their beliefs
in order to follow God? Why or why not?

November 24 ~ Role Expectations

But you are a chosen race, a royal priesthood, a holy nation, God's own people,
in order that you may proclaim the mighty acts of him who called you out of
darkness into his marvelous light. Once you were not a people, but now you are
God's people; once you had not received mercy, but now you have received mercy.

—1 Peter 2:9-10

251

Before we were married, Bill and I discussed our desire to have an equal partnership where society's expectations did not penetrate how we responded to each other. We've discovered the difficulty of those early desires. Despite our efforts, we often slip and enact those roles and even expect them. We've also discovered a point of tension. As much as I love being a mom, I hate that I am expected to be the primary caregiver. As much as Bill doesn't mind sharing the role of "breadwinner," he hates having to live up to the expectation that he must have the higher-paying job.

We are discovering that our identity as a couple is not rooted in societal norms but is defined by God's call to take on the role of "God's people." This means daily choosing to model the kingdom of God. Seeing through this lens allows our frustrations with societal expectations and roles to be minimized so that the call to serve God can be our first priority.

God, thank you for calling both of us to live as your people. Help us see ourselves within this identity you have given us. Amen.

Talk It Over: *In what ways do you fit society's role expectations? How do you feel about that? How do you define your identity as a couple? Do you find it difficult to define yourselves in light of God's call to both of you? Why or why not?*

November 25 ~ Success

Not that I am referring to being in need; for I have learned to be content with whatever I have.

—Philippians 4:11

"Success" is a tough notion to define. Does it mean financial security, a promising career, or generally being "better" at life than most of one's contemporaries? And even if one of these "successes" is achieved, it can be an ephemeral achievement—money can disappear as the economy slows, and good jobs can become dead ends or cease to exist at all. The reality is that none of us knows what unexpected setbacks await to rock our seemingly "in control" lives.

We are learning that our definition of success is constantly changing. We have had to learn (again and again!) how to be content in *all* kinds of circumstances—both "successful" and "unsuccessful." This is an issue with which we continually struggle, and one that constantly reminds us to look for God's grace in unlikely places.

God, strengthen our marriage as we seek to understand your grace in both successful and unsuccessful times. Amen.

Talk It Over: *What definitions of success did each of you bring into your relationship? How have these changed over time? What key experiences can you identify in which you had to be content with something less than full "success" in an area of your life? How have you recognized God's grace during these times?*

November 26 ~ Taking Off the Masks

Therefore, since we are surrounded by so great a cloud of witnesses, let us also lay aside every weight and the sin that clings so closely, and let us run with perseverance the race that is set before us.

—Hebrews 12:1

The word *personality* comes from the Latin word *persona,* which means "mask"—as in the masks worn by stage actors portraying different characters in a play. Just like actors play multiple roles, so also we sometimes mask ourselves to suit the situation. Whereas most of us are guilty of doing this, hiding behind masks is a poor foundation upon which to build a marriage.

Marriage is complete only when the most basic, primary part of oneself is given to one's partner. This act of intimate self-giving and vulnerability cannot take place as long as one or both spouses are hiding behind masks, leaving the relationship vulnerable to the inevitable difficulties of life.

It's simply impossible to discard all our masks in one fell swoop. Rather, with the help of our spouses, we slowly peel them away one at a time and expose the vulnerable living flesh underneath. And then, with our partners' support and God's grace, we learn to live without needing to pick them up and wear them again.

Dear God, thank you for the patience of my spouse as I remove the layers under which I have hidden myself little by little. Give me the courage to reveal my true self, and give my spouse the love to receive me as I truly am. Amen.

Talk It Over: What masks have you spent your life cultivating? How have these influenced your marriage? Where are you in the process of sharing your most intimate, personal self with your partner? What areas are most difficult to open to your spouse? Which are easiest?

November 27 ~ Telling the Truth in Love

Whoever speaks the truth gives honest evidence, but a false witness speaks deceitfully. Rash words are like sword thrusts, but the tongue of the wise brings healing.

—Proverbs 12:17-18

"You seem to be gaining an unhealthy amount of weight."

"I'm concerned about your smoking habits and want you to quit."

"You've been excessively angry (or grumpy or moody or depressed) for the past few weeks. It's hard to live with you right now. How can I help?"

"I really don't like that haircut or that outfit or those earrings."

Is there a way to say such things without hurting the feelings of one you love? Honesty can hurt, yet honesty—*if given and received in love*—has the potential to nourish a relationship. As a couple, neither of us has the upper hand in these situations. These "difficult spots" require honest love and sensitivity rather than condescending judgment.

We love our spouses by honestly and sensitively caring for their well-being.

God, give us the sensitivity to speak honestly to each other and to truly receive the loving honesty that we receive. May it not divide us but strengthen us. Amen.

Talk It Over: When does honesty in your relationship hurt? Have you ever felt that your spouse was offering condescending judgment rather than love? When? How can your spouse speak to you so you can receive his or her honesty? When do you hesitate to speak honestly to your spouse? Why? How do you believe your choice affects your relationship?

November 28 ~ The Long Run

I press on toward the goal for the prize of the heavenly call of God in Christ Jesus.

—Philippians 3:14

We live in a "gotta-have-it-now" society. From the latest high-tech gadgets and fashion trends to success and satisfaction in every part of life, our culture tells us that we are incomplete if we do not have all of these "things."

This worldview has a tendency to make its way into our marriage relationships as well. How often have you wondered, whether individually or jointly: *What's wrong with our marriage? Why do we face so many frustrations and setbacks in our relationship? Why can't we seem to "have it all" now?*

Unlike popular culture, though, marriage isn't a short-term arrangement, waiting for the next fad to hit. Marriage begins with the promise to be in the race together for the long run, not for a brief sprint. Although our culture may tell us something is wrong if we don't "have it all" now, the truth is that we're aiming for an enduring end that promises to be so much more lasting than the superficial and ephemeral "good life" we hear so much about. Our marriage is called to be a microcosm of God's kingdom—a reality that has already started to grow, but whose ultimate fulfillment we look forward to in hope.

God, open our eyes to see with you enduring love in our relationship, even when the "here and now" is more difficult than we anticipated. Amen.

Talk It Over: When has short-term thinking affected your marriage? What were the results of this kind of mind-set? Describe your image of an enduring relationship. How does it differ from the "have-it-all-now" mind-set of our culture?

November 29 ~ Wanting Different Things

Love never fails.

—1 Corinthians 13:8a (NIV)

Before we got married, I asked Bill what we would do if somewhere along our journey we decided that we wanted different things from life. I wanted to allow him to be whomever he needed to be to be happy. The flip side of this was the potential for my own pain if his choice for happiness excluded me. To address our concerns, we consciously chose to make a lifetime commitment to stand by each other in a way that constantly would seek the happiness of the other. In the same way that I would seek love and happiness for him, he would seek love and happiness for me. True love makes sacrifices and compromises. Love never fails.

God, thank you for the love between us that allows us both to be happy. Amen.

Talk It Over: *When do you seek your partner's happiness? What sacrifices and compromises have you made for your spouse's happiness? How did you feel about making those decisions? Do you ever seek your happiness before your partner's? When and why? Have you ever felt that you and your partner were headed along different paths? How did/can you work to return to your lifetime commitment to each other?*

November 30 ~ When People Change

Listen, I will tell you a mystery! We will not all die, but we will all be changed.
—1 Corinthians 15:51

When we married, Bill felt called to enter the pastorate. I was applying to Ph.D. programs in clinical psychology. But somewhere along the way, things changed. Today Bill is an editor, and I'm an ordained minister. We often laugh about how different things would have been had we followed our early vocational goals.

Our "changing" (or should I say "emerging"?) selves have often been a point of frustration for us. We say, only half joking, that we married someone completely different. How do we grow to love this "other"?

I like to think that we are both constantly being changed into the likeness of God. With life's changing circumstances, we emerge as individuals who get a larger taste of God's presence. To be able to see God in Bill's emerging person gives me the strength to believe that I am blessed to be in relationship with this changing individual.

May you know marital love in the constant changes of life!

God, thank you for your presence with us as we grow and change in our life together. Amen.

Talk It Over: *How have you and your spouse changed since you married? How do you feel about these changes? How are you able to observe your spouse's changes as transforming him or her into God's image? Do you see yourself changing more and more into God's image?*

December

GROWING IN YOUR MARRIAGE AND YOUR FAITH

Robert and Jeanette Lauer

December 1 ~ Marriage Is God's Gift

Then the LORD God said, "It is not good that the man should be alone; I will make him a helper as his partner."

—Genesis 2:18

*T*here, at the dawn of creation, God gave us the gift of marriage because we all need partners in life. The single Hebrew word translated "helper as his partner" is also used of God as God relates to us. To accept God's gift of marriage, then, is to relate to your spouse in the same supportive way as God relates to you.

Paul made the same point when he wrote that marriage is like the relationship between Christ and the church (Ephesians 5:32). Marriage is God's gift to enrich us. It is a sacred trust, to be nurtured and guarded. Dedicate this month to accepting God's gift with gratitude and growing in both your marriage and your faith.

Lord, show us through this month how we can strengthen our marriage and our faith. Amen.

Talk It Over: *Come up with at least two specific things you can do to strengthen your marriage and two things you can do to strengthen your faith (individually or together) in the coming months.*

December 2 ~ Learn from Each Other

I will instruct you and teach you the way you should go.

—Psalm 32:8a

"Why can't God just give me a simple set of directions for living the Christian life?" a young woman asked. She wanted a quick-assembly project but found that being a Christian is a lifelong process of learning. God is continually instructing and teaching you through the scriptures, the Holy Spirit, and other people—including your spouse.

A devout Christian man in a fifty-year marriage put it this way: "I have learned more about what it means to be a Christian from my wife than from anyone else. She looks at people with the eyes of Christ and cares about them with the heart of Christ. She inspires me to try to be the same kind of good and faithful servant that she is."

Lord Jesus, help us as we strive to teach each other and learn from each other what it means to be your servant. Amen.

Talk It Over: *Take turns describing a Christian virtue in your spouse that you admire and would like to emulate.*

December 3 ~ A Congregation of Two

"For where two or three are gathered in my name, I am there among them."
—Matthew 18:20

Your marriage is a sacred union. You were married in the name of Jesus. He brought you together and continues to abide with you. You remain united through his grace and power. Your relationship is special because you constitute a congregation of two members. Your life as a couple is truly a sacramental act.

To think of your relationship in such terms is to keep your marriage in a state of high spiritual alert. You will be more open to God's instruction. You will be more careful about how you speak and behave with each other. And you will rejoice, for the source of all joy is ever with you.

258

Lord, you are with us always as you have promised. We rejoice in you and in each other. Amen.

Talk It Over: *Talk about the implications of regarding yourselves as a congregation of two. In what ways does this affect your activities, the atmosphere of your home, and the ways you relate to each other?*

December 4 ~ Spiritual Intimacy

I will take you for my wife in faithfulness; and you shall know the LORD.

—Hosea 2:20

In both the Old and New Testaments, spiritual intimacy is likened to the relationship between husband and wife. Since the two are alike in so many important ways, you can use your marital intimacy to model your spiritual intimacy, and vice versa. Take, for example, faithfulness. Hosea notes that faithfulness builds both spiritual and marital intimacy. Faithfulness deepens intimacy because it is a measure of your commitment. To be faithful to God is to give God highest priority in your life. To be faithful in your marriage is to give your spouse priority over any other human consideration. And because you are God's gift to each other, faithfulness to your spouse is one way to fulfill your faithfulness to God.

Help us, Lord, to become ever more intimate with you and with each other. Amen.

Talk It Over: *Discuss various ways in which your intimacy with each other is like your intimacy with God, and how you can use each kind of intimacy to build the other.*

December 5 ~ The Blessing of Sharing

"I have called you friends, because I have made known to you everything that I have heard from my Father."

—John 15:15b

Jesus came that we might have abundant life (John 10:10). This can happen only as we are intimate with God and each other. Jesus spoke of intimacy when he called his disciples "friends" and noted that the essence of intimacy is sharing. Jesus shared everything he heard from his Father with his disciples.

Because the marital relationship is like that between Christ and his church, you are called to share with each other. By sharing your feelings, dreams, needs, and fears, you become intimate friends with God and with each other. Such friendship is the heart of a relationship that fills the soul with abundance.

O God, help us freely share ourselves with you and with each other so that we may truly be intimate friends. Amen.

Talk It Over: *Talk about the things each of you finds difficult to share and ways you can help each other be more open and more comfortable in your sharing.*

December 6 ~ A Safe Place to Share

O LORD, you deceived me, and I was deceived; you overpowered me and prevailed.

—Jeremiah 20:7 (NIV)

Jeremiah accused God of acting like a deceptive tyrant! Like the psalmist David, who often asked God to curse his enemies, Jeremiah did not hesitate to express his feelings to God. Obviously, both felt safe in venting their feelings—the kind that we as Christians often don't admit we even have.

Perhaps that's why Jeremiah and David were so intimate with God, for intimacy demands an open sharing, not a pious veneer of words. But you can only be open when you feel safe. God won't be shocked by your honesty. God already knows how you feel. You can safely share your darkest thoughts with God. Make this the model for your marriage, so you can safely share anything with each other.

Dear Lord, help us be gracious like you so that we may safely share with each other any of our thoughts or feelings. Amen.

Talk It Over: *Discuss together what you can do to make your marriage a safe place for sharing.*

December 7 ~ Bridled Honesty

If any think they are religious, and do not bridle their tongues but deceive their hearts, their religion is worthless.

—James 1:26

When dealing with God, you should be totally honest. When dealing with each other, James points out, you need to practice a bridled honesty. There should be a shutoff valve between your brain and tongue. Not everything that comes into your mind should be spoken to your spouse.

For example, you may have moments when you dislike your spouse or find someone else sexually attractive. These are transient and don't represent your true feelings. So it would be hurtful to express them to your spouse. With God, the ideal is to be totally open and honest. With each other, the ideal is this: You *can* say anything, but you *never* say everything. You practice unbridled honesty with God and a bridled honesty with each other.

Show us, O Lord, how to speak the truth in love with each other and how to be completely open with you. Amen.

Talk It Over: *Discuss with each other how to know what kinds of thoughts and/or actions should be bridled or shared totally.*

December 8 ~ Building Commitment

Greet Prisca and Aquila, who work with me in Christ Jesus, and who risked their necks for my life.

—Romans 16:3-4

Prisca and Aquila, a husband-wife team, were a committed couple. Whenever we encounter them in the scriptures, they were working together for

261

the cause of Christ, even at the risk of their own necks. They were committed to each other and to the Lord. They illustrate that husband and wife can work together to build their spiritual as well as their marital commitment.

When you work together in some kind of Christian ministry to others, you will find your commitment to both God and each other growing stronger. Couples build their commitment when they do such things as teach Sunday school as a team, visit shut-ins, or sponsor a youth group. And as your commitment deepens, your spirits will soar.

Jesus, Savior, give us daily opportunities to serve you and use our service to nurture our commitment to you. Amen.

Talk It Over: *How can you engage in some kind of Christian ministry as a couple on a regular basis? Discuss it with your pastor.*

December 9 ~ Living with Differences

An argument started among the disciples as to which of them would be the greatest.
—Luke 9:46 (NIV)

It's not surprising that the disciples argued over selfish matters. They were only human, plus they differed in many ways. Their group included, among other things, a tax collector, a political zealot, a chronic skeptic (Thomas), and several fishermen. Still, they learned to live with their differences and become one in Christ.

Similarly, every Christian marriage has two people who must learn to live with their differences and become one flesh. Accept and respect these differences, but also use them to learn and grow. For instance, an extravert can teach an introvert how to be more social, and the introvert can teach the extravert about the riches of the interior life. Each will thereby be richer and better prepared to serve God.

O God, help us accept and celebrate our differences and show us how to use them to increase our intimacy with each other and with you. Amen.

Talk It Over: *Select a way in which you differ and discuss how you can use it to learn from each other and to grow as Christians.*

December 10 ~ Loving with a Difference

Therefore be imitators of God, as beloved children, and live in love, as Christ loved us.

—Ephesians 5:1-2

Agape, or Christian love, means to act in behalf of the well-being of others. It stresses what you do rather than how you feel. Jesus, for example, felt anger toward religious bigots of the day and frustration over his disciples' slowness to believe. But these feelings didn't keep him from acting on their behalf and giving himself for the sins of the world.

The measure of your love for each other and for God, therefore, is what you do, not how you feel. You practice agape love when you attend worship, pray, are kind and patient, listen sympathetically, and forgive even though your feelings might urge you to do something different. That's why we call it "loving with a difference." It's the kind of love you see in Jesus.

Lord, may your love so fill us that it will spill over into our love for each other and for others. Amen.

Talk It Over: *Map out a plan for showing Christian love to someone in need, especially someone who is struggling or who has few friends.*

December 11 ~ One Up, One Down

Praise be to the God and Father of our Lord Jesus Christ . . . who comforts us in all our troubles, so that we can comfort those in any trouble with the comfort we ourselves have received from God.

—2 Corinthians 1:3-4 (NIV)

Life is a series of ups and downs. Ups are "feeling good" times. Downs are "feeling low" times. They occur because of struggles, problems, frustrations, or even biorhythms. Usually, a couple's ups and downs don't occur simultaneously. At times, one of you may be up while the other is down. When that happens, put Paul's words into practice. Comfort your mate.

Giving comfort is not offering unwanted advice or proposing quick-fix solutions. You comfort when you listen carefully, support patiently, and

263

encourage gently. In the process, you will grow spiritually and your marriage will be strengthened.

O God of comfort, we commit ourselves to comfort each other with the same comfort we have received from you. Amen.

Talk It Over: *You and your spouse may not find the same kinds of things comforting when you're in a down time. Discuss what you each need from the other when you're feeling low.*

December 12 ~ When You're Both Down

Cast your burden on the LORD, and he will sustain you; he will never permit the righteous to be moved.

—Psalm 55:22

There will be times when you both feel low. You may have a problem at work, troubles at church, money worries, concerns about children, or conflict in your relationship. It's no longer a matter of one comforting the other but of both needing comfort.

What then? Respond to the invitation to cast your burden on the Lord. Remind yourselves of God's promise to sustain you. In other words, share your concerns with the God who loves you, and claim God's pledge to help you through your troubled time. A down time is not a sign that God has abandoned you; it is an invitation to entrust yourself to God's care.

Lord, remind us whenever we are both feeling down to bring our burdens to you and find in you the strength we need to get through it. Amen.

Talk It Over: *Ask other Christian couples to share with you how their faith sustained them when they were feeling down. Use their experiences as encouragement for yourselves.*

December 13 ~ Children of a Forgiving God

"And forgive us our debts, as we also have forgiven our debtors."

—Matthew 6:12

264

We are the children of a forgiving God. Whenever we confess, God is faithful and just to forgive our sins (1 John 1:9). But Jesus said there is a condition: we must forgive those who have trespassed against us (Matthew 6:14-15).

To be forgiven is to be set free. To forgive is to act like God and set others free. The more readily you forgive, the godlier you become. So practice forgiveness relentlessly with each other, knowing that each of you needs both to forgive and to be forgiven. And keep in mind that forgiveness doesn't mean the hurtful behavior was OK (just as God's forgiveness doesn't mean it was OK to sin). It means you have restored your relationship and are working together so that the hurtful behavior is not repeated.

O God, help us be as ready to forgive each other as you are to forgive us. Amen.

Talk It Over: *Discuss what you can do or say to make it easier to be quick to forgive each other.*

December 14 ~ God Our Teacher

"But the Advocate, the Holy Spirit, whom the Father will send in my name, will teach you everything, and remind you of all that I have said to you."
—John 14:26

"Teach me your paths," David prayed to God (Psalm 25:4). His prayer is echoed in Jesus' promise that God's Spirit will teach us all things. The point is that spiritual growth is not like a sudden surge into a new realm. Rather, it's a slow process of being taught and learning how to walk in God's paths.

God our Teacher instructs us in many ways. God speaks through the Bible, through your consciences, through worship, through prayer and meditation, and through each other. As a couple, you have the advantage of having two minds and two hearts to pursue an answer to the question: Where is God leading us? You are fellow students in God's school of Christian living.

Forgive us, Lord, when we stray from your way. Continue to teach us how to walk in the paths of righteousness. Amen.

December 15 ~ Sharing Insights

Let the word of Christ dwell in you richly; teach and admonish one another in all wisdom.

—*Colossians 3:16a*

"What do you think this passage means?" a man asked his wife as they left a Bible class. He was not fully satisfied with the teacher's explanation. They talked about it as they drove home, and each provided their own spiritual insights.

They were able to teach each other because they weren't concerned about knowing the "true" or "correct" interpretation of the passage. They simply shared with each other what the passage meant to them. And as they shared, they had new thoughts and gained new insights. Teaching each other in God's school isn't like an expert sharing knowledge with a student. Rather, it's like two students working together to understand and grow as they share their thoughts and experiences.

Lord, as we teach each other by sharing our thoughts and experiences, let your Holy Spirit work through us to teach your way for us. Amen.

Talk It Over: Cultivate the practice of reading a short Bible passage (one or more verses) and discussing what it means to each of you.

December 16 ~ Teaching by Example

Be imitators of me, as I am of Christ.

—*1 Corinthians 11:1*

One way to teach is by example. For Paul, this meant he imitated Christ so that new converts could imitate him. Paul had found one of the most effective ways to teach someone how to live the Christian life.

266

In your calling as each other's "teacher," therefore, think first not about what you should say, but about what you should do—namely, strive to imitate Christ. As you imitate Christ, you give each other a concrete and inspiring example to follow. A good way to begin is to choose one quality of Jesus and work on developing that in your life. For instance, strive to be as forgiving or as compassionate with everyone around you as Jesus was with those around him.

Jesus, you have set an example for us. Give us grace to follow your example and so be an example to each other. Amen.

Talk It Over: *What particular quality of Jesus would each of you like to cultivate more in your life? Talk about ways you can do this and how you can help each other achieve your goals.*

December 17 ~ Teaching with Gentle Words

But we were gentle among you, like a nurse tenderly caring for her own children.
—1 Thessalonians 1:7b

At times, you teach each other how to grow spiritually by using gentle words. A husband noted once, "I didn't realize I was being curt with people until my wife pointed it out." His wife, he said gratefully, was gentle with him: "She didn't yell at me or tell me to stop being so insensitive. She just took me aside one day and said, 'I think you came across as curt with that couple. I know you didn't mean to be. Could I make some suggestions?'" Had she berated him, he would have become defensive. But he responded to her gentle approach and changed his behavior.

When you teach by words, follow Paul's advice and this woman's example. Be gentle, like a nurse caring for a child. It's very effective.

Thank you, Lord, for reminding us to be gentle with each other as we strive to grow in grace and knowledge. Amen.

Talk It Over: *Share appreciation for times when your spouse's gentle words were helpful to you. Then try to come up with several other examples of ways you might "teach" each other with gentle words.*

December 18 ~ High Expectations

They are like trees planted by streams of water, which yield their fruit in its season.
—Psalm 1:3a

God's children, the psalmist said, are like trees that grow and yield fruit. In other words, spiritual growth is natural for us; it's to be expected that as Christians we will yield fruits of righteousness.

Cultivate such an expectation. Expect each other to become spiritually mature—not in the sense of exerting pressure, but in the sense of having confidence in God and each other that it will happen. Social scientists have found that the expectations of others are a powerful influence in our lives. Expect a child to do well at something, and your expectation will help make it happen. Expect your mate to grow spiritually, and your expectation will encourage and help him or her to do so. High expectations are the soil in which you both can grow into spiritual maturity.

Help us, O God, to hold the high expectations for each other that will nurture our growth in Christ. Amen.

Talk It Over: *Set some goals for spiritual growth for the coming year; then discuss how you can help each other achieve these goals.*

December 19 ~ The Power of Questions

Once when Jesus was praying alone, with only the disciples near him, he asked them, "Who do the crowds say that I am?"
—Luke 9:18

The Gospels are full of questions. Some were questions raised by Jesus, and some were questions asked of Jesus by others. Regardless of who raised it, each question provided an occasion for Jesus to teach a spiritual truth.

Asking questions provides an excellent opportunity to stimulate discussion, to learn from each other, and to hone spiritual insights. Pepper your conversations with questions. For example, you can question each other on matters of doctrine (What do you believe about heaven?), perplexing situations (What does it mean to love a boss who lies to his employees?), and social issues (What should we do to help the poor?). By raising these

268

kinds of questions, you are enlisting each other's aid in your joint quest for spiritual maturity.

May your Spirit guide us, Lord, both in the questions we raise and the discussions we have. Amen.

Talk It Over: *Draw up a list of questions you would like to pursue with each other. Refer to the list when you have some time to talk together.*

December 20 ~ Count Your Blessings

I give thanks to my God always for you because of the grace of God that has been given you in Christ Jesus.
—1 Corinthians 1:4

Giving thanks is an interesting way to begin a letter that goes on to address such problems as divisions, conflict, abuses of Communion, and sexual immorality in the church. But this was exactly what Paul did. He first reminded the Christians at Corinth of how they had benefited him. Even in the midst of difficulties, he was grateful to them.

This approach also works well in marriage. Although you shouldn't ignore problems, we urge you to spend sufficient time giving thanks. Compliment each other, express appreciation to each other, and speak often about the many ways in which God has blessed you. Giving thanks will nurture both your marriage and your faith.

Thank you, God, for making us rich through your grace and the love we have for you and each other. Amen.

Talk It Over: *"Count your blessings," says an old hymn. Talk about all the ways in which you feel blessed by each other and by your faith.*

December 21 ~ Putting Faith to Work

So, whether you eat or drink, or whatever you do, do everything for the glory of God.
—1 Corinthians 10:31

"Use it or lose it" is as true for faith as for many other things. The way to strengthen and nurture your faith is to use it in all situations in your life, including your marriage.

One way to put your faith to work in your marriage is to accept that every aspect of your life together—such as eating, arguing, playing, and doing household chores—is of concern to God. This is why couples say grace before eating, pray for guidance in resolving disagreements, and consider household chores a way to serve God while helping each other. In "whatever you do," then, use your faith. You will feel increasingly closer to God and ever more bound to each other.

Lord, be ever present in our minds that we may do all to your glory. Amen.

Talk It Over: *Do you agree that every aspect of your life together is of concern to God? Discuss how you can use your faith to add a spiritual dimension to both the routine and special experiences you share as a couple.*

December 22 ~ Practice, Practice

So let us not grow weary in doing what is right, for we will reap at harvest time, if we do not give up.

—Galatians 6:9

Deciding to put your faith to work in your marriage is a first step. The second step is to keep at it until it becomes almost instinctive. In other words, just as you must practice to gain other kinds of skills in life, so also you need to practice living out your faith. Practice Christian virtues until they become your nature.

Here's a wife's testimony: "I'm not a sensitive person by nature, and I'm often insensitive to my husband's needs. But I no longer excuse my insensitivity by saying, 'That's just the way I am.' I keep reminding myself that as a Christian I need to be more sensitive. And although I still have a way to go, I'm making progress."

O God, help us practice Christian virtues with each other until they become a part of our nature. Amen.

Talk It Over: *Identify a Christian virtue that you need to practice more fully in your relationship, such as forgiveness, edifying words, or sensitivity. Discuss ways you can help each other do this.*

December 23 ~ Be Kind

And be kind to one another, tenderhearted, forgiving one another, as God in Christ has forgiven you.

—Ephesians 4:32

Kindness is a marriage-enriching Christian virtue. To be kind is to take on one of the qualities of God, for Jesus taught that God is kind (Luke 6:35). And Paul noted that in kindness, God our Savior appeared to save us (Titus 3:4-5), not because of our worthiness but because of God's mercy. God's kindness, then, means that God takes the initiative.

Similarly, to practice kindness in your marriage means to take the initiative in doing things that help your spouse. "I was in a grumpy mood, snapping at everybody," a wife said. "My husband just came up to me, gave me a hug, and smiled. This told me that he knew I'd had a rough day and he was there for me. His act of kindness turned my day around."

Kind and loving Savior, we commit ourselves to be kind to each other as you have commanded. Amen.

Talk It Over: *Discuss your ideas of what kindness is; then agree that you will consciously practice kindness with each for the next week.*

December 24 ~ Be Patient

Love is patient; love is kind; love is not envious or boastful or arrogant or rude.
—1 Corinthians 13:4-5a

Jesus came in the "fullness of time" (Galatians 4:4), hundreds of years after the prophets foretold his coming. Christmas reminds us to be patient with God, because God's schedule is not the same as ours. We expect instant responses and quick fixes. But faith grows as we accept God's schedule and God's ways, for we're trusting God to do what is best rather than what we prefer at the moment.

Patience will also strengthen your marriage. Don't always insist on your own schedule, your own way, your own preferences. For instance, if your spouse doesn't reform a bad habit as quickly as you'd like, continue to patiently encourage him or her. You'll actually facilitate the process of change. Badgering creates resistance, but patience creates goodwill and cooperation.

Forgive our impatience, O God, and teach us to wait upon you and upon each other. Amen.

Talk It Over: *Who are the most patient people you have known? What can you learn from them about exercising patience in your own lives?*

December 25 ~ The Mind of Christ

Finally, beloved, whatever is true, whatever is honorable, whatever is just, whatever is pure, whatever is pleasing, whatever is commendable . . . think about these things.

—Philippians 4:8

As a Christmas gift to each other, spend a few days thinking about what it means to have the mind of Christ. The more you think with the mind of Christ, the more you grow spiritually. One way to have the mind of Christ, Paul noted, is to focus on the true, the honorable, the just, the pure, and whatever is pleasing or commendable.

Apply this teaching to your marriage. You and your spouse are each married to a flawed person. You can focus on the flaws, or you can focus on the things you find pleasing and commendable. If you focus on the flaws, you'll sink into dissatisfaction. If you focus on positive qualities, you'll look at each other through the eyes of Christ and rejoice in the richness of your marriage.

Thank you, Lord, for all the qualities we treasure in each other; we commit ourselves to focus on them. Amen.

Talk It Over: Share a few things you find pleasing and commendable in your marriage.

December 26 ~ Assume the Best

Jesus answered, "Neither this man nor his parents sinned; he was born blind so that God's works might be revealed in him."

—John 9:3

When they encountered a man who was blind, the disciples assumed the worst—the man or his parents had sinned. Jesus assumed the best: it was not a matter of sin, but of an opportunity to glorify God. To assume the best, then, is to think with the mind of Christ.

In marriage, assuming the best means to put a positive rather than a negative spin on things your spouse says and does. For instance, assume your spouse's irritability is a passing state rather than a permanent problem. Even if the behavior is troublesome, you can assume that the intentions were good. Perhaps your spouse's criticism of something you say or do is an effort to help rather than a put-down. In all things, try to assume the best about each other. That's what Jesus is doing.

As you assume the best about us, Lord Jesus, so help us assume the best about each other. Amen.

Talk It Over: How can you help each other learn to assume the best?

December 27 ~ How Can I Serve You?

"For the Son of Man came not to be served but to serve, and to give his life a ransom for many."

—Mark 10:45

Jesus focused on serving God by serving people. His approach was not, "What can you do for me?" but, "What can I do for you?" To have the mind of Christ, then, is to approach others with the attitude, "How can I serve you?"

273

It's an attitude you can adopt as a couple as you deal with others, and one you can adopt in your dealings with each other. For example, how can you, as a couple, help the person struggling through a divorce, a sense of loss, or financial problems? It will help if you begin each day by reminding yourselves that you are called to serve each other and called as a couple to serve others. Be alert for every opportunity that God brings your way.

Thank you for coming to serve us, Lord. We give ourselves to serving you by serving others. Amen.

Talk It Over: *What can you do to serve each other? What can you do as a couple to serve others?*

December 28 ~ Worship Together

O come, let us worship and bow down, let us kneel before the LORD, our Maker!
—Psalm 95:6

For the remainder of this month, we'll reflect on worshiping as a couple. The church service, of course, is part of your worship experience. But we'd like you to broaden your notion of worship and think about ways to worship daily.

One purpose of worship is to sense God's presence. God is always with us, but we don't always sense this. To increase your awareness of God's presence, commit to remind each other about the spiritual significance of everyday experiences. Noticing the flowers in your garden, for instance, will remind you of God's promise to care for you (Matthew 6:28-30). If you work together in this way, you will increasingly be aware that God is at work in the world and in your lives.

We are grateful, O God, that you are with us always. Use our experiences to continually remind us of your presence. Amen.

Talk It Over: *Revisit your experiences of the past week or so. In what ways were you aware of God's presence, and what was God trying to say to you through these moments and experiences?*

December 29 ~ Devoted to Prayer

Devote yourselves to prayer, keeping alert in it with thanksgiving.
—Colossians 4:2

A second way to worship is to pray together. You can pray at any time and anywhere. Jesus once went to a mountain and spent the entire night in prayer there (Luke 6:12). Prayer can be a natural part of your friendship with other Christian couples. We were once driving with another couple, talking about the blessings we all enjoyed, when the woman turned to her husband and exclaimed, "Say a prayer of thanksgiving right now!" And to me, the driver, she added, "You don't have to close your eyes, Bob!"

You can pray together before meals, including meals in a restaurant. You can pray together in the morning and/or the evening in your home. You can join hands in a public situation and silently pray for something or someone there. Devote yourselves to prayer. Opportunities are everywhere.

Teach us, Lord, how to talk with you regularly as a couple so that prayer may adorn our marriage. Amen.

Talk It Over: *Discuss how you can add more times of couple prayer to your daily lives. Make specific plans to do it.*

December 30 ~ Songs of Faith

And with gratitude in your hearts sing psalms, hymns, and spiritual songs to God.
—Colossians 3:16c

Songs are a third form of worship. The first Christians continued the Jewish tradition of singing the psalms in worship, adding new hymns that reflected their faith in Christ. Through the centuries, Christians have sung about their faith in many situations—from those herded to death in the Roman Colosseum to those in our time who gather in churches each Sunday. It's hard to imagine a worship service today without the glory of music filling the sanctuary.

Buy a hymnal or songbook or a praise and worship CD for your home. Sing together as a way to praise and worship together at home. If you can't sing, select a hymn or song and read the words as a devotional. Every song of faith is an inspiring sermon that will nurture you spiritually.

We thank you, Lord, for music and for Christians in the past and present whose music helps us worship you. Use these songs to sanctify our thoughts and illumine our paths. Amen.

Talk It Over: *Select a favorite hymn, or a favorite praise or worship song, and read the words carefully. Discuss how they reflect biblical teachings and what they imply for your life together.*

December 31 ~ Celebration

Praise the LORD! Praise, O servants of the LORD; praise the name of the LORD.
—Psalm 113:1

To praise God is to worship God. To celebrate the goodness and mercy of God is an act of worship. Celebration can be a part of your worship even during times of struggle. As James put it: "My brothers and sisters, whenever you face trials of any kind, consider it nothing but joy, because you know that the testing of your faith produces endurance . . . so that you may be mature and complete, lacking in nothing" (James 1:2-4).

Why not end each day in worship by reflecting on the many ways in which God has blessed you, and then giving thanks for them? Celebrate your faith, your marriage, your life. "Praise the LORD, who is good and whose steadfast love endures forever" (Psalm 136:1).

We praise you, O God, and pray that our marriage may be a lifelong celebration of your goodness in bringing us together. Amen.

Talk It Over: *List the ways in which you are blessed. Be certain to include the ways in which God has nurtured you during times of struggle.*